# CONVERSATIONAL
# SOCIOLOGY

This book is dedicated to the memory of co-author
Paul D. Richardson, who passed away before realizing his dream of
seeing it published; and to our families, students, and society, particularly
those who have fought to promote the understanding and
acceptance of cultural diversity.

# CONVERSATIONAL SOCIOLOGY

## An Intercultural Bridge Where East Meets West

Julio C. Caycedo
and
Paul D. Richardson

THE CASLON COMPANY

First published in 1995 in the United States of America by
THE CASLON COMPANY
Middletown, New Jersey

**Library of Congress Cataloging-in-Publication Data**

Caycedo, Julio César.
  Conversational sociology : an intercultural bridge where East
meets West / by Julio C. Caycedo and Paul D. Richardson.
    p.   cm.
  Includes bibliographical references and index.
  ISBN 0-391-03937-7
  1. Intercountry marriage.  2. Taiwanese—United States.
3. Marriage—United States.  4. Marriage—Taiwan.  5. Intercultural
communication.  6. Sociology.  I. Richardson, Paul D., 1911–1995.
II. Title.
HQ1032.C39       1995
306.84'5—dc20                                                    95-10145
                                                                      CIP

Printed in the United States of America

# CONTENTS

# PREFACE

The main objective of an over-ambitious author is to write a book that the reader will pick up eagerly, linger with profitably, and lay down reluctantly. Such a book, of course, could not have a universal appeal across the literary field. An avid reader of romantic novels, for example, may not accept a "who-dun-it" mystery with the same degree of enthusiasm as a love story. By the same token, a reader obsessed with the love for fiction is not going to be easily convinced to become immersed in factual writings.

Although the scientific-literary gap is difficult to bridge, we hypothesize that a scientific study written in a popular vein would have a broader appeal than if it were restricted by the straight jacket of precise terminology on a highly professional level. Since sociology is a scientific study of human relationships, it provides a fertile field for testing our hypothesis. Although *Conversational Sociology: An Intercultural Bridge Where East Meets West* is not purely scientific, it makes heavy demands upon our academic background in sociology. Furthermore, relaxing the scientific restrictions enables us to capitalize on up to thirty years of teaching sociology, extensive multi-cultural and multi-class experiences, and our roaming imagination.

Perhaps an analogy will illustrate this point. In plying one's trade as an electrician, it is essential to measure and cut conduit, a protective pipe for wires feeding the lights or other electrical appliances. Any measurement within a quarter of an inch was acceptable. Such a margin of error was quite a contrast to the machinist's measurements which had tolerance limits of 1/1000th of an inch. The electrician's measurement is an approximation—but adequate—whereas the machinist's measurement is precise. Likewise, the following work is somewhat of a "roughing-in plan" providing an adequate coverage without becoming bogged down in detailed precision. We make a conscientious effort to place the study on three levels of appeal. This book is designed to challenge the lay person, to stimulate the sociology student, and to interest the sociology scholar through this unique approach.

*Conversational Sociology: An Intercultural Bridge Where East Meets West* is illustrated with a study of the attitudes of Chinese college students toward inter-

---

1. The term America(s) as used in this book refers to people from the U.S.

cultural marriage, particularly between Chinese and American[1] Caucasians. An attempt is made to give the reader a better understanding of sociological concepts by applying these concepts to the various aspects of the study.

If this innovative approach receives a wide reception, perhaps others will realize that a highly technical vocabulary is not imperative to share ideas. The common sense approach is designed to broaden the appeal of the field of sociology beyond the limits of an introductory text-book or the college classroom. To accomplish this purpose, the main emphasis is placed upon an understanding of human relationships, rather than upon the science that studies these relationships, as sociology is often characterized. For this reason, the materials are presented in a popular vein to satisfy the needs of the casual reader, the sociology student, and the sociology scholar.

No apologies are offered for any deviations from the standard methodology used in a soundly based scientific sociological study. The main purpose of the book is not to defend sociology as a science, but to stimulate interest in the study of the subject-matter of sociology. The aim is not to array a battery of authoritative opinions to support a particular position, but to express opinions formed through numerous years of graduate study, college teaching, and multi-cultural as well as multi-class experiences—ranging from being a common laborer to becoming an academe and from living in the West (North and South America) to living in the East (Taiwan and Thailand).

# INTRODUCTION

A book that attempts to present a scientific subject in a popular vein could be labeled a "half-breed": An offspring of a mixed marriage between a literary composition and a scientific research paper. The material must be presented in an appealing language which does not violate the scientific meaning. The strategy is simply to cruise in the middle of a communication stream with the ripples of literary language gently lapping against the craft on one side and the discriminating scientific terminology battering it on the other side.

The study of sociology provides a fertile field for an attempt to blend the channels of expression of literature and science because sociology studies culture scientifically, while literature reflects it. Sociology is mostly concerned with the effect of various types of literature, and other forms of mass media, have on the reader. Literature, on the other hand, manipulates the emotions of readers to produce a particular effect on them. Whereas sociology deals with reality, literature, in many instances, provides an escape from reality. In literature, human relationships are a means to an end. If the writer presents them in an appealing manner, the goal is achieved. In sociology, however, human relationships are an end in themselves: They are the object of study.

*Conversational Sociology: An Intercultural Bridge Where East Meets West* uses the ordinary means to achieve the specialized end. The title suggests that the scientific study of human relationships—a streamlined definition of sociology—is presented in ordinary language. The work could just as well be entitled *A Tinker's Sociology*, because the method used in this book is very similar to the one used by a tinker. For example, the tinker will replace a precisely calibrated electrical fuse with a common copper coin. Such a practice is highly inadvisable because the penny does not offer protection against a fire hazard as the fuse does. The practice does enable the tinker to find the trouble spot, however, by observing where the electrical sparks are flying—he sometimes can locate the source of the problem before the house burns down. As in the case of the tinker, this book uses simple techniques to deal with the complex subject of sociology. The aim is to accomplish the task without destroying the scientific structure of the subject. The first section of the book is devoted to the discussion of this delicate task.

A comparative approach is used throughout the book. The thesis is that through contrasting various social phenomena, their meanings are made clearer. It is not possible to appreciate warmth, for example, unless cold has been experienced. A person inexperienced in evaluating jewelry is not able to judge the purity of a genuine diamond without comparing it to one of cruder quality. In another context, such as that formed by comparing it with a glass bauble, the meaning of purity as a quality of a diamond becomes even more evident. The meaning of purity becomes more and more refined as the evaluator makes additional comparisons.

Likewise, through comparing the function of a sociological concept in one context, such as traditional China, with its operation in another, such as the United States, the concept's meaning becomes clearer. As will be discussed more fully later, a concept devoid of a context is meaningless.

It follows that as the context becomes more complete, the meaning of the concept becomes clearer. For example, the term interaction, in isolation, has no meaning. However, when its function as a part of the mate selection process is revealed, it becomes meaningful. Additionally, when social interaction is viewed as a part of the mate selection process in the social context of traditional China, it becomes more understandable. By also relating social interaction, in the same way, to the social context of the United States, the reader is given even a better understanding of the sociological concept of social interaction.

The main purpose of this book is to give the reader a basic understanding of a condensed version of the field of sociology. To accomplish this task, a research study concerned with the "Attitudes of Chinese[1] College Students toward Intermarriage with American-Caucasians" is used to illustrate the sociological concepts presented in the book. That study focuses on the mate selection process as it presently functions in Taiwan. By presenting the field study in Section I, the textual materials are arranged in a manner that differs from the usual presentations. Normally, the background is first established in order for the reader to gain a better understanding of a scientific study. Such a procedure is proper if the main objective of the presentation is the interpretation of the findings of the fieldwork. In this way, the study is the objective and sociological knowledge is the means to this end. In *Conversational Sociology: An Intercultural Bridge Where East Meets West*, a reversal of this procedure is used. Since a better understanding of sociology is the main purpose of this book, the research study becomes the means by which this goal is attained. The first approach is purely descrip-

---

1. Throughout this book, the term Chinese refers to the Chinese identified with Taiwan, Nationalist China, or the Republic of China; mainland Chineses, or mainland China, refers to Communist China; traditional China refers to pre-Communist China.

tive, providing the reader with another morsel of knowledge to be tucked away for future reference; whereas the approach used in this book is analytical. To know that the attitude of the Chinese toward intercultural marriages is more favorable in urban than in rural areas, is descriptive; however, to know why the attitude is more favorable in one social setting than in the other, is analytical.

Another reason for presenting the scientific study near the beginning of the book (following the discussion of the importance of language in Chapter 1 and scientific methods in Chapter 2) is because research is the heart of sociology. A scientific study of human relationships, which is a streamlined definition of sociology, is not possible without fieldwork resulting in primary data, or the use of secondary data (fieldwork done by someone else) such as other sociological studies, census materials, or vital statistics. The presentation of scientific methods in Chapter 2 serves as an introduction to the study of attitudes toward intercultural marriages set forth in Chapter 3.

In the first part of Chapter 4, the classification system especially devised for this book is presented. An adequate, but not a detailed, treatment of selected key sociological concepts which are basic to an understanding of the discipline, and are essential in the study of Chinese/U.S. Caucasian marriages, is also given. In the latter portion of that chapter, the key concepts are interwoven into a logically closed social system. In this way, the reader is able to see the interrelationships of the various concepts as a whole. The arrangement also provides a framework in which the function of the mate selection process can be seen more clearly, and the field of sociology can be understood more fully.

Section II of the study is concerned with the process of mate selection as it functioned in traditional China and is functioning in the United States today. By comparing its operation in these two social environments, the purpose of the mechanism is understood better, and the meaning of the concepts becomes clearer as they are viewed in the two contrasting types of societies. That section also points out the positive and negative influences operating in the traditional Chinese culture (and the United States' social environment) on the mate selection process.

Section III shows the impact of social change on the attitudes of Chinese college students toward intermarriage with American-Caucasians. Through this analysis, emphasis is placed upon changes in the major social institutions in the Republic of China since World War II as possible causes of any variations that may be apparent in the comparison of the *traditional* Chinese model with the *present day* Chinese model. The thesis is that the study of the practice of choosing marital partners in Taiwan, against the backdrop of social change during the past four decades, will provide the reader with a basic understanding of the process, as it interacts with other forces in society.

The value of such a work as this is commensurate with the interest of the reader. The lay person is introduced to the basic sociological concepts, which serve as salient points of orientation in the study of the field of sociology. By interweaving these concepts into a social system, the influential relationship that each has with the others is clearly shown giving the novice a view of the forest, rather than a glimpse of the individual trees. For example, the concept "authority" is better understood when it is considered in relationship to the family, the political, or the religious institutions than when it is presented as a single, isolated term. The meaning of each individual term can be understood more clearly when seen in relationship with other terms. The term family is understood more fully when its type of authority is distinguished from that of the government. Through this method, the lay person is introduced to a condensed version of the discipline of sociology.

The beginning sociology student (including those who speak English as a second language), the student of Asian studies, the student of marriage and the family, and the student of sociolinguistics will also find this book valuable as supplemental reading to text-books in those fields. For one thing, the sociological concepts are viewed from a different perspective, since the research study of the attitudes of Chinese college students toward intercultural marriage serves as a focal point from which the sociological principles radiate. For another thing, the key terms selected for the study are organized into a closed social system which provides a clearer illustration of their meaning. Finally, the comparison of the traditional and contemporary patterns of mate selection reveals the impact of social change on social processes.

If in no other way, the advanced student in sociology will find value in the research study itself. First, the study reveals the vulnerability of an extremely staunch social structure, such as that of traditional China, to social change. Second, it deals with the influence of internal, as well as external, forces hammering out modifications in the deeply entrenched social institutions.

In addition to the contributions of the research study, other materials may be of value in refining the advanced student's definitions of essential sociological concepts.

# SECTION I

## SCIENTIFIC TERMINOLOGY AND METHODS

In Section I, a distinction is made between the language of literature and the terminology of science. Also, the use of the scientific method in field studies is discussed. Chapter 1 emphasizes the importance of precision of language in scientific presentations. In addition to considering sociology as a science, Chapter 2 serves as an introduction to the field study which provides the foundation for this book. A discussion of the methods involved in scientific research is also included. A description of the scientific tools used in gathering and analyzing the field study materials is given in Chapter 3. This explanation of the techniques is followed by an analysis of the findings derived from the questionnaire. The core of the book centers in Chapter 4, where a unique classification is used to categorize the key concepts and laws in analyzing the mate selection process and in providing a framework for the study of sociology. The last part of this chapter plays an important role in the book by weaving the key concepts into a logically closed social system which reveals the intricate pattern of the interrelationships existing between and among sociological concepts.

# 1

## The Importance
## of Language as a Tool
## of Precision

The fact that a system of communication is the foundation of culture and is, therefore, a prerequisite of society, makes it imperative to discuss the importance of language as a literary and scientific tool before considering its products in the form of sociological concepts. A communication system consists of symbols expressed on various levels of understanding. Symbols are objects, motions, or sounds representing something else. For present purposes, they are classified as crude, refined, and sophisticated symbols.

The crude symbols form the lowest level of communication, such as sounds or motions which can be understood universally. A newborn infant crying, an adolescent moaning in pain, or an adult flinching in fear convey uniform messages across all cultural or national boundaries. The refined level of communication attaches meaning to objects and gestures. It is more particularized, culturally, than the crude symbol. An infant, old enough to sit up and explore, sees in its national flag nothing more than a colorful piece of cloth that serves as a plaything, a coverlet, or an object on which to cut teeth. As the infant grows older, s/he learns the significance of the symbol of loyalty and sacrifice purchased with the lives of multitudes of individuals. Classical dances, especially in Oriental countries, impart historical accounts of their country by the use of gestures. The handshake, nodding the head, or shaking a clenched fist are refined symbols conveying particular meanings in various cultural contexts.

The sophisticated level of communication expresses meaning through symbols, either oral (i.e., vocabulary) or written (i.e., alphabet), which have been devised to convey thought in a particular culture. These symbols are less readily understood universally than those on the lower levels of communication. For this reason, it is essential to discuss the importance of language as a conveyer of thought rather thoroughly for the purposes of this presentation.

## LANGUAGE AS A BRIDGE OF COMMUNICATION

Just as we have various types of bridges for roadways—draw bridges, suspension bridges, pontoon bridges, swinging bridges, etc.—communication bridges could likewise be classified according to types. For example, the bridge leading from ignorance to knowledge could be termed the "lore" bridge. The span connecting a hazy expression to a clearly-defined, concise statement could be named the "precision" bridge. The gap cross-over between superstition and fact could be labeled the "reality" bridge.

This section of Chapter 1 attempts to straddle the linguistic fence separating the fertile fields of literary expressions from the unimaginative fields of matter-of-fact scientific presentations. To illustrate the differences in the use of language in the two fields, the following quotations drawn from two of the oldest and most standardized forms of literature (the King James Version of the Holy Bible and Shakespeare's writings) are compared to sociological maxims.

In the Sermon on the Mount, Jesus says, "Be ye therefore perfect, even as your Father which is in heaven is perfect" (Matt. 5:48). The message contained in this passage is to establish a code of ethics patterned after the scriptures and to live according to it.

Some sociologists would say, "Conform to the norms." Norms are expected or required patterns of behavior in certain social situations. They have developed into ideals through the trials and errors of individuals as members of society. In attempting to conform to the norms, the individual is striving toward perfection.

In the same Sermon Jesus says, "Where your treasure is, there will your heart be also" (Matt. 6:21). That is to say, whatever is of most importance to a person will be given top priority in a program of endeavor.

The sociologist would say, "Personal values are of paramount importance to the individual."

Shakespeare has Polonius say to Laertes, "To thine own self be true and it follows as night the day thou canst not be false to any man." Otherwise, the advice is to follow the dictates of your conscience in dealing with others, or, "Do unto others as you would have them do unto you" (Matt. 7:12).

Some sociologists would say, "The conscience is formed by the internalization of norms." If these norms are firmly implanted, they compel us to behave according to the demand of the requirement.

As can be seen, for many centuries, according to both the Bible and Shakespeare, language is a vehicle that has conveyed the same message in different ways.

The messages in the above mentioned literary quotes, as well as other literature and arts, give expression to our feelings; while science gives an exact, objective report of data. The communication nuggets of literature become scientific concepts in sociology. Further, literature varies descriptive terms to avoid monotony, while scientific terms are used repeatedly because each term has a precise meaning. For example, in literature the terms desegregation and integration can be justifiably interchanged to provide variety in the presentation. The process of desegregation could be illustrated by welding a variety of metals to form a single ring with each metal maintaining its own identity. The process of integration, by contrast, could be shown by melting all of the metals together into a single substance, each metal losing its original identity.

The Supreme Court Act of 1954 broke down the spatial barriers between the races with the purpose of weakening the social barriers. The Act represents a new approach in attempting to solve the race problem. Prior to 1954, the efforts of reformists focused on the elimination of discrimination between the races in an attempt to gradually phase out segregation. The Supreme Court reversed this procedure by declaring segregation in the schools illegal in order to lessen the sting of discrimination. Possibly, the decision of the Supreme Court was based on the "foxhole philosophy" that developed during World War II. Just as there are no "atheists in foxholes," neither is racial prejudice evidenced in similar emergency situations.

This attempt to bridge the gap between literary and sociological presentations requires the use of nomenclature which appeals to the literary advocate without alienating the sociological student. The scientific terminology is tinged with colorful variations without distorting the scientific meaning. Semantics, then becomes secondary to the conveyance of thought, which is the function of language. Communication designed for a wide receptive field must, of necessity, be in more general terms than that directed toward a highly specialized audience. Hence, the challenge in the present study is to select vehicles of communication general enough to appeal to the layperson but specific enough to scientifically identify social phenomena.

The following example is helpful in demonstrating the use of a vocabulary to bridge the gap between the inspirational phraseology of literature and the disciplined expressions of sociology. For example, a literal account of a tinker who was unable to repair a toaster would be phrased, "The frustration of the would-be repairman, who unsuccessfully tried to restore the toaster to working order, was expressed in a barrage of four letter words that would embarrass even those who are deeply inured to the use of profanity." The scientist's statement would be, "The unskilled artisan's failure to repair the toaster resulted in an expression of frustration through the use of profanity."

A compromise of the two statements is expressed by, "The tinker, who lacked the technological expertise to repair the toaster, expressed his frustration in colorful terms unacceptable in polite society." All of these statements say the same thing, but the appeal of the context varies according to the interests of the reader.

## LANGUAGE AS A BRIDGE OF UNDERSTANDING

Language is a mechanism by which an idea conceived by one person can be transported into the thinking process of another. It is a mechanism because it forms a vital link in the thought process. Words are the foundation stones on which the most complex ideas rest and, on the other hand, they also provide a basis for the simplest expression. A tot that says "Daddy" is doing more than seeking the attention of the father. The child is enlisting a communication partner who, normally, s/he has learned will respond, and bridge the gap between the thinking of the two.

Words are more vital to human thought than they are as a medium of expression or as a method of communication. They are vital factors in our thought-process. In fact, the thoughts we have are determined to a large extent by the vocabulary we command. To understand sociology, or any other science, we first must have the basic concepts sharply defined in order to muster our thoughts. Meaning results only as we relate one person, thing, event, or situation to another person or their combinations, and these relationships can only be shown through a set of conceptual tools.

Language is not only important to sociology as a tool for refining thought, but it is even more important as the mechanism of human communications. Sociology is concerned with man's relationship to his physical and social environment. Whatever progress he has made in either of these environments can be directly attributed to his system of communication. Language is one of the things which fixes the unsurpassable gulf existing between the lowest form of man and the highest form of animal. It is the basis of culture. It is the means by which mankind has blazed an ever-widening trail through the wilderness of ignorance and superstition. Through the system of human communication, relationships between individuals, groups, and nations have been improved. A better understanding of the linguistic systems of others gives us a better understanding of the users of a particular system, and in this understanding lies the possible solution of many critical problems facing our world today.

The growth of a better understanding among persons has been stunted, and the development of a closer cooperation between them has been arrested, because, for one thing, the machinery of human communication has not functioned smoothly. It is operating with ever-increasing efficiency, through extensive traveling and through such instruments as the United Nations, but there are still points at which it is ineffective.

In addition to a knowledge of the meaning of the term itself, a context is essential to the understanding of a particular concept. The context of some type is necessary to provide a word with its true and significant meaning. This means that a word can have a similar meaning only in a similar context. The length and explanatory content of the context is determined by the nature of the term. The more abstract the term, as a rule, the more meticulous the context must be.

A few examples will reveal the wide range of meaning a single word can have in various contexts. We usually think of the verb "carry" as meaning to convey or transport an object by our hands or a vehicle. But we can also "carry" the war into Asia, "carry" a customer on our books, "carry" a town by force, "carry" an election, "carry" a state or nation in an election, "carry" an audience with us, "carry" our head high, "carry" weather reports in our newspapers, and "carry" hardware in our drugstores. These are only a few meanings of the transitive form of the verb. Numerous additional meanings could be conveyed in other contexts.

More than this, the same word in the same context, but viewed from different conceptual frameworks, conveys different meanings. The sentence, "He carried the ball," could have two exactly opposite meanings. In a football game, it could, and usually does, mean that the player made a gain for his team. In a basketball game, it always means that the player and his team drew a penalty. In colloquialism "He carried the ball" means that he took the lead or initiative in a lively discussion or a particular development.

One other reason for communication failure is the emotional meanings of words. The meanings that we give to words are products of our total experiences. Since no two people have exactly the same total experiences, and since these words reflect the differences in experiences, a single word never has exactly the same meaning to different persons. A single word, therefore, not only is used to indicate an object, but it is frequently used to suggest an emotional attitude toward that object. For example, while some people assign the dignified title of an "officer of the law" to a policeman, others more colloquially refer to him as a "cop." There are those who even assign him the stigmatized title of "pig." All three of these terms are laden with meanings that can be traced from strong, respectful approval to strong disgusting disapproval.

Every word identifying a subject is colored by our experiences in association with the object, relationship, ideology, and other topics. A baseball bat, for example, is a means of livelihood for the "designated hitter" in professional sports. However, it is a weapon for the antagonist, a stick of firewood for the desperate camper, an instrument of the devil for the fundamentalist minister because it is a means of violating the Sabbath, and on and on.

## LANGUAGE AS A SCIENTIFIC TOOL

To understand any science, it is imperative to have certain fundamental points of reference that serve as centers from which exploratory expeditions into the labyrinth of vital and properly distributed locations could be made. A general view of the area of the discipline could be gained through such expeditions. With a generalized understanding of a particular science, the explorer is better prepared to make a detailed study within a specialized area of that science, which is to be done later in the book.

This part of Chapter 1, as indicated in the introduction, selects certain basic sociological concepts that are strategically located in a general system of sociology. In this way, a framework is constructed for the study of attitudes toward intercultural marriages. These linguistic pegs may also serve as points of orientation, or a framework, into which sociological knowledge may be classified. This is not to say, however, that a comprehensive knowledge of sociology is dependent upon nothing more than a well-ordered system of sociological concepts with a clearly defined terminology. The discipline is much more complex than that.

For one thing, sociology has structural as well as functional aspects. Auguste Comte, often referred to as the founder or father of sociology, was the first to make such a division by labeling the structural aspect as "social statics" and the functional aspects as "social dynamics." The treatment in this part of Chapter 1 is concerned with both the structural and functional, as well as other, aspects of sociology. Those concepts associated with the various aspects of society have been grouped together for consideration in the special classification system presented in Chapter 4. The frame of reference for present purposes is constructed in Chapter 3 through the organization of the sociological concepts into a logical system upon which a general theory of sociology may be built. Such an organization weaves the individual concepts into the system as a whole. It is mainly in this theoretical framework that a better understanding of sociology can be attained and its data interpreted.

The frame of reference and concepts of sociology must be broader and more comprehensive than those required for most other disciplines because of the discipline's interrelationships with other social sciences (i.e., anthropology, economics, geography, political science, psychology). Sociology is not solely concerned with the relationships that are common to these disciplines, but it is also concerned with the elements that are peculiar to itself. In a word, sociology is concerned with man in both his physical and social environments. This means that sociology has a vital relationship of mutual dependence with the other social sciences.

This can be seen by selecting basic concepts that serve as pivots or foci about which social systems, such as those in traditional China and Nationalist China, as presented in this book, will be constructed. An understanding of these basic concepts of sociology is essential to an understanding of the discipline, but the conceptual understanding is a means to an end and not an end in itself. So, to provide pivotal points in a social system alone, is not adequate to present a basic understanding of sociology, but it does provide the means to sharpen the analytical tools with which a more clear-cut understanding of sociology may be carved.

It does not matter how refined these analytical tools are, or how elaborate the frame of reference is. If the concepts are not applied to the social situation, the treatment is descriptive. Although they are essential to an understanding of sociology, to simply know the meaning of each concept is not adequate to understand the field of sociology. This requires the application of the tools to the practical situation. When this is done, the study becomes analytical. It answers the question, "Why?" In addition to explaining the meaning of the concepts, as will be done in Chapter 2, they are applied to the process of mate selection later in this book.

# 2

## Sociology as a Science

The term sociology is defined according to the backgrounds of various individuals. There are two significantly different opinions by academic stalwarts well acquainted with the field. One set of scholars looks upon sociology as a dignified discipline well qualified to be recognized as a science. Another set looks upon the discipline as a parasite feeding off of the physical sciences by claiming its knowledge is validated by the use of the scientific method.

To spend time discussing whether or not sociology is a pure science, a behavioral or social science, a pseudo-science, or a parasitical science is to seek knowledge for knowledge's sake. The importance of sociology is not so much in what it is, but in what it does. Its contribution to the field of knowledge is not determined by its definition, but by the reliability of its findings. A cake baked in an oven heated by a wood burning stove can be just as tasty as one baked in an electric or gas oven. It is the quality of the product that counts, not the name of the contrivance by which it is produced. Likewise, it is the accuracy of sociological predictions that are of importance to science, not the label of the mechanics through which they are reached.

The main value in considering the qualifications of sociology as a science is for purposes of classification, which is of importance to any field of knowledge. For this reason, a brief discussion of the nature of science, and whether or not sociology has the prerequisite to be identified as science, is warranted.

### DEFINITION OF SCIENCE

Science is a methodical approach to the study of empirical data resulting in a collection of organized reliable knowledge. The knowledge is collected using the scientific method, which is a procedure designed to eliminate subjective influences to the fullest possible extent. No matter how meticulous the method, or how qualified the investigator, it is not possible to make an absolutely pure scientific study, because the individual's judgment is involved in various stages of the procedure. If in no other way, the selection of terms in formulating the conclusion makes it impossible to present the findings in terminology that is completely free from bias. As pointed out in Chapter 1, every word in our vocabulary is colored by our experiences. Consequently, the results of an experiment by one scientist cannot be presented in such a way that they will have, ultimately, the same meaning to another. Although the difference may be infinitesimal, and therefore insignificant, it nevertheless exists. "Pure" science, then, is a matter of degree and not of kind.

The scientific method is the methodical means by which the data are accumulated and tested. It includes observation, the collection of pertinent materials, establishing and testing hypotheses, drawing conclusions, and classifying the findings. The body of knowledge must be reliable, valid, and organized. Reliable knowledge is that which can be verified. It means that if another examiner makes the same study under the same circumstances, the results will be the same. Valid knowledge is that which measures what is intended. The knowledge is organized through classification of the findings.

## LEVELS OF CERTAINTY IN SCIENCE

There are three levels of certainty in science. The hypothesis represents the most questionable of these levels. It is a statement of opinion formulated for testing purposes in using the scientific method. The hypothesis is not a pure guess, but is based upon some support. For example, the hypothetical statement that "there is closer companionship between father and son in urban areas than in rural areas" is supported by a comparison of the family types in each of the areas. Social distance is more likely maintained between father and son in the rural patriarchal family for disciplinary purposes. In this type of family, the mother usually acts as the intermediary between father and son. In the urban areas, however, the family is more likely to be democratic and the association of father and son is likely to be personal and direct. The hypothesis is then tested. If the educated guess proves to be correct, the hypothesis is supported. If the evidence fails to support the statement, the hypothesis is then rejected. A rejected hypothesis is just as valuable to science as an accepted one, because it usually rules out any further investigation of that particular area of exploration.

If the hypothesis is substantiated, and is verified by additional studies, by the same or other examiners, then the theory can be established that "the democratic form of family structure cultivates father and son companionship." A theory is simply an explanation. In the example just given, the democratic family explains the reason for companionship between father and son. A theory is a statement with substantial supporting evidence. The more support a theory receives, the stronger it becomes. There are many theories attempting to explain the creation of man. In fundamentalist religious groups, the Biblical theory is strongly supported. In scientific circles, and among some of the intellectual elite, the evolutionary theory draws strong support. With each turn of the archeological spade, this theory appears to be gaining strength.

The hypothesis has some support, the theory has more support, and scientific law has the most support. A scientific law is a statement that is true beyond any doubt in the light of present-day knowledge. Newton's law of gravitation illustrates this point. To step off of a second-floor balcony without the benefit of a stairway, or any other technological support, will cause one to fall at a rapid rate of descent. Likewise, the law of the universe controls the heavenly bodies that move in a changeless pattern, which enables interested viewers to look forward to seeing Halley's Comet every seventy-five years after it has made its regular tour of the universe.

One reason for the questionable scientific status of sociology is because human behavior is the main focus of its study. Most social scientists would argue that since the innate drives of individuals are conditioned by culture, various persons will react in different ways to the same stimulus. For example, suppose a pollster trying to determine the outcome of an election asked the question, "Whom do you intend to vote for in the election?" One respondent may not answer the question because it is a personal matter. Another respondent may be offended and deliberately give the wrong answer as an expression of his irritation. A third respondent, who has no intention of voting, but feels it is his patriotic duty, may express his intention to vote for one of the other candidates, rather than being embarrassed by admitting he does not intend to exercise his legal rights.

On the other hand, animals of the same species, driven by instinct, will react in similar ways to the same stimulus. A gun-shot, or a loud bang, would cause most rabbits to scurry for protected cover.

Although there may be some question about the validity of sociological knowledge based upon individual responses, statistical knowledge in sociology is reliable. Scientific sociological studies have made it possible to predict, with a high degree of accuracy, the number of marriages that will end in divorce in certain geographical areas or under certain conditions. Because studies show common characteristics in successful, as well as unsuccessful, marriages, sociologists can predict the probability of success in instances where the common characteristics are favorable. These anticipated developments, however, are generalities, which means that the outcome of a particular marriage cannot be predicted. Some marriages in which the mates conform to the ideal pattern of a successful marriage end up in a divorce court, whereas some couples break every rule in the book and still form a lifelong, happy, marital relationship.

However questionable sociological knowledge may be, sociology qualifies as a science because it uses the scientific method and its accumulated knowledge is organized and reliable. Sociological knowledge is scant for two major reasons. One is that the discipline is comparatively young, dating from the middle of the nineteenth century. The emphasis on research in the United States has a life span of a little more than a half-century. From this point of view, sociology is still in its infancy compared to such a field as biology which has been recognized as a science for more than two thousand years.

The other reason for the dearth of sociological knowledge is the painstaking methods of, and the time and expense involved in, scientific research in the field. As an example, one field study in Washington County, Kentucky (by one of the authors of this book), was designed to determine how farm practices were spread. It seems that this would be a simple task. Just ask this farmer and that one how they learned when and how to plant, cultivate, and harvest corn. The study was not that simple. It required a twenty-five page questionnaire, or schedule, which took almost an hour to complete. In addition to the work involved, to get a busy farmer to take an hour to give the required information to a stranger formed a barrier to garnering the knowledge.

Sociology in the present day is generally recognized as a social, or a behavioral, science. Perhaps these qualifying terms appease those who are reluctant to classify it as a pure science. Nevertheless, since sociology uses the scientific method, and since its comparatively meager body of knowledge is organized and to some extent reliable, it can be labeled an adolescent science without the qualifying terms of social or behavioral. If the determining criteria of classifying sociology as a science include the accuracy of prediction, as mentioned above, then as sociological research methods are refined, its body of knowledge will become more reliable. As it expands, the discipline will become more fully recognized as a pure science.

Interest in the study of human relationships dates back far beyond the birthdate of sociology. For over two thousand years, social thinkers have been curious about the behavior of human beings. Plato's *Republic*, based upon his knowledge of human behavior, presents a detailed program for developing an orderly society. Augustin's *City of God*, written over five hundred years ago, is another attempt to explain and control human behavior. Many other ancient, as well as medieval, social thinkers were concerned with explaining human behavior. The difference between these early efforts to understand society and those of sociologists in modern times is that sociologists use the scientific method to study human behavior.

Interest in understanding society was heightened by a number of staggering developments in European societies during the nineteenth century. One of the major developments was the accelerated pace of the Industrial Revolution as it shifted into high gear, about the beginning of that century. Industrialization caused a mass exodus of rural dwellers to the cities, which depleted the manpower of the countryside. It also placed a heavy strain upon the social structure of the cities. The social institutions were not designed to absorb the heavy burdens placed upon them by the rural to urban migration. As a result, in the cities, slums developed, poverty became rampant, and order turned into chaos. In France, some of these social problems developed as a consequence of the French Revolution that ushered in the nineteenth century.

A number of the social thinkers of that day were coping with the problems developing as a result of this societal upheaval. One of them in France, Auguste Comte, developed the thought that the social problems should be attacked in an orderly fashion such as that used by pure science. About the middle of the nineteenth century, he published *Cours de Philosophie Positive*. His book was translated in the latter part of that century as *The Course of Positive Philosophy*. This work gave birth to the method that distinguished social thinkers from sociologists.

Comte held that thought developed in three stages. In the first stage, he argued that explanations of events in the earliest forms of society leaned heavily upon theology. According to this line of thought, the preliterate would believe that the "man in the moon" was placed there by God for burning brush on Sunday. In the present day, he is placed there by space rockets. In the second stage of thought, Comte held that with the accumulation of knowledge, explanations of natural phenomena were based upon reasoning or logic. According to him, the more advanced societies of his time were on the brink of the third stage, which he labeled positivistic philosophy. This stage was to be created by the application of the scientific method to study human behavior. In so doing, Comte advanced interest in human behavior from social thought, based upon the deductive method, to sociology based upon the inductive method. The deductive method starts with the general and goes to the specific. An example would be, "All believers in God are good." Since this person believes in God, s/he is good. The inductive method, on the other hand, starts with the specific and goes to the general. For example, if this person believes in God, he is a moral man. If that person believes in God, she is a moral woman. It then follows that others who believe in God are also moral. Therefore, all believers in God are moral persons.

Because of his contribution to the field, Comte is sometimes referred to as the father or founder of sociology, as previously mentioned. It is not possible to give full credit to a single individual for, or assign a particular date as the origin of, a significant change in the trend of thought. No matter how catastrophic the shift in thought may be, those credited with founding every major movement have drawn heavily upon existing ideas. They have just rearranged the patterns. No matter how competent the leader, or how pregnant the idea or ideology, the time must be right, meaning that social conditions have to make the potential adherents receptive to such a change, or the movement will die aborning or in early infancy. Many examples of this could be given, but suffice it to say that Comte conceived and gave birth to his new approach to the study of society in a time when different methods were desperately needed for this purpose. Social turbulence was battering society on all sides. His "positivism" was well received as a possible means of understanding and solving the prevalent social problems.

No matter who is responsible for the origin or the success of this new discipline; sociology, as well as other social sciences, plays a major role in modern society. More emphasis needs to be placed upon the study of human relationships in order to narrow the gap between the rapid development of technology and the means to control it. Defensive and offensive missiles are poised in major nations to pinpoint targets thousands of miles away and with a single strike wipe out major segments of the population. National leaders are nervous, and the populous is drenched in fear, because adequate controls are not available to avert such a catastrophe. High-powered automobiles race down the highways needlessly snuffing out the lives of thousands of persons each year because effective social controls are not in operation.

It is good to know how to predict with unerring accuracy that 200,000 years from now the earth's physical environment will be affected by the harmonious movements in the boundless universe. It is better to know the means by which more harmonious relationships can be developed within our own social environment. It is good to know how to change the course of a satellite millions of miles in space by the touch of a button. It is better to have the know-how to redirect the life of an individual in such a way that a social liability is converted into a social asset.

Sociology is one of the disciplines designed to improve social conditions. A fuller understanding of this particular scientific field can be gained by logically organizing the fundamental concepts into a structure in which the study of sociology may be framed. Such a basic system may be used for purposes of classification of additional sociological knowledge and as a point of orientation for future elaboration. An orientation of this nature will serve the beginning student as a standard by which the levels of abstraction can be changed and prevent the confusion of these levels. It will also provide a referent which will keep the student constantly aware of empirical knowledge. Clear thinking results when tangible events are tied into our thoughts.

## VARIABLES IN SOCIOLOGICAL RESEARCH

Variables are indispensable tools in the sociological researcher's kit. The selection of certain variables defines the problem and the findings are determined by a study of the variables. A variable is anything that changes, or is different, over time, by localities, between or among individuals, and between or among social groups. Industrialization is an example of a variable changing over time as well as in different regional localities. In most college classrooms, sex, age, academic class, academic standing, religious belief, and family background are some of the variables existing among individuals. Academic class is a variable existing between a freshman introductory course and a senior seminar. The subject matter, the degree of specialization, and the size of the class are examples of other variables between the two social groups. In sociological studies, variables are not limited to differences in cultural characteristics. Studies involving the effects of the climate on geographical terrain, along with other things, are variables in a sociological research project.

In some sociological research, certain variables are fixed or held constant in order to eliminate their influence on the variable under study. For example, to hold the academic class constant, the researcher would make the study in either the freshman or senior class. Then, whatever variation there may be in the subject variable it could not be caused by the academic class difference. If the researcher wanted to hold sex constant as well, then the study would include only males or females in the senior or the freshman class being studied. This is to say that variables can be explained only with other variables, not with constants. Since the sex and the class are the same for all respondents, that is held constant, the change in the variable being studied cannot be explained by them. It cannot be said that the grade varies because this student is a freshman, if that is the class selected, because all of the respondents are freshmen.

Variables can be either independent or dependent. The independent variable wields an influence over the dependent variable, so it is recognized as the cause. The change in the dependent variable depends upon the action of the independent variable. The same variable can be dependent, or the effect, in one situation and independent, or the cause, in another. This can be illustrated by using the student grade as the dependent variable which is dependent, usually, by the amount of effort applied by the student. On the other hand, the grade is an independent variable because the ranking of the student in the academic placement system is dependent upon the grade point average.

Sometimes it is difficult to identify a variable as either dependent or independent. An air conditioner is a dependent variable in the sense that the increase in the room temperature activates the thermostat causing the air conditioner to turn on. As the air conditioner runs, it is an independent variable causing the room temperature to drop. The identification assigned to the variable is determined by the purpose of the study. If the interest is in ranking the efficiency of the air conditioner at different room temperatures, the air conditioner is the dependent variable. Its efficiency is affected by different settings. If the study is intended to show how effectively the air conditioner cools the room at different thermostat settings, then it is the independent variable, causing the room temperature to drop at different rates according to the setting of the thermostat.

If a change in the independent variable causes a change in the dependent variable, then a causal relationship exists between the two, which can be either positive or negative. A positive relationship exists when the two variables change in the same direction at the same time, such as when the divorce rate increases as the marriage rate increases or the divorce rate decreases as the marriage rate decreases. A negative relationship exists when one variable decreases as the other one increases. As the divorce rate goes up, the marriage rate goes down. The rate of change in one variable does not have to be to the same degree as in the other variable.

The degree of change in the relationship is measured by the correlation coefficient. For example, if the marriage rate increased ten percent from 1981 to 1982 and the divorce rate increased at the same rate during that period, then this forms the strongest possible positive relationship which reveals a correlation coefficient of +1.0. If, on the other hand, the marriage rate decreased at the same rate that the divorce rate increased during the same period, then this forms the strongest possible negative relationship revealed by a correlation coefficient of -1.0. In other words, the correlation coefficient ranges from 0.0 to 1.0, either in the positive or negative direction. The positive or negative sign in front of the numeral has nothing to do with the strength of the relationship. It merely indicates the direction, either positive or negative. It is the numerical figure that indicates the strength of the relationship. This means that a correlation coefficient of +.85 is no stronger than a correlation coefficient of -.85. Furthermore, a correlation coefficient of -.85 indicates a stronger relationship than a +.65.

Even though the correlation coefficient shows the strongest possible relationship, +1.0 or -1.0, this does not necessarily mean that a change in one variable causes the other to change to the same degree, and in the direction indicated by the sign. The relationship may be purely coincidental. To illustrate this point, if the number of cigarettes sold in Spokane, Washington, increases by ten percent one year and the price of onions in Bermuda increases by ten percent that same year, this does not necessarily mean that one variable caused the other to change. In Bermuda, however, the increase in the price of onions may provide the means for the onion grower, or the merchant, to buy more cigarettes causing the purchase rate to rise. The function of the correlation coefficient, then, is to show the strength of the relationship between two variables, indicating whether or not further study is warranted to determine whether the relationship is causal or whether it is coincidental.

In addition to coincidence, there are three other possible explanations for a positive or negative relationship revealed by a correlation coefficient. One of these is that "A" may cause "B," or the increase in the marriage rate may cause an increase in the divorce rate. Or, "B" may cause "A" to change, which means that the increase in the divorce rate may cause the marriage rate to increase. The third possible explanation is that "C," some outside influence, may cause both "A" and "B" to increase. As an example, studies show that both the marriage rate and the divorce rate increase during wartime or during an economic boom.

## THE CONTINUUM

The continuum is a viable measuring instrument in determining the qualities of a variable. As stated in the introduction, the comparative approach is used in this book. The sociological continuum makes possible a comparison of variables which reveals the predominant characteristics in that particular variable creating the possibility of placing it in one category or another in a classification system. It should be noted that the lines separating the various niches in a classification system are arbitrarily drawn. As an example, suppose students were being classified as above average, or below average, and that a numerical grade from 75.00000 to 84.99999 is assigned as the grade range of the average student. Theoretically, a student with a grade of 84.99999 is classified as average, while a student with a grade of 1/100,000th of a point higher, 85.00000, is classified as above average. For all practical purposes, there is no significant difference in the academic performance of the two, but the arbitrary demarcation has placed them in widely differing brackets.

A continuum is a connecting line between two imaginary extremes. These two extremes cannot exist in actuality or the measuring instrument is of no value. The continuum can be likened to a college examination which is difficult enough so that no one can make a hundred, and with at least one question simple enough for everyone to answer, so that no one gets a zero. The questions in between would be graduated on the basis of difficulty. The students can then be evaluated on the basis of mastering the material because they are all somewhere between the two extremes. A fourth grade examination in geography would not be helpful in evaluating fourth grade geography teachers in a large city where the same text is being used, because most, if not all of them, would make a hundred. Neither would a high level examination in any particular field in graduate school serve as an evaluation of fourth graders in that subject because all, or most, of them would get a zero.

Perhaps the usefulness of the continuum as a measuring device can be demonstrated with a simple illustration by classifying communities on the basis of rural characteristics and urban characteristics. To keep the illustration simple, suppose only three distinguishing, objective characteristics are selected to determine the placement of communities "A," "B," "C," and "D" along the rural-urban continuum. In community "A," the predominant occupation is farming, the land is mainly acquired through inheritance, and most of the families are large. Since all of these are rural characteristics, community "A" would be placed near the rural extreme of the continuum. If community "B" is predominantly rural according to two of the three characteristics, then it would also be placed in the rural section, but closer to the middle dividing line than community "A." If community "C" has only one of the rural characteristics, it would be predominantly urban, but not to the extent of community "D" which has none of the rural characteristics. The illustration is oversimplified because community "A" which is predominantly rural as far as all three characteristics are concerned, may have only fifty-five percent of the labor force in farming, while community "B" with only two of the rural characteristics predominantly may have ninety-five percent of its labor force in farming. Without going into details, adjustments are made to allow for such rating difficulties.

## NUMERICAL MEASURES OF SOCIAL PHENOMENA

In popular usage, the numerical average is considered a representative figure, which is derived by totaling all of the quantities and dividing the sum by the number of items in the distribution. In scientific usage, the result is referred to as the arithmetic mean. The arithmetic mean, in itself, may be misleading. An exaggerated example of a distortion of this nature is shown by averaging the income of ninety-nine factory workers making $10,000 annually with the $1,000,000 income of the owner. The total income is $1,990,000, divided by 100 gives an average income of $19,900. An unemployed person seeing the figure may conclude that this area is a good place to look for work. Also, the businessman concludes that his higher priced product would find a good market there.

In order to get a more accurate numerical picture, two additional measures need to be applied. One is the median, which is the mid-point in a number of figures arranged in numerical order. In other words, the median divides the numerical data into two equal parts with half of the items being higher and the other half being lower than the numerical quantity of the median. In the example given before, the median would be the 50th item which would be $10,000. The other measure necessary to get an accurate numerical picture is the mode, which is the quantity, or item, which appears most frequently in the distribution of figures. Again, in the illustration, $10,000 appears ninety-nine times more frequently than the other figure in the illustration, making it the mode in the example, and the distribution is skewed.

When the mean, median, and mode are identical, the distribution results in a normal curve. Some professors use this method in their grading system. The grades are distributed evenly on the different levels, with as many "F's" as "A's," the same number of "D's" as "B's," and the average grade "C" representing the mode. When the results are plotted on a graph, the distribution forms a symmetrical bell shape.

## THE SOCIOLOGICAL RESEARCH SAMPLE

Sampling is a technique used in research to curtail the cost and the expenditure of time and effort to survey the individuals who can reveal information regarding the subject being studied. In sociological research, it is a process which enables the investigator to view the characteristics of a large contingent of persons without interviewing each of the members. A valid sample is one in which those selected are representative of the whole group involved in the area of interest being studied. Those selected are the respondents, and the "whole group" is referred to as the population.

There are two critical selections that are necessary in gathering data for a sociological study through sampling. The first of these is the selection of the population from which the sample is to be drawn. This chore is dependent upon the definition of the research problem. Suppose, for example, the focus of the study is dating practices of teenagers. The population would have to consist of those acquainted with the behavior patterns of those in this age group. Therefore, limiting the field of possible respondents to a retirement center in Florida and selecting the members from every fifth household for interviews, would not be too productive. Likewise, a typical picture of the patriarchal traits in the family of an oil well driller could not be accurately drawn by interviewing bathers on the beach, or residents of Miami Beach, Florida. Just as the sample has to be representative of the research population unit under study, the population selection has to be representative of the general society.

The high school provides a fertile field for teenage studies. This still represents a broad scope. To get an accurate account of dating practices of teenagers, samples would have to be drawn from a wide variety of high schools. The schools in the ghettos of New York are different in many ways from those in an elite suburb of the same city. Those in the rural areas of Mississippi, or any other state, are different from schools in Northern Virginia. Consolidated schools differ from either rural or urban schools. Dozens of other comparisons could be made.

A logical assumption could be made that since there is a wide variation in high school enrollments, the dating practices would differ among teenage students in these schools. Hence, it is impractical to attempt to draw a typical picture of the entire high school population in the United States. Usually, the study is narrowed to a particular segment of the high school (in this case) population. Consequently, the topic becomes more specific such as, "Dating Practices of High School Teenagers in the Ghettos of New York." When studies are made of practices in ghettos in other cities, or in different types of schools, comparisons can be made and used for whatever purposes intended. The researcher's population then becomes the segment of the high school population being studied.

After delineating the population, the researcher then gives attention to the size of the sample. The size of the sample is not the main determining factor in the accuracy of the findings, but it does vary according to the nature of the study. There is a negative relationship between the homogeneity of the selected population and the size of the sample. That is, the sample taken in a population with similar characteristics, such as isolated rural areas in the United States, would not have to be as large as one dealing with the same practice in the population mixture, or the heterogeneity, of a large city. The size of the sample is also dependent upon the techniques used in gathering the data. This will be illustrated after a discussion of the sampling methods.

The random sample is a frequently used technique, which makes certain that every individual in the population has an equal opportunity of being selected. This procedure is similar to drawings for door prizes where stubs of tickets are put into a container of some kind, thoroughly mixed, and the number is selected by someone not able to see the contents. To be a pure random sample, the stubs have to be thoroughly mixed, otherwise the stubs of the late-comers' tickets have a better chance of being drawn than those who arrived early.

The first number in a series to be used in a random sample is determined in the same way. If the sample is to consist of ten percent of the population, then ten balls, or cubes, or slips of paper, numbered from one to ten are placed in a container, mixed, and one number is drawn. If the number six is drawn, for example, this marks the beginning point in the selection. From whatever list of names being used to select the sample, the sixth, sixteenth, twenty-sixth, and every tenth number following is used to compose the sample. If the first number is not selected by chance, the researcher arbitrarily rules out the possibility of selecting any name of the other ninety percent of the population. If another study is to be made using the same list of names, and the number six happens to be drawn again at random, the same persons are included in the sample. If the number is not used as a beginning point in the selection, because it is the same number that was used in establishing the first sample, then the researcher arbitrarily denies ten percent of the persons whose names are in the list an equal opportunity of being drawn.

The telephone provides a quick and simple method for gathering information for a study. The random sample selected from the telephone directory is valid in some studies, but for others it is distorted. If the purpose is to determine the effectiveness of the telephone in maintaining family relationships, then the use of the telephone directory does not result in a distorted sample. Even then, caution should be used to select only non-business telephone users, because very few business phones are used for this purpose. If the purpose of the study is to determine the life-style of the average U.S. resident, then the telephone sample is distorted because the life-style of those who can afford a telephone differs from that of those who cannot afford one.

A random sample taken in the center of a shopping mall in the middle of the day to get the public's opinion on a particular civic matter is distorted because it denies most of those at work an equal opportunity of being selected. If the purpose is to get the opinion of shoppers regarding inflation then it is a valid sample. Many other examples could be given to illustrate the difference between a valid and an invalid random sample. To emphasize the point made earlier, the distinction between the two types of samples is the degree of opportunity available for each member of the population to be selected. In a pure random sample, any one individual has the same chance of being selected as any other member.

A stratified-random sample refines the pure random sample by providing a technique that insures a more typical picture of the population. This is a proportionate sample in which members within various categories of the population are represented in the same proportion in the sample. Within the proportionate categories of the population, respondents are selected at random. For example, suppose the purpose of the study is to describe the characteristics of a typical student on a particular university campus with a total of 3,700 students—2,000 freshmen, 1,000 sophomores, 500 juniors, and 200 seniors. In such a distribution, using the pure random sample, the likelihood of drawing a freshman is ten times as great as the likelihood of drawing a senior. The chance of drawing a freshman or a sophomore is fifteen times as great as the chance of drawing a senior. Consequently, in a pure random sample, there is a strong possibility that no senior would be included in the sample, which would distort the typical picture.

By using the stratified-random sample, the researcher makes certain that seniors will be represented in the same proportion as they appear in the total student distribution. If a ten percent sample is desired, then ten percent of the students in each academic class will be selected at random. The results of such a selection are shown in Figure 2.1.

There is a much greater possibility of getting a representative sample by using the stratified-random sample than by using the pure random sample. However, even this type of sampling does not guarantee a fully representative sample because of variations on each of the academic levels. There may be more females than males in one or all of the classes. Furthermore, the senior class will possibly have more students in the upper social class because their parents can afford to keep them in school for a longer period than the parents of those in a lower social class.

Because of the certainty that all categories will be represented, the stratified-random sample can be smaller than the pure random sample. In any case, the size of the sample is not as important to the validity of the sample as is the technique used. The U.S. Census uses a twenty percent sample to get detailed information from individuals. Normally, researchers follow this pattern in selecting samples for their studies.

---

FIGURE 2.1: Distribution of Total Student Enrollment in a 10% Stratified Random Sample

|            | Number of Students Enrolled | Number of Students in 10% Sample |
|------------|-----------------------------|----------------------------------|
| Seniors    | 200                         | 20                               |
| Juniors    | 500                         | 50                               |
| Sophomores | 1,000                       | 100                              |
| Freshmen   | 2,000                       | 200                              |
| Total      | 3,700                       | 370                              |

---

After defining the problem and selecting the sample, the next step in the research project is to gather the data. The information may be gathered through participant-observation or non-participant observation. In the former method, the researcher identifies with the group to be studied enabling him to get a more complete account of the subject matter than can be had by a nonparticipant observer. The investigator can either participate in the group anonymously or reveal his identity. If he does not reveal his position or the purpose involved to the group, then the ethical question of whether or not the information was gathered through deceit arises. If the researcher does make himself and the purpose known, then the behavior of the member of the group may be affected by this knowledge.

The nonparticipant observer has the option of gathering the information through the use of a questionnaire or by interviewing the respondents. The questionnaire has a number of advantages over the interview. It can be mailed to respondents or distributed in a classroom for students to take home and bring back, or it can be distributed and filled out in a public place, while the researcher waits for the respondent to complete the form, thus saving the investigator the time of conducting an interview. The disadvantage of these methods is the high attrition rate involved. A researcher can expect about a twenty-five percent return of the questionnaires mailed to respondents.

The main advantage of a questionnaire over the interview is the degree of objectivity. This difference could be illustrated by comparing an examination composed of true or false questions to one containing discussion questions. Suppose a portion of the materials covered prior to the examination dealt with the relationships within a patriarchal family, and one of the questions asked the students to discuss these relationships. In the presentation of the lectures, the instructor had emphasized the importance of the dominance-submission pattern of interaction, the role of the mother as the intermediary, and filial piety. On the examination, he ranks the value of each part of this thirty-point question equally (ten points for each part). If a student fails to mention the dominant-submission pattern in answering the question, the grade would be lowered to twenty points for that part of the examination. Further, suppose that the instructor became ill and was not able to give or grade the examination, and the Department Chair assigned a graduate student to carry out these responsibilities. The graduate student considered the dominance-submission pattern as the core of the question, and if this aspect were not included, the answer was practically worthless. So, in grading the papers, he assigned a value of 20 points to this aspect of the relationship and five points to each of the two other aspects. Thus, in the graduate student's evaluation, the student leaving out the dominance-submission aspect was given ten points credit by the graduate student for the answer to the question, compared to the twenty points he would have received if the instructor had graded the exam. The subjective influence caused a variation in the evaluation of the answer.

The true or false type of test breaks the question down into smaller details. For example, each aspect of the discussion question just illustrated would be broken down into more detailed parts. Such a true or false statement as "the dominance-submission pattern of interaction is prevalent in the patriarchal family relationships" is one detail of a patriarchal family. Perhaps five similar statements would be made for each of the three parts in the discussion question. Regardless of the grader's subjective opinion, then, the answers would be evaluated on an objective basis.

The interview technique is carried out on a face-to-face oral basis, which differs from that used with the questionnaire. Through the personal contact, such things as the facial expressions, gestures, and hesitancy in answering the questions, on the part of the respondent, may provide the interviewer with additional insights regarding the answers, making them more complete. Such expressions may also bias the interviewer's interpretation of the response.

There are two types of interviews. One is structured and the other is unstructured. The unstructured interview is carried out in two ways. The first is by note taking in the presence of the respondent, while the second method is to jot down notes immediately following the interview, but not in the presence of the respondent. Individuals responding to questions are a little reluctant to reveal everything when the answers are being written down in their presence. Somehow, this represents a permanent record, whether the interviewer uses all of the materials or not. Consequently, the response is not as likely to be complete as when the interviewer waits until the interview and the face-to-face contact have been terminated before making any notes.

The structured interview is one in which the questions are written into a schedule with space provided to record the respondent's answers. The questions should be asked in the same sequence so the respondent's train of thought will be similar. The responses are more limited than in an unstructured interview, but there is less opportunity for bias in the use of this technique.

No matter which method is used, caution is required to frame the questions in such a way as to avoid misleading the informant or distorting the findings. Emotionally tinged terms such as upper-crust, social climbers, and the dregs of society, or the emotionally laden terms such as Commies, Japs, and White Trash, should be avoided. Limited response questions, like the true or false statements illustrated previously, should not be used. In determining the range of income, for example, the question should be open-ended. A question such as, "Is your annual income $5,000 to $10,000, $10,000 to $25,000, or $25,000 to $50,000?" leaves no opportunity for responses for those with incomes under $5,000 or over $50,000. Although few respondents would need the additional brackets, they, nevertheless, should be provided for those possibilities. A question for which there is more than one answer should not be asked. An example of this type of question would be, "Do you think that bars and lunch rooms should close at midnight?" Although some respondents may think that bars should close at midnight, they may, however, feel lunch rooms should stay open all night. Also, do not ask questions to which the answer is obvious. It is evident how every student will answer the question, "Would you rather take the examination or flunk the course?"

The purpose in presenting materials in this chapter has been to briefly consider the scientific aspects of sociology and the measures and procedures used in research studies. In the next chapter, scientific measures and procedures used in sociological research will be applied to the field study of attitudes toward intercultural marriages involving Chinese and American-Caucasians.

# 3

## Intercultural Marriage:
## Attitudes of Chinese College Students
## toward Marriage with
## American-Caucasians

Defining a problem in sociological research is a process of gradually reducing a broad field of material into smaller and smaller areas until the effort is focused on a manageable unit. The field study presented in this chapter is a product of such a process.

The first step in this procedure is to select a general area of interest from the expansive knowledge available in the particular field of concentration. The family was selected as the broad area of interest in the present study, which was further narrowed to a consideration of the Chinese and American families. Further reductions in the scope of interest resulted in singling out one of the processes by which families are established, mate selection, as it functions in Taiwan.

### INTRODUCTION

Taiwan provides a unique social milieu for the study of intercultural marriages. For one thing, ". . . Taiwan is a part of China, a natural offshoot, a present incarnation of a marvelously complex tradition" (Ahern & Gates, 1981, p. 7). The firmly established social structure of mainland China provided the framework from which the Republic of China has developed as an independent nation, albeit with the reunification of the vast mainland country as one of its primary objectives. The major social institutions imported to Taiwan, however, have been geared to maintaining a unified China, not recapturing it. Since major social institutions are intricately intertwined, with change in one affecting the whole social structure, Taiwanese political goals have had to be adjusted to meet social demands.

The twin processes of industrialization and urbanization have resulted in widespread changes in the Republic of China. First, the redistribution of the population has created a distinctly different way of life between rural and urban areas. Second, formal education is more essential in an industrial society than in one based upon an agrarian economy. Third, the increase in income that accompanies industrialization alerts life styles. A survey of the extant literature describing the development of Taiwan reveals that all three of the foregoing manifestations of social change have recently occurred and are still under way.

It should be noted that at the time the governmental center of Nationalist China was shifted to Taiwan (1949), the newly formed country consisted of a traditional Chinese society. The phenomenal changes to that traditional social structure, toward a modern society, have occurred in a startlingly brief span.

This study of intercultural marriage, then, is couched in the politically oriented ideological struggles, which were often fraught with experimental maneuvers, to achieve the nation's goals. Undeniably, Taiwan has experienced "repeated political redefinition" during the twentieth century (Ahern & Gates, 1981, p. 13); consequently, the political structure has become somewhat flexible, enabling the government to cope with the new demands being made upon it.

The patriarchal extended family, deeply imbedded in the social structure of traditional China, is another element of the social context in which the present study is placed. Traditionally, the authority of the male head of the kinship group was unquestioned. The independent peasants, however, have not always granted the political leaders the same degree of authority. In fact, Welty (1984) argues that the government has frequently been regarded with deep suspicion. The differences in the extent of authority in these two major social institutions—extended family and the national political system—and their differing degrees of structural rigidity provide the study on intercultural marriages with two differential perspectives.

The field study on intercultural marriages is more of a preliminary excursion into the area of intercultural marriages rather than a thoroughly exhaustive effort, for it raises more questions than it answers. Nonetheless, the study presents some valuable findings that are based on more than adequate quasi-scientific support. For example, the survey of literature available reflects the trends and shows the impact of social change on the major social institutions in the Republic of China. The study is especially useful in comparing the attitudes of parents with those of their children and in charting the effects of social change on these attitudes. An additional contribution of the study is its documentation of present-day attitudes of Chinese college students toward intercultural marriages with American-Caucasians.

The study of Chinese intercultural marriage is narrowed to the possibilities of marriage with American-Caucasians for a number of reasons. For one thing, the population of the United States is predominantly Caucasian. Additionally, for maximal cultural contrast, marriages between native Chinese and American-born Chinese were excluded from the study, as such marriages would not be considered interracial by those who still maintain that there is more than one race of homo sapiens. The third reason for narrowing the focus is to limit the number of variables in the comparison and, thus, to minimize confusion on the part of respondents in completing the questionnaire.

The classification of the materials on the basis of the three aforementioned major social changes provides a foundation for the three hypotheses developed in this study. The first hypothesis posits that the attitudes of the most highly educated Chinese social group are more favorably inclined toward intermarriage between Chinese and U.S. Caucasians than the attitudes of those from lower educational levels. The second hypothesis postulates that the attitudes of college students in the highest income bracket are more favorable toward intermarriage between Chinese and U.S. Caucasians than the attitudes of those in the lowest income bracket. Finally, the third hypothesis maintains that the attitudes of college students from urban areas are more favorable toward intermarriage between Chinese and U.S. Caucasians than the attitudes of those from rural areas.

The educational measures used in the study distinguish respondents on the basis of education, sorting the respondents into freshmen and seniors. Although the three-year educational gap may appear to be insignificant, quite a bit of sophistication takes place between the freshmen and senior levels in college, especially in Taiwan. This is particularly true in a society that is as family-oriented as the Chinese culture is. One may contend that in such a society, the thoughts of pre-college students strongly reflect family interests. As their horizons are broadened through college education, however, personal and extra-familial interests become more and more important, especially in the selection of a marital partner.

The second educational measure is based upon the number of years of schooling completed by the parents. The highest educational level includes parents who both have a college degree. One parent with a college degree and the other with a high school education, and parents both having a high school education, are placed in the middle category. A parent with a high school education married to a mate with less education is placed in the low educational category, as are those parents with both having less than a seventh-grade education.

The arbitrary dividing line set between those in the higher and those in the lower income brackets is placed at an annual income of NT $200,000, which at the time this study was conducted was approximately U.S. $5,000. This is around 50% higher than the per capita income for Taiwan at the time data for this study were collected (June, 1985). The estimate of NT $200,000 is based upon the reasoning that parents who can afford a college education for their children have a higher per capita income than those who cannot.

The varying life-styles in rural and urban areas affect the attitudes toward intercultural marriage. The rural-urban classification of students is based upon the arbitrary population figure of 2,500. College students reared in population centers of 2,500 or above are classified as urban, and those reared in areas of dispersed population, or in villages of less than 2,500, are classified as rural.

## QUESTIONNAIRE CONTENT

The first section of the questionnaire deals with background data such as the respondents' academic class, marital status, and whether the place of residence is in a rural or an urban area. This section also solicits information on the respondents' family background. Parents' occupations, educational levels, and income brackets, as reported by the students, are the specific items intended to assist in analyzing the students' attitude toward intermarriage. Additionally, two questions are framed to determine whether or not the student is the offspring of a mixed marriage.

The second section of the questionnaire is designed to reveal the attitude of the Chinese respondents toward intermarriage with American-Caucasians. Although it is assumed that most of the students are yet unmarried and that the majority plan to marry within their own ethnic group, an important part of the questionnaire attempts to assess the respondents' willingness to enter into intercultural, interreligious, or international marriages. Another topic covered by that section of the questionnaire is the attitudes of friends toward the respondent dating or marrying an American-Caucasian. A question is framed, also, to determine the students' preferences, if any, besides their own race in the selection of marital partners. Other questions deal with the respondents' preferences regarding place of residence, cultural traits of offspring, and comparison of perceptions of Chinese and American-Caucasian mates. Questions involving factors of adjustment to such a marriage are also posed.

The third area probed in the study considers the influence of the family on intercultural mate selection. There, an effort is made to determine the degree of parental control over the respondent and the attitudes of the parents, according to the respondent, regarding the marriage of their offspring to an American-Caucasian. Other inquiries are designed to attempt to establish the degree to which the American-Caucasian mate would be integrated into the respondent's family of orientation.

A key question on social change constitutes the last section of the questionnaire and is designed to elicit the opinion of the respondent as to whether the attitudes toward Chinese/American-Caucasian marriages is changing in Taiwan.

## QUESTIONNAIRE DISTRIBUTION

Many developments (i.e., travel, student exchanges, and influence of the media) have narrowed the racial and cultural gaps between the Republic of China and the United States and have made intercultural marriages more acceptable in the present than in the past. Intercultural exchanges, higher educational levels, occupational propinquity, and compatibility of interests have contributed toward a greater tolerance of racial and cultural differences. In other words, social nurture is becoming more important in mate selection than biological inheritance. In fact, the mates crossing over race lines in marriage may be more compatible, because of common cultural characteristics, than mates transcending social class lines.

As a means of determining the attitudes of Chinese college students toward intermarriage with American-Caucasians, selective samples were drawn from seven different Taiwan universities. In an effort to make the sample as representative as possible, at the university level, different types of universities in various geographical areas of Taiwan were selected. The urban college student samples were drawn from two major cities, Taipei in the north and Taichung in the central part of Taiwan. Two universities in each of these cities were selected, accounting for 58% of those who responded to the questionnaires and returned them. The remainder (42%) of the questionnaires returned came from students in two Changhua universities in the central section of Taiwan and from one university in the southern part of the island, located in Tainan.

Representative classes (one or two) of students from each of these seven universities were selected, and the professors of those classes were asked to distribute, oversee, and collect the completed questionnaires. As a result of this procedure, 549 questionnaires were distributed and all were returned.

## DESCRIPTIVE ANALYSIS OF THE FINDINGS

Of the 549 questionnaires that were returned, only 515 were included in the analysis. The other thirty-four were excluded because several questions were left unanswered. Although one or two questions were left unanswered by ninety-nine of the participants, these questionnaires were included in the analysis since they were still considered of value in the study. A more detailed description of their characteristics and attitudes follows.

## EDUCATION, INCOME, AND PLACE OF RESIDENCE

Of the 515 respondents, 303 were freshmen and 212 seniors. On the parental income level, 280 are classified as low and 212 as high, with twenty-three not answering. On the basis of residence, 146 come from rural areas and 367 from urban centers, with two not responding. The distribution is well balanced on the basis of parental education, with the majority, 202, both having high school diplomas.

## ETHNIC PREFERENCES IN INTERMARRIAGE

The questions regarding ethnic preference in marriage to a non-Chinese were posed by this study to ascertain the willingness of Chinese college students to marry outside of their own cultural group as much as to reveal actual preference. The questions were placed near the beginning of the questionnaire to confront the students with the main purpose of the study and with the stark realization that intermarriage is possible.

Table 3.1 reveals that the Chinese prefer Caucasians—Americans and Europeans—two to one over Asians as marriage partners. Preferences were expressed by 486 out of the 515 respondents, indicating that the thought of marrying outside of their own ethnic group has not only been entertained, but has been considered in terms that may be quite astonishing.

TABLE 3.1: Preference of Respondents in Selecting Mates Other Than Their Own Ethnic Group by Educational Level, Parental Income, and Residence

| Category | American-Caucasians | | Europeans | | Japanese | | Other Asians | | Total | |
|---|---|---|---|---|---|---|---|---|---|---|
| | No. | % | No. | % | No. | % | No. | % | No. | % |
| Freshmen | 64 | 23 | 100 | 36 | 76 | 27 | 40 | 14 | 280 | 100 |
| Seniors | 74 | 36 | 75 | 36 | 42 | 20 | 15 | 7 | 206 | 99 |
| Low Income | 71 | 26 | 93 | 34 | 80 | 20 | 33 | 12 | 277 | 101 |
| High Income | 67 | 32 | 82 | 39 | 40 | 19 | 20 | 10 | 209 | 100 |
| Rural | 34 | 25 | 48 | 36 | 32 | 24 | 21 | 16 | 135 | 101 |
| Urban | 104 | 30 | 127 | 36 | 88 | 25 | 32 | 9 | 351 | 100 |
| Average | 69 | 29 | 87 | 36 | 60 | 23 | 27 | 11 | 243 | 101 |

Except for the seniors, there is a significant percentage difference evident in the preference for Europeans over the American-Caucasians. Without further study, only hypothesizing can suggest the possible reasons for all respondents, other than seniors, preferring Europeans over Americans as marital partners. Perhaps the romantic reputation of some European countries, or more probably, the wound caused by the severance of diplomatic relationships with the Republic of China by the United States, which has not yet healed, may explain these findings. Perhaps also an examination of new ideas and values during the initial years of college has led students, by the time they are seniors, to reconsider their traditional values in a more favorable light.

ATTITUDES TOWARD INTERMARRIAGE

Three types of intermarriages were selected for analysis in this study. Interracial, international, and interreligious aspects of marriage are usually involved when a Chinese marries an American-Caucasian. Three measures were used, as shown in Table 3.2, to determine the attitudes of Chinese college students toward such unions. Respondents who definitely would, or would consider, crossing over racial, national, or religious boundaries in marriage were classified as favorable. Those who said they might cross over these lines were categorized as neutral. Finally, those who thought it unlikely that they would, and those who definitely would not, intermarry were classified as unfavorable.

According to Table 3.2, freshmen are more willing than seniors to cross over national and religious lines in marriage. Interracial marriages are equally acceptable to both groups. Freshmen are a little more, and seniors much more, willing to marry into another race than to enter into either international or interreligious marriages. Evidently, the deeply entrenched religious and nationalistic beliefs are much more of a deterrent to intercultural marriages for both freshmen and seniors than race is.

Students in both the lower and higher income levels look more favorably upon interracial marriages than upon either of the other two types of intercultural marriages. Again, both groups consider interracial marriages with about the same degree of favor: fifty-six percent for those with high incomes and fifty-seven percent for the low income students. The low income respondents look more favorably upon international and interreligious marriages than those on the high income level. Possibly, those on the higher income level have stronger political and religious bonds than those on the lower income level. This could be a vestige of the gentry loyalty carried over from mainland China.

TABLE 3.2: Attitudes toward Intermarriage Involving Chinese American-Caucasians by Education, Income, and Residence

| Education Level: | Favorable | | Neutral | | Unfavorable | |
|---|---|---|---|---|---|---|
| | Freshmen No. % | Senior No. % | Freshmen No. % | Senior No. % | Freshmen No. % | Senior No. % |
| Interracial | 155 57 | 114 56 | 86 31 | 55 28 | 37 13 | 30 15 |
| International | 143 52 | 83 43 | 82 30 | 65 33 | 49 18 | 47 24 |
| Interreligious | 148 54 | 94 47 | 78 28 | 53 27 | 50 18 | 51 26 |
| **Income Level:** | Low | High | Low | High | Low | High |
| Interracial | 154 57 | 115 56 | 79 29 | 62 30 | 39 14 | 28 14 |
| International | 133 50 | 93 46 | 79 30 | 68 33 | 53 20 | 43 21 |
| Interreligious | 143 53 | 99 48 | 70 26 | 61 30 | 55 21 | 55 22 |
| **Residence:** | Rural | Urban | Rural | Urban | Rural | Urban |
| Interracial | 65 49 | 204 60 | 47 35 | 94 27 | 22 16 | 45 13 |
| International | 54 41 | 172 51 | 44 34 | 103 30 | 33 25 | 63 19 |
| Interreligious | 64 48 | 178 52 | 36 27 | 95 28 | 33 25 | 68 20 |

Table 3.2 reveals that those living in urban areas accept all three types of intermarriage more readily than those living in rural areas. The gap in the comparative figures is much wider when residence is considered than the differences in either education or income. The rural dwellers look with less favor upon international marriages (41%) than the other two types of intercultural marriages. The strong traditional ties in rural areas probably accounts for this.

An overall comparison of the favorable and unfavorable categories reveals that freshmen, those with low incomes, and urban residents look more favorably upon entering into all three types of intercultural marriages than seniors, those with high incomes, and rural residents do.

PEER APPROVAL OF INTERCULTURAL DATING OR MARRIAGE

An overwhelming majority of the respondents felt that their friends would approve of them dating an American-Caucasian. According to Table 3.3, those in the high income bracket expect a slightly higher degree of approval than those in the low income bracket. This is the only category in which any noticeable difference is seen. Very little difference is evident in the freshmen-seniors and rural-urban categories in intercultural dating.

It is clearly apparent, from Table 3.3, that a much higher percentage of friends (31%) disapprove of the respondent marrying an American-Caucasian than those (6%) dating one. A significantly higher percentage of the rural residents (36%) disapprove than those (6%) in urban areas, or in any other category. The high income group shows the highest percentage of friends approving dating (96%) and marriage (74%), compared to the other categories. Approval of the respondent marrying an American-Caucasian is about the same for freshmen as it is for seniors.

TABLE 3.3: Attitude of Friends toward Respondent's Dating or Marriage to an American-Caucasian by Education, Income, and Residence

Percentage of Those Responding

| Dating: | Approve No. | % | Disapprove No. | % | Don't Know | % of Total |
|---|---|---|---|---|---|---|
| Freshmen | 178 | 94 | 12 | 6 | 90 | 32 |
| Seniors | 122 | 93 | 9 | 7 | 75 | 36 |
| Low Income | 163 | 92 | 15 | 8 | 100 | 21 |
| High Income | 137 | 96 | 6 | 4 | 65 | 31 |
| Rural | 87 | 94 | 6 | 6 | 42 | 31 |
| Urban | 213 | 93 | 15 | 7 | 123 | 35 |
| Average | 150 | 94 | 21 | 6 | | |
| Marriage: | | | | | | |
| Freshmen | 79 | 70 | 34 | 30 | 163 | 59 |
| Seniors | 52 | 69 | 23 | 31 | 130 | 63 |
| Low Income | 70 | 66 | 36 | 34 | 168 | 61 |
| High Income | 61 | 74 | 21 | 26 | 125 | 60 |
| Rural | 39 | 64 | 22 | 36 | 74 | 55 |
| Urban | 92 | 72 | 35 | 28 | 219 | 63 |
| Average | 65 | 69 | 28 | 31 | | |

In looking at the total picture, as portrayed in Table 3.3, an average of 94% of the students responding thought that their friends would approve of them dating an American-Caucasian, whereas 6% thought their friends would disapprove. Disregarding returns of respondents who did not profess to know the attitudes of their friends regarding dating an American-Caucasian, 62% percent thought that their friends would approve and 4% would disapprove; thirty-four percent did not know whether their friends would approve.

The average percentage of the friends approving the respondent marrying an American-Caucasian is considerably lower than those approving dating. The average percentage approving is 69, while 31% disapprove. When all 515 returns are considered, 27% of the respondents thought that their friends would approve of them marrying an American-Caucasian, 12% thought that their friends would disapprove, and 61% expressed no opinion.

A possible explanation of the high percentage of respondents who indicated they did not know whether their friends would approve is that they had not discussed with their friends the idea of intermarriage and, moreover, had given little thought to serious dating or marriage. Taiwan statistics show that only 4% of males fifteen to twenty-four years of age were married in 1980, while 12% of the females in the same age bracket had mates (Budget, Accounting, & Statistics: Executive Yuan, 1983, p. 15). Also, deeply entrenched nationalistic loyalty and religious beliefs might have strengthened the voice of their conscience when thought was given to dating or marrying an American-Caucasian.

## CHARACTERISTICS OF CHINESE AND AMERICAN-CAUCASIAN HUSBANDS

The respondent's perceptions regarding some characteristics of Chinese and American-Caucasian husbands are compared in Table 3.4 to attempt to determine any significance differences in the perceived roles of the husbands with contrasting cultural backgrounds. Variations of major import in the characteristics would possibly serve to discourage marriage between Chinese and American-Caucasians. Only those expressing opinions are included in the table. The averages of all categories show that 41% expressed no opinion as to the dominance of the husband, 15% did not know whether the Chinese or American-Caucasian husband displayed more affection for the wife, and 32% did not know which husband was more tolerant.

The data indicate that a highly significant number of the respondents in all three categories believe that the Chinese husband is more domineering than the American-Caucasian husband. The highest percentage (79%) characterizing the Chinese husband in this way is registered by students living in rural areas. The seniors rank highest (33%) in thinking the American-Caucasian husband in more dominant.

Approximately twice as many respondents feel that the American-Caucasian husband expresses more affection for his wife than the Chinese husband. Seventy-seven percent of the seniors recorded this opinion while 38% of the freshmen think that the Chinese husband gives more evidence of affection for his wife.

In indicating whether they feel the Chinese or the American-Caucasian husband is more tolerant, the opinions of the respondents are a little more balanced. In all categories, however, the respondents feel that the Chinese husband is more tolerant than the American-Caucasian husband. Such responses should be expected with the wide reputation the Chinese have for the attribute of patience. The highest percentage (40%) rating the American-Caucasian husband as more tolerant than the Chinese husband is registered by the respondents in the low income bracket, compared to 31% of those in the high income bracket who support this position.

TABLE 3.4: Respondents' Opinions Regarding Chinese or American-Caucasian Husbands' Role by Education, Income, and Residence

Percentage of Respondents Expressing Opinions

| Husband's Trait | Chinese | | American-Caucasian | |
|---|---|---|---|---|
| Educational Level: | Freshmen | Seniors | Freshmen | Seniors |
| More Domineering | 72 | 67 | 28 | 33 |
| More Evidence of Affection | 38 | 23 | 62 | 77 |
| More Tolerant | 61 | 68 | 39 | 32 |
| Income Level: | Low | High | Low | High |
| More Domineering | 73 | 76 | 27 | 24 |
| More Evidence of Affection | 37 | 26 | 63 | 74 |
| More Tolerant | 60 | 69 | 40 | 31 |
| Residence: | Rural | Urban | Rural | Urban |
| More Domineering | 79 | 72 | 21 | 28 |
| More Evidence of Affection | 30 | 33 | 70 | 67 |
| More Tolerant | 67 | 63 | 33 | 37 |

By considering the differences in the perceived characteristics of the Chinese and American-Caucasian husbands, it can readily be seen that significant adjustments would need to be made in marriages that cross over these cultural boundaries. A summary of the greatest and the least differences of opinions, as shown in Table 3.5, emphasizes this observation.

The smallest difference in the opinions of the respondents, as shown in this Table is seen in the comparison of tolerance on the part of the Chinese and American-Caucasian husbands. Twenty percentage points separate the opinions of respondents in the low income group. The widest gap shows a difference of 58 percentage points when the dominance of the Chinese husband is compared to that of the American-Caucasian husband for students from rural areas. Seventy-nine percent of the respondents residing in rural areas feel that the Chinese husband is more domineering than the American-Caucasian husband, while only 21% of the respondents living in rural areas think that the American-Caucasian is more domineering.

TABLE 3.5: A Summary of the Differences of Opinions Shown in Table 3.4

| | Percentage Widest Difference | | Percentage Narrowest Difference | |
|---|---|---|---|---|
| | Chinese | American-Caucasian | Chinese | American-Caucasian |
| More Domineering | 79 | 21 | 67 | 33 |
| More Evidence of Affection | 23 | 77 | 38 | 62 |
| More Tolerant | 69 | 31 | 60 | 40 |

In spite of the wide differences in the responses comparing the perceived characteristics of Chinese and American-Caucasian husbands, approximately 50% of all respondents expressed a willingness to cross over the cultural boundaries of race, religion, and nationality. This was shown in Table 3.2 and the discussion that followed.

PARENTAL OBJECTION TO OFFSPRING'S DATING AND MARRIAGE

Two educational measures are used to attempt to determine the degree of parental objection to the respondent marrying an American-Caucasian. One of these is based upon the academic level of the respondent and the other registers objection on the basis of the parents' educational level.

According to Table 3.6, parents differ between themselves in their opinions toward their offspring either dating or marrying an American-Caucasian. In the opinions of the respondents, an average of 15% of both parents would object to their offspring dating an American-Caucasian, compared to 28% of the respondents believing that only one parent would object. The subject of marriage is viewed a little more strongly, with more respondents assuming that both parents would object to their offspring.

TABLE 3.6: Parental Objections to Offspring's Relationship with an American-Caucasian by Education, Income, and Residence (Percentage)

|  | Dating | | | Marriage | | |
|  | Objection | | No Objection | Objection | | No Objection |
|  | One | Both |  | One | Both |  |
|---|---|---|---|---|---|---|
| Freshmen | 6 | 13 | 61 | 24 | 17 | 59 |
| Seniors | 29 | 17 | 54 | 38 | 23 | 39 |
| Low | 30 | 14 | 56 | 35 | 21 | 44 |
| High | 24 | 14 | 61 | 31 | 23 | 46 |
| Rural | 33 | 19 | 48 | 37 | 27 | 6 |
| Urban | 25 | 13 | 62 | 31 | 19 | 50 |
| Average | 28 | 15 | 57 | 33 | 22 | 46 |

marrying an American-Caucasian (22%), or that at least one parent would object (33%).

Over half (52%) of either one or both of the parents in rural areas are reported to object to their offspring dating an American-Caucasian, and 64% object to a marital arrangement. These are the highest percentages of objection registered in any category. The highest percentage of parents with no objection to their offspring marrying an American-Caucasian, amounting to 59%, is listed in the freshmen tabulation. This compares to 36% of the parents living in rural areas who have no objection to such an arrangement.

In comparing the categories in Table 3.6, it is seen that there is more perceived parental objection (either one or both parents) to their offspring dating an American-Caucasian in the opinions of the seniors (46%) than is registered by the freshmen (39%). Parents of seniors are also believed to object much more rigorously (61%) to their offspring marrying an American-Caucasian than freshmen's parents (41%).

PARENTAL EDUCATIONAL LEVEL AND OBJECTIONS

As Table 3.7 indicates, there appears to be a negative relationship between the educational level of the parents and objection to their offspring marrying an American-Caucasian. The statistics show that only 36% of the parents, when both had a college degree, object to such a relationship. In cases where both parents have a sixth grade education or less, 57% of them were expected to object.

TABLE 3.7: Parental Objection Based upon Parents' Educational
Level (Percentage)

| Educational Level | One Parent | Both Parents | Neither Parent |
|---|---|---|---|
| Both College | 25 | 11 | 64 |
| One College and | | | |
| One High School | 26 | 24 | 50 |
| Both High School | 36 | 18 | 46 |
| Mixed | 34 | 23 | 43 |
| Both Six Years or Less | 36 | 21 | 43 |

Only 11% of the parents with college degrees were judged by respondents to agree in objecting to their offspring marrying an American-Caucasian. The strongest agreement on this point (24%) is between parents with one having a college degree and the other a high school diploma. Agreement among parents with mixed educational levels, and those with less than seven years of schooling, was reported by respondents to be just about as strong.

CHANGE IN ATTITUDES TOWARD CHINESE/AMERICAN-CAUCASIAN MARRIAGES

As Table 3.8 indicates, an average of all categories shows only 4% of the respondents feel that there is still strong opposition toward Chinese/American-Caucasian marriages. The freshmen, lower income group, and rural dwellers seem to think that there is more opposition to such marriages in comparison to the opinions of seniors, upper income level, and those living in urban areas concerning this matter.

Respondents with the opinion that there is little or no opposition to marriages between Chinese and American-Caucasians are pretty well balanced in all categories. The highest percentage (40%) with this opinion is found among the rural dwellers. Thirty-five percent of the respondents in the high income bracket expressed little or no opposition to intercultural marriages.

ANALYZING THE HYPOTHESES

No statistical test was conducted to ascertain if the difference of means of the variables involved in the hypotheses of this study was significant. However, a simple analysis is made here by drawing pertinent excerpts from the preceding data and summarizing them according to the categories of each of the hypotheses we proposed earlier—dealing with education, income, and residence. Whereas interpretation of the preceding tables compared data between or among categories, in this section comparisons are made within each category.

TABLE 3.8: Respondents' Opinions Regarding the Change in the General Attitudes in Taiwan Regarding Intercultural Marriages since World War II by Education, Income, and Residence (Percentage)

|  | Strongly Opposed | Some Opposition | Little or No Opposition |
|---|---|---|---|
| Freshmen | 5 | 57 | 38 |
| Seniors | 3 | 60 | 36 |
| Low Income | 5 | 56 | 39 |
| High Income | 3 | 62 | 35 |
| Rural | 9 | 50 | 40 |
| Urban | 2 | 63 | 36 |
| Average | 4 | 58 | 37 |

*The Educational Hypothesis*

Table 3.9 compares the responses of freshmen and seniors on the basis of selected criteria. The table shows that more than half of the freshmen and seniors are willing to enter into interracial marriages. The percentages are about equal. Freshmen, however, are much more willing than seniors to cross over national and religious boundaries. Both groups are less willing to enter into international and interreligious marriages than interracial marriages. Both the freshmen and seniors are more willing to marry across religious lines than they are to marry one whose nationality differs from theirs.

There is a significant difference between the willingness of the seniors to marry interracially (57%) than to marry internationally (43%) or across religious lines (47%). Perhaps this is because of the heavy emphasis Confucius placed upon ethnocentrism.

There is not much difference in the willingness of freshmen to intermarry in any of the three categories. Two possible reasons exist for the discrepancies between the freshmen and the seniors. The first one is that the freshmen may not have been as fully indoctrinated with Confucianism as the seniors have and are, thus, more willing to enter into interreligious marriages. The second reason is that the higher educational level is more concerned with nationalism and that seniors are thus less willing to enter into international marriages.

Very little difference exists between the opinions of the peers of the freshmen and those of the seniors regarding respondents dating or marrying an American-Caucasian. There is an understandably significant difference in the opinions of the peers between the approval of dating and in approving marriage. Ninety-four percent of the peers of both freshmen and seniors approve of dating an American-Caucasian, compared to approximately 70% in both groups who would approve marriage.

Less than half of the respondents' parents, of both freshmen and seniors, are believed to object to their offspring dating an American-Caucasian. Fewer parents of freshmen (39%) are believed to object to such a relationship than the parents of seniors (46%). The objections of the freshmen's parents to marriage is slightly higher (41%) than dating (39%). The parents of seniors, however, are reported to object much more strongly to marriage (61%) than dating (46%).

---

TABLE 3.9: Comparison of Freshmen and Senior Respondents: The Educational Hypothesis

| Willingness to Cross Cultural Boundaries in Marriages: | Percentages | |
|---|---|---|
| | Freshmen | Seniors |
| Interracial | 56 | 57 |
| International | 52 | 43 |
| Interreligious | 54 | 47 |
| Average | 54 | 49 |
| Total | 162 | 147 |
| Peer Group* of: | | |
| Dating | 94 | 94 |
| Marriage | 71 | 69 |
| Parents with No Objections** to: | | |
| Dating | 61 | 54 |
| Marriage | 59 | 39 |
| Total Percentage Points Favoring Marriage | 292 | 255 |

*Of Those Responding
**One or Both Parents

---

For comparative purposes, the percentages in the three types of intercultural marriages—interracial, international, and interreligious—are added together. The result shows that freshmen are much more willing to enter into all three types of intercultural marriages than seniors are. The former had a total of 162 percentage points, compared to 147 for the latter.

When these percentage points are added to those of peer approval of marriage (71 for the freshmen and 69 for the seniors), plus the percentage points of parents having no objections to their offspring marrying an American-Caucasian (59 for the freshmen and 39 for the seniors), the percentage points total 292 for the freshmen and 255 for the seniors.

Based on these findings, the hypothesis stating that "the attitudes of the most highly educated Chinese social group are more favorably inclined toward intermarriage between Chinese and U.S. Caucasians than the attitudes of those from lower educational levels" is rejected.

---

TABLE 3.10: Comparison of Respondents on Basis of Low and High Income Levels: The Income Hypothesis

| Willingness to Cross Cultural Boundaries in Marriage | Percentage | |
|---|---|---|
| | Low | High |
| Interracial | 57 | 56 |
| International | 50 | 46 |
| Interreligious | 53 | 48 |
| Average | 53 | 50 |
| Total | 160 | 150 |
| Peer Group Approval* of: | | |
| Dating | 78 | 96 |
| Marriage | 71 | 75 |
| Parents with No Objection** to: | | |
| Dating | 56 | 61 |
| Marriage | 44 | 46 |
| Total Percentage Points Favoring Marriage | 275 | 271 |

*Of Those Responding
**One or Both Parents

---

*The Income Hypothesis*

Half or more of the respondents whose parents have low incomes, according to Table 3.10, are slightly more willing to enter into all three types of intercultural marriage than those with parents in the high income bracket.

The order of priorities for both groups, on the basis of income, is the same that registered on the basis of education. That is, interracial and interreligious marriages are more preferable than international marriages. Only 50% of those on the low income level are willing to marry internationally compared to 57% who look favorably upon interracial marriages. Those on the high income level are less willing to cross national and religious boundaries than those on the low income level. Over half of both groups are willing to marry interracially.

Since the gentry in traditional China included more of those on the upper income level than those on the lower, possibly their nationalistic spirit makes them less willing to enter into international marriages than those on the lower income level.

An average of all three types, as seen in Table 3. 10, shows 53% of the respondents with parents in the low income bracket are willing to marry interculturally compared to 50% in the high income bracket. Almost all (96%) of the peers of those on the high income level are said to approve of the respondents dating an American-Caucasian, compared to 78% on the low income level. The gap is not as great between the two income levels as far as peer approval is concerned regarding marriage. The data show that 75% of the peers of those on the high income level approve of the respondents marrying an American-Caucasian, compared to 71% of those responding on the low income level.

More parents with high incomes, compared to those with low incomes, have no objections to their offspring either dating or marrying an American-Caucasian. The percentages for those with low incomes are 56 and 44, respectively, compared to 61% of the high income parents with no objection to dating and 46% with no objection to marrying an American-Caucasian.

An analysis of the income hypothesis reveals that slightly more of the respondents whose parents are in the low income bracket, an average of 53, with total percentage points amounting to 160, are more willing to marry interculturally than high income bracket respondents, whose average is 50%, with 150 percentage points. A slight difference is noted when the assumed parental attitudes toward their offspring marrying an American-Caucasian are considered. Forty-four percent of the low income parents and 46% of the high income parents are thought to have no objection to such marriages.

The total percentage points for the respondents with parents having low incomes is 275 compared to 271 for those having parents in the high income bracket. On the basis of this index, the hypothesis postulating that "the attitudes of college students in the highest income bracket are more favorable toward intermarriage between Chinese and U.S. Caucasians than the attitudes of those in the lowest income bracket" is neither supported nor rejected. The total score is, for all items and purposes, balanced. This means that additional research is needed before any definite conclusions can be drawn as to the effect of parental income on the attitudes of Chinese college students toward intermarriage with an American-Caucasian.

TABLE 3.11: Comparison of Respondents on the Basis of Rural and Urban Residence: The Residence Hypothesis

| Willingness to Cross Cultural Boundaries in Marriage | Percentage | |
| --- | --- | --- |
| | Rural | Urban |
| Interracial | 49 | 60 |
| International | 41 | 51 |
| Interreligious | 48 | 52 |
| Average | 46 | 54 |
| Total | 138 | 163 |
| Peer Group Approval* of: | | |
| Dating | 94 | 94 |
| Marriage | 66 | 73 |
| Parents with No Objections** to: | | |
| Dating | 48 | 62 |
| Marriage | 36 | 50 |
| Total Percentage Points Favoring Marriage | 240 | 286 |

*Of Those Responding
**One or Both Parents

*The Residence Hypothesis*

Rural dwellers, according to Table 3.11, are much less willing to enter into all types of intermarriages than those living in urban areas. The average percentage for those living in rural areas is 46 compared to 54 for urbanites.

As in the cases of the educational and income levels, both rural and urban residents are more willing to enter into interracial marriages than either international or interreligious marriages. All respondents, in either rural or urban areas, prefer to enter interfaith marriages over international ones.

There is not too much difference among rural dwellers in their willingness to cross over racial boundaries (49%) compared to religious boundaries (48%). The difference among urbanites, however, is more significant. Sixty percent would enter into interracial marriages, compared to 52% who would marry into another religion.

The approval of peers, of those responding to the question about dating, is the same for both rural and urban dwellers. Almost all respondents (94%) are of the opinion that their peers would approve of them dating an American-Caucasian. The percentage of peers approving such a marriage, however, is significantly lower. Sixty-six percent of those living in rural areas and 73% of the urbanites are of the opinion that their peers would approve of the respondent marrying an American-Caucasian.

A much higher percentage of parents living in urban areas are thought to have no objection to their offspring dating or marrying an American-Caucasian than parents living in rural areas. While the percentage of urban parents not objecting to the interdating and intermarriage of their offspring is 62% and 50% respectively, the percentage of rural dwellers having no objections to these practices by their children is 48% and 36%.

Tradition undoubtedly is a major factor in the significant gap existing between the attitudes of those living in rural compared to those living in urban areas. As noted earlier, the culture transported from mainland China to Taiwan was originally very traditional. Forty years or so do not provide enough time to radically change values and behavior patterns of the past, especially in rural areas.

An analysis of the residence hypothesis indicates that far more respondents living in urban areas, versus rural areas, are willing to marry interculturally. The respective averages are 54% and 46%. The percentage points for those living in rural areas is 138 for intercultural marriages, compared to 163 in urban areas. When peer group opinions and parents with no objections are included, the percentage point total for rural residents is 240, compared to 286 for urban residents. Based upon the percentage figures, the hypothesis positing that "the attitudes of college students from urban areas are more favorable toward intermarriage between Chinese and U.S. Caucasians than the attitudes of those from rural areas" is strongly supported.

*Synthesis*

The foregoing analysis of the hypotheses reveals that freshmen are more willing to marry American-Caucasians than seniors. Respondents with parents in the lower income bracket look a bit more favorably upon Chinese/American-Caucasian marriages than those in the higher income bracket, and those in urban areas are more likely to marry an American-Caucasian than rural dwellers. The total percentage figures are as follows:

|  | Low Index |  | High Index |
|---|---|---|---|
| Seniors | 255 | Freshmen | 292 |
| High Income | 271 | Low Income | 275 |
| Rural | 240 | Urban | 286 |
| Total | 766 |  | 853 |

According to the previous discussions, and the above distribution, the residence hypothesis is the only one supported by the responses. The educational hypothesis is rejected and the income hypothesis is balanced between acceptance and rejection. Classifying the index values as positive for support of the hypothesis and negative for the failure to support it, an overall estimate of the attitudes of Chinese college students toward marrying an American-Caucasian can be determined.

| Category | Index Value |
|---|---|
| Freshmen-Seniors | -37 |
| Low-High Income | - 4 |
| Rural-Urban Residence | +46 |
| Total | + 5 |

When the results of the tests of all three hypotheses are combined, as shown in the preceding figures, the overall attitudes of Chinese college students toward marriage to an American-Caucasian are pretty well balanced between the favorable and unfavorable. The slight difference, however, does not undermine the value of this study. Further explanatory analysis, which is not within the scope of this chapter, is essential to pinpoint the precise reasons for the relatively narrow gap between the attitudes of college students in each of the categories. The present work, nevertheless, makes it possible to present some conceivable reasons for the differences.

DISCUSSION

As previously pointed out, this study raises more questions than it answers. One such question is why are freshmen more willing to enter into intercultural marriages than seniors. Normally, a college education extends the horizons of the student, broadening the tolerance limits. Such an experience is usually conducive to probabilities of intercultural marriage. Evidently, this is not the case in Taiwan. Since Chinese higher education is saturated with nationalism, perhaps the three additional years of schooling by the seniors have exposed them more to Confucianism and led them to develop an attitude of ethnocentrism, making them less willing to cross over national boundaries in marriage. The evidence presented earlier in Table 3.9 supports this hypothesis by showing that 52% of the freshmen are willing to enter into international marriages compared to 43% of the seniors. This is a wider gap than is shown in either the interracial or interreligious marriages.

Literature on the subject supports the foregoing assumption. For example, "The [Taiwanese] government requires the use of teaching materials in history and geography to expound the real meaning of the nation. General education should be based upon the teachings of Dr. Sum Yat-sen to cultivate in children and youth the eight national moral virtues: loyalty, filial piety, kindness, love, faith, righteousness, harmony, and peace" (Lih-wu Han, 1982, p. 223). It stands then to reason that the higher the educational level, the more indoctrinated the individual becomes and, thus, the less inclined s/he is to consider the possibilities of international marriages.

One question raised by a study of the income hypothesis is why Chinese college students on both the high and low income levels appear equally willing to marry an American-Caucasian. Perhaps this willingness stems from a blurring of social class lines, as wealth in Nationalist China becomes more equally distributed than in traditional China.

A number of changes in the economic institution, both internal and external, have weakened the endogamous structure of mate selection on both the high and low income levels. One of the internal forces broadening the geographical base of exposure to members of the opposite sex is the development of marketing areas. Marriage choices in Taiwan

> still depend on social knowledge of prospective partners and their families. Such knowledge can be obtained through relationships that derive from marketing activities, thus creating a link between marketing areas and marriage partners.

> An immediate effect of changed marketing habits, as occurs when a new standard town develops, is a disruption of existing marriage patterns, which is often followed in a decade or so by the emergence of new marriage patterns within the new marketing area. (Ahern & Gates, 1981, pp. 120-121)

Clearly, new marketing patterns have introduced heterogeneity into the relationships of persons of the opposite sex, thereby increasing the opportunity for exogamous marriages among all income brackets. International trade, which has mushroomed in recent years between Taiwan and other countries, involves heterogeneous relationships more fully. Such a development, especially with the United States, has undoubtedly contributed to the development of a more favorable attitude toward Chinese/American-Caucasian marriages on both economic planes included in the hypothesis.

Finally, the residence hypothesis that students in urban areas accept Chinese/American-Caucasians more readily than those in rural areas is strongly supported by this study. The question on this issue is why the trend toward a more ready acceptance of such marriages, as compared to high-low educational and income levels, has been so much slower in developing in rural areas than among the urban dwellers.

The degree of traditional control in male/female relationships is probably the most significant difference between the rural and urban segments of society. Social change in the more traditional rural areas tends to be evolutionary, rather than revolutionary. Consequently, the mate selection process is little affected. On the other hand, in urban areas, where social change is more rapid, socially normative structures are weaker and the established mate selection practices are much more likely to change.

The traditional bonds of society are still strong throughout Taiwan, as a unifying force, and even link Chinese communities across the world into a single entity. Although one aim of traditional Chinese society is to perpetuate the traditions of China throughout Taiwan, more success in doing so has been achieved in rural areas than in urban centers, according to the evidence presented by this study. The lag in social change in the rural areas of Taiwan, when compared to urban areas, follows the generally accepted pattern of social change in rural and urban areas across the world. That is, rural culture changes much more slowly than the urban culture.

Although some scientific measures were used in an attempt to determine the attitudes of Chinese college students on Taiwan toward marrying an American-Caucasian, much more research needs to be undertaken before undeniable conclusions can be drawn. The foregoing study simply presents indications of the trend in these attitudes.

In spite of the fact that many classical studies of the traditional Chinese family have been used as ideal models studies of the family, little research appears to have been undertaken to reveal the evolving Chinese family structures on Taiwan. We are not aware of other studies that have been conducted on the topic of this chapter.

One value, then, of the foregoing treatment is that the focus of the study has been shifted from the rigid, traditionally extended Chinese family to the nuclear-type family emerging on Taiwan. A unique feature of this study is that the emphasis is upon the process involved in establishing the Chinese family rather than concentrating on the structure and/or the function, as is the case in most, if not all, studies of the Chinese family. The main value of the study presented in this chapter centers on the questions it raises regarding findings in this unique field. The conclusions drawn are more appropriately labeled tentative assumptions than established facts. They do indicate, however, that there are more favorable than unfavorable attitudes among Chinese college students on Taiwan toward marriage with an American-Caucasian. As can be seen in Table 3.12, respondents favoring intercultural marriage averaged 213 in number, compared to 78 who looked upon such marriages unfavorably. In other words, 73% of those expressing a position considered intercultural marriages favorably, while 27% considered them unfavorably.

The findings reported in this chapters are supported by the following logical assumptions based upon the literature dealing with the development of Taiwan.

TABLE 3.12: Summary of Total Responses Regarding Intercultural Marriages to an American-Caucasian

Intercultural Marriages:

| | Favorable | | Neutral | | Unfavorable | | Total | |
|---|---|---|---|---|---|---|---|---|
| | No. | % | No. | % | No. | % | No. | % |
| Interracial | 232 | 56 | 125 | 30 | 59 | 14 | 416 | 100 |
| International | 196 | 47 | 132 | 32 | 88 | 21 | 416 | 100 |
| Interfaith | 211 | 51 | 117 | 28 | 88 | 21 | 416 | 100 |
| Average | 213 | 51 | 125 | 30 | 78 | 19 | 416 | 100 |

For countless decades the Chinese family has been a model for Western scholars. It has been presented by various studies as the epitome of stability, exhibiting in bold relief the characteristics of familialism. In traditional China, the family is the basic unit of society, within which the individual's identity is subsumed, even lost. "The success or failure of an individual reflected upon the family and increased or decreased its prestige.... In this sense traditional China was composed of a large number of families rather than of individuals" (Welty, 1984, p. 219). With the individual locked so securely into the family unit, individual interests were submerged in and secondary to the family interests, and intercultural marriages were discouraged.

The establishment of factories altered the social structure of Taiwan drastically. At first, the influence of this economic development was confined to the cities, but the government's interest in diversifying the rural economy resulted in the establishment of factories in the villages. Factories spreading south from Taipei attracted young people from the countryside, freeing them from family discipline. The factories also offered females an opportunity to free themselves from the confining limits of household duties. In fact, since 1950 women have migrated from the rural areas in greater numbers than men (Han, 1982). The draining of youth, but especially young women, from the family through residential and personal mobility has weakened family structure and has broadened the tolerance limits of intercultural marriage. In addition, the strong parental control over the youth has been lessened by competing socializing influences. No longer is the Chinese family the sole socializing agency, but the scouts, school organizations, and mass media, often in opposition to the family values, are socializing the child. Such changes make intercultural marriages more acceptable.

The political institution is tightly intermeshed with the family in both traditional China and the Republic of China today. In fact, these are the only two social institutions included in the five basic social relationships implementing "right action" as defined by Confucius. "These five relationships are: ruler and subject, father and son, elder brother younger brother, husband and wife, and friend and friend. All of these except the last involve the authority of one person over another" (Welty, 1984, p. 168).

This means that for almost two thousand years since "Confucianism was adopted as the orthodox Chinese philosophy" (Welty, 1984, p. 162) the capstone of the hierarchy of authority was the state. Welty states that because the Confucians believe the state to be an extension of the family, the same attitudes toward authority and obedience are valued in the family as well as in the state. In the days of the Empire, the emperor and all his officials were referred to as the parents of the people. President Chiang Kai-shek embodied this fatherly figure until his death in 1975 (Han, 1984). Extending familial boundaries to the state level establishes a national political enclosure that is difficult to penetrate through intercultural marriage.

One of the forces at work today in the Republic of China that is chipping away at the shell of national unity (which perpetuates traditional practices) is the cultural interchange through international relationships with several nations. These have subjected the Republic of China "to exogenous political elites with exogenous policy objectives" (Ahern & Gates, 1981, p. 14). The close ties established with the United States during the latter half of the twentieth century have also led observers to interpret "Democratization as 'Taiwanization,' [which] when rephrased means Chinese political values in the language of Western democracy" (Ahern & Gates, 1981, p. 205).

Compromise in the political arena was ushered in by the establishment of the Republic of China, which followed almost fifty years of political upheaval as the Chinese struggled to formulate a political philosophy and establish political institutions which would combine both Western and Chinese elements necessary to meet the changing needs of Taiwan. Sun Yat-sen's "Three Principles of the People" became guiding precepts for the new Republic of China. Comparable with Lincoln's government of the people, by the people, and for the people, the Three Principles embrace "the ideals of nationalism, democracy, and people's livelihood" (Han, 1982, p. 8). The adjustment of the Republic of China's political institution in the direction of that of the United States, along with the frequent associations of diplomats between the two countries, bred familiarity, developed a better understanding of each other's culture, and broadened the tolerance limits regarding international marriages.

The prevalent religion in the Republic of China, Buddhism, is an integrator of society. "Anthropologists have explored the use of local popular religion as both a source and an emblem of the solidarity of local communities" (Ahern & Gates, 1981, p. 34). "It is now well known that Taiwanese communities are similarly linked by hierarchies based on kinship, ritual, marketing practices, and political or administrative organization" (Ahern & Gates, 1981, p. 164). The central power of this cohesive force is the conception of the state as the extension of the family, which is linked to religion through ancestral worship. This tightly interwoven nucleus discourages intercultural marriage because it dilutes the ideology.

A number of changes in the religious structure, however, have made the Chinese more receptive to evolving cultural traits. One of these is the shift in emphasis upon ancestor worship, in traditional China, to the observance of an ancestor memorial service in Taiwan (Welty, 1984, p. 213). Another change is that Article 13 of the Constitution of the Republic of China asserts that "the people shall have freedom of religious belief" (cited by Han, 1982, p. 32). This more tolerant religious structure is conducive to intercultural marriage. A third change in the religious structure began in 1911, as Confucianism "lost its favored position with the institution of the Republic of China…, when a mixture of Confucianism and Western liberal thought as propounded by Sun Yat-sen, the father of modern China, became the official political theory of the state" (Welty, 1984, p. 165). Such alterations in the traditional religious structure open the possibilities toward a more receptive view of intermarriage.

Also weakening the influence of Confucianism was the advent of Nationalism. As mentioned before, Sun Yat-sen's Three Principles of the People incorporated Lincoln's philosophy of government of, by, and for the people. The democratic flavor of Nationalist China's political foundation, promulgated through the schools, strongly contributes to a mutual appreciation of individual free choice in mate selection.

One of the objectives of education in Taiwan is to broaden the horizons of individuals, giving them a better understanding of other cultures. "For social education, people should be taught to keep abreast of the current international situation..." (Han, 1982, p. 223). "With a view to strengthening cultural ties with friendly nations, the government has subsequently signed cultural cooperation pacts with various countries to promote exchange of publications, teachers, students, and fellowships" (Han, 1982, p. 235).

In order to achieve this goal, education has been emphasized at different academic levels. The tuition-free program was extended in 1968 from six years of schooling to nine years. College enrollment increased from 6,665 in 1950-51 to 348,437 in the 1981-82 school year, representing an increase of over 5,000 percent. In addition, the Republic of China has encouraged foreign students to come to Taiwan for educational purposes, and has developed programs to enable Chinese students to study in other countries. In 1980, there were 7,200 foreign students from fifty different countries studying in Taiwan. At the same time, there were 5,933 Chinese studying in 21 different countries (Han, 1982, p. 235). According to the December 7, 1984, issue of the *China Post* (a Taipei, Taiwan, newspaper published in English), there were 21,960 Chinese students in American universities alone. Such exposure to other countries, through better understanding as well as spatial proximity, weakens ethnocentric attitudes and increases the possibility of intermarriage.

In traditional China, the gentry and the peasantry represented the only two levels in the stratification system; each level was, relatively speaking, closed to the other class. Formerly, since the peasant had to spend all of his time in eking out an existence for his family, there was little time for study leading to an improvement in social status. About the only chance a peasant had of achieving the gentry class level was through the pooled resources of a community. "It was not uncommon for a bright peasant boy, educated through group effort, to pass the examinations and embark upon a government career. This achievement immediately placed him and his family in the gentry class" (Welty, 1984, p. 200).

Although vertical mobility was possible for the peasant, the gentry consolidated their social position through marital alliances, which perpetuated the gap between the two classes.

> Gentry families tightened the bonds among themselves through expedient marriages. Connections among the gentry were extremely important and marriages a convenient method to arrange alliances between strategically placed families. Since all gentry families engaged in such practices, the web of interconnected families eventually covered most of the officials in administrative positions. (Welty, 1984, p. 204)

Education, however, finally opened the gentry class to the peasant. These and other changes in the Chinese socio-economic structure, both internal and external, have weakened the endogamous structure of mate selection in Taiwan. The development of the marketing area, with its expansion of the mate selection social and spatial areas, has already been discussed. "The widespread acceptance of factory work as a respectable occupation for young women" (Ahern & Gates, 1981, p. 186) further extended their social horizons.

All of these forces affecting the individual's choice of marriage partners appear to have conditioned the Chinese to accept exogamous marriages more readily. Once the wall of endogamy has been breached, a further widening of the gap is made easier. External forces, especially those in the United States (for our purposes in this discussion) have effectively extended the tolerance limits in mate selection.

Chinese investment in the United States provides yet another powerful force in extending the social boundaries of mate selection. Business interests have attracted Chinese to the United States to the extent that Chinese enclaves have been established in most large cities and in many smaller ones. "Chinatowns" in New York and San Francisco are especially prominent. Although the spatial segregation of such a subculture encourages endogamy, the anonymity of the large city, the prevalent impersonal relationships that relax normative controls, and occupational propinquity beyond the ethnic group boundaries are all conducive to intermarriage between Chinese and American-Caucasians.

All of these developments have brought about adjustments in the modern social institutions. In addition to the restructured social institutions, many other forces affect attitudes toward intercultural marriages in the Republic of China. Tradition and ethnocentrism have been diluted through industrialization, migration, and urbanization.

As stated earlier, the purpose of this study is not to present undeniable evidence that intercultural marriages are more acceptable today in Taiwan than four decades ago, but to indicate the trends in the attitudes a selected sample of college students have toward intermarriage with American-Caucasians. Enough evidence has been mustered in the foregoing study, buttressed by the logic based upon the literature, to make the logical deduction that social adjustments have been made and are still in progress toward the creation of a social milieu which places more emphasis on individual interests and, therefore, makes the Chinese college student more receptive to intermarriage at present than in the past.

# 4

## Sociological Conceptual Tools for Analyzing Attitudes toward Intercultural Marriage

The task of establishing a clearly defined terminology of a study such as this, as described in Chapter 1, may be illustrated by a sales distribution map of a large manufacturing firm. At a glance, the colored code reveals the geographical area of the greatest volume of business. The extent of the transportation systems can be seen, and the manufacturing center can be located with some degree of accuracy. By knowing the product, we can have some idea of the type of consumers served. But back of the simple distribution map lie reams and reams of statistical data, long sessions of planning, high-level administration, and a complex network of technology. In a word, back of the simple distribution map lies the whole history of the firm.

In like manner, behind each of the linguistic pegs to be presented in this chapter lies the whole history of the English language. According to *A New English Dictionary* (Vol. I, p. xviii, 1977):

> The vast aggregate of words and phrases which constitutes the vocabulary of English-speaking men presents, to the mind that tries to grasp it as a definite whole, the aspect of one of those nebulous masses familiar to the astronomer, in which a clear and unmistakable nucleus shades off on all sides, through zones of decreasing brightness, to a dim marginal film that seems to end nowhere but to lose itself imperceptibly in the surrounding darkness.

Each word in this "vast aggregate" has been hammered out by man's continuous struggle to give expression to his thoughts. The vocabulary mushrooms as the thoughts defy imprisonment through the tools of expression.

A concept is a cloak for an idea. It is an abstract drawn from a broad area of knowledge. Democracy as a concept refers to more than a form of government. It covers the way of life of a society which governs itself according to the principles of such an ideology. In other words, to include every area of meaning denoted by the concept, democracy would be an interminable, if not impossible, task. Likewise, a complete treatment of each concept discussed in this chapter would require a complete book or more. For example, in order to get a comprehensive view of the term sociology, a student needs to spend several years in graduate school studying numerous books. If there is a desire to narrow the interest down to a specialized area, such as rural sociology, more time must be spent in graduate study. Consequently, the coverage of a concept ranges all the way from a concise definition to a study consisting of several years in graduate school.

The classification system of sociological materials for present purposes is designed to break the mass of material down into individual traits. Each trait can then be treated in the broader context. As an example, the authority of the father over the son is a trait in the complex of filial piety, which is a trait in the complex of the patriarchal family, which is a trait in the complex of the family institution, which is a trait in the complex of the social structure, which is a trait in the complex of society, which is a trait in the complex of world order. In viewing the traits in the various complexes, their meanings become clearer.

Another need to be satisfied by classifying sociological data is to arrange the material according to the purpose being served. Using a technological example, information dealing with the operation of an automobile is organized differently from that concerned with the maintenance of the car. Using only a few major topics, the difference is shown in the following example.

### A. Operation of the Automobile

| Efficiency | Safety Measures |
|---|---|
| 1. Gradual application of brakes | 1. Brake application distances at various speeds |
| 2. Proper tire pressure | 2. Depth of tire tread |

### B. Proper Maintenance Measures

| Tire Maintenance | Brake Maintenance |
|---|---|
| 1. Rotate tires regularly | 1. Keep brake fluid at normal level |
| 2. Proper air pressure in tires | 2. Adjust brakes regularly |

As can be seen, both presentations include the subject tires and brakes, but each category is arranged in a different order.

The classification scheme used for the purposes of this book is especially designed to satisfy both of the previously mentioned needs. In the first place, it provides a basis for the discussion of the interrelationships of social phenomena, including that of the cultural trait to its complex. The terms appearing in the classification system are reduced to manageable units and are considered essential to an understanding of sociology.

The second need is satisfied by arranging the concepts in such a way as to reflect the social milieu in which the attitudes of college students toward intercultural marriages are formed. To accomplish this, five major categories are set up in the special classification system. These divisions, captioned by coined terms, emphasize the salient aspects of the study.

Before describing the classification system depicted in Figure 4.1, a brief explanation of the sequence of the major categories, and an explanation of the headings will be helpful. There is a logical urge to discuss the statisphere in laying a foundation for the presentation of other social phenomena. As mentioned before, the classification system is designed especially for the purpose of this book.

The rigid social structure of traditional China, which could well be symbolized by the Great Wall, provides the focus for the concepts denoting the framework of various social entities. Because of the implied immobility, this category is called the statisphere. The functional aspects of society are labeled the dynasphere, which relates to the catastrophic adjustments made in the social structure of Nationalist China in its abrupt shift from the mainland to Taiwan. The psychosphere is related to the strong loyalties of the Chinese to their ideology saturated with Confucianism.

The major social institutions are highlighted in the discussion on social change. To emphasize the importance of these fundamental facets of society, they are placed in a separate category of the classification system under the title instisphere. Because social institutions form the bulwark of society, a whole chapter is devoted to the discussion of each in relationship to their structure in traditional China and their influence on the mate selection process. Since social institutions involve all other spheres of social phenomena, they are treated separately in Section III.

It should be noted that the various categories in Figure 4.1 overlap, which is common to all classification systems. For example, a social group, listed in the category statisphere, also serves certain functions which would classify it as a trait in the dynasphere. Both the structural and functional aspects are different in the primary group as compared to the secondary group. Furthermore, socialization listed in the dynaspheric category occurs in social groups listed in the statisphere. The various social institutions are also socializing agents of society. In other words, the categorization of the social phenomena is based upon the emphasis, or predominant characteristics of each item. Each of the major categories, subcategories, and sub-sub-categories could be further subdivided. Such a detailed classification scheme, however, is not essential for present purposes.

Only those concepts considered most essential to an understanding of sociology, and to an analysis of intercultural marriages, are listed in the various categories of Figure 4.1.

FIGURE 4.1: Classification System for the Purpose of Studying Chinese College Students' Attitudes toward Intermarriage with American-Caucasians

| STATISPHERE | DYNASPHERE | PSYCHOSPHERE | INSTISPHERE | TECHNOSPHERE |
|---|---|---|---|---|
| *Culture* | *Society* | *Socialization** | Family* | Transportation |
| | | Agencies | Structure | Land |
| *Social Structure* | Social *Interaction* | Family | Authority | Water |
| | | Peer Group | Patriarchal | Air |
| *Social Groups** | *Social Control** | School | Matriarchal | |
| Primary | Norms | Mass Media | Democratic | Electronics |
| Intimacy | Folkways | | | Communications |
| Personal | Mores | Stages | Function | |
| Informal | Laws | Infancy | Economic | Social Mobility* |
| | | Childhood | Protective | Vertical |
| Secondary | Deviation of | Adolescent | Education | Horizontal |
| Comparison | Norms | Young Adult | Socialization | Residential |
| Advantages | | Mature Adult | Emotional | Personal |
| Disadvantages | *Social Change* | Elderly | Bonds | Ideational |
| | | | | |
| Social Role | | *Values* | Religion | |
| and Status | | Attitudes | Education | |
| | | | Political | |
| | | | Economic | |

Note: Only items pertinent to this book are listed. Italicized concepts are those used in constructing a logically closed social system.
*Only one example of an expanded classification system is presented for illustrative purposes.

## THE STATISPHERE

A more detailed study of the classification concepts shows that the statisphere is composed of items indicative of the structural aspects of society. Although the term connoted to identify this category implies that the concepts are static, this is not the case. They are placed in this category because their structural characteristics are more predominant than their functional characteristics. The social groups, for example, both the primary and secondary types, are vitally functional in a society, and are, therefore, dynamic. The definition of social group, however, revolves around structures. A social group consists of two or more persons in reciprocal interaction with a common interest which is structured. Because structure is the predominant distinguishing criterion between primary and secondary groups, social groups are placed in the statisphere. While the primary group is informal, the secondary group is formal. Figure 4.1 also represents a classificatory system for culture, which as other concepts, such as society, entails all of the sociological phenomena to be discussed in the book. Since culture, as will be seen later, is considered the relatively static aspect of society, it is listed in the statisphere. Social structure, as the term implies, logically fits into this category. Social role is a pattern of behavior prescribed by social status. Therefore, both role and status are properly placed in the statisphere.

As can be seen in Figure 4.1, sociological terms are discussed in the contexts in which explanations of the concept can best be given, rather than being placed in the structure of an established pattern as is the customary practice.

All three hypotheses dealt with in the field study discussed in Chapter 3 are placed in the statisphere classification. One of these deals with the *social structure* in rural and urban areas. Another tests the attitudes of Chinese college students toward intercultural marriages according to their educational level. The third considers attitudes on different income levels. Both income and education are measures of *social class.*

The major topic in the statisphere, *social groups,* is dealt with throughout the book. The peer group, family, and religious groups, especially, form an important part of the discussion.

## THE DYNASHPERE

The dynasphere is the active arena of the special classification system. The category includes the main processes in a sociological system. The concepts constituting the dynasphere can be considered the functional aspects of society. Perhaps it would be helpful to show the interrelationships between structure (or the statisphere), function, and process. The structure provides a framework within which the function is carried out. The function is what a social unit does. The process determines the degree of efficiency of the social unit in carrying out its function. In looking at Figure 4.1, it can be seen that the *norms* sub-classified as folkways, mores, and laws are the instruments through which the process of *social control* is carried out. If these norms are effective, the process of social control operates at a high level of efficiency. If they function poorly, then the level of efficiency is low.

Usually, social norms are treated along with the concept of culture in most introductory sociology texts and would, therefore, be placed in the statisphere. In the discussion on classification of concepts, however, it was pointed out that terms are arranged in the order that best serves the purpose of this particular presentation. Consequently, social norms are treated as measures of social control in the dynasphere for two reasons. The first reason is because of the effectiveness of social control measures in China through religious and family influences. Pressures are applied by both of these sources in the regulation of mate selection practices. The prominent role played by social control, in this respect, is emphasized by treating it in a separate category from the concept culture. The second reason, which is of significance in the mechanics of the special classification system, is that social control is a process, not a product. This means that it is predominantly dynamic rather than structurally static, and is, therefore, listed in the dynasphere.

Society is both a process and a structure. The emphasis in this book is upon society as the enactment of culture, or the dynamic aspect of culture, therefore, it is placed in the dynasphere. Social interaction, as the term implies, is a dynaspheric cultural trait. The questions in the field study presented in Chapter 3 concerning the discussion with family members, or friends, regarding intercultural marriage reflects social interaction. Social control is a process with the function of maintaining or restoring order in a society. The extent to which respondents obey their parents and the answer to the question regarding embarrassment in being seen in the company of an American-Caucasian of the opposite sex, which is in the questionnaire, deals with the effectiveness of some social control.

Social change is a process that is constantly affecting alterations in society, so it is properly placed in the dynasphere. The respondent's response as to the degree of difference in the Chinese attitude toward intermarriage measures social change in Taiwan to some extent.

## THE PSYCHOSPHERE

The psychosphere is the mental category of the classification system. In essence, it is the heart of the study of attitudes, which are mentally formed opinions. Concepts in the psychosphere play a major role in society. As will be seen later, they are intricately interwoven with concepts in the other categories. The items listed in the psychosphere actually represent the "soul" of society.

Although *socialization* is a process, it is appropriately placed in the psychosphere because it is the means by which the mental image of the self is developed. Like other concepts, it could be listed in the dynasphere. As indicated earlier, this special classification system is designed to meet the needs of this particular book. Because socialization is the means by which the norms are internalized, reinforcing tradition, which is the mainstay of pre-Communist China, the concept belongs in the dynasphere. Values and attitudes are also representatives of mental images.

The answers as to whether the Chinese or the American family would accept the offspring of an intermarriage more fully, and the willingness to marry in spite of national and racial barriers, give some idea of the extent of socialization. Among the values discussed in the book, ethnocentrism is evidenced to some degree by answers to questions reflecting bias, such as preferences in language to be spoken, and customs to be observed, by the children as products of a mixed marriage. The strong loyalty to the Republic of China, and the high level of morale of the Chinese, are presented as depicted in the reading materials, as are knowledge, beliefs, and other subjects that are included in the psychosphere. As indicated in the discussion of the instisphere, a complete chapter is devoted to each of the agencies of socialization.

Social values is another concept usually tied in with the discussion of culture in the introductory sociology texts. Here, again, the purpose to be served by the classification system places this specific concept in the psychosphere. The heavy emphasis upon nationalism and the loyalty of the Chinese to the Republic of China make social values a significant concept in the mate selection process, which makes it a psychospheric cultural trait.

## THE INSTISPHERE

The instisphere includes the most rigid elements in the social structure. These consist of various forms of social controls, or regulatory norms, interwoven around certain basic needs of the members of society. The structure of each social institution is formed by a network of social norms, which prescribes the way the function is to be carried out. The structures of the social institutions vary more widely from society to society than the functions do, because the functions of social institutions are to meet basic needs which are similar in various societies.

Social institutions are classified on the basis of the needs they satisfy. Generally, five major social institutions are recognized as essential in satisfying the prerequisites, or the needs, of a society which must be met in order for the society to exist. A society must have some means of replacing the members it loses through death; the family satisfies this need through reproduction. Also, in modern society, the political institution partially satisfies this need through immigration. There must be a means of producing and distributing goods and services; the economic institution serves this function. Communication is essential for the existence of society; this is provided through the educational institutions. A system of social control is necessary to maintain order, which is the very essence of society; religious and political institutions pool their resources in satisfying this prerequisite. In addition to its internal function of regulating the behavior of its members, the political institution satisfies society's need for protection from external forces through a defense system. Additional needs met by the social institutions will be discussed more thoroughly later.

### THE TECHNOSPHERE

The technosphere is actually the core of the study of intermarriage between Chinese and Americans. Without modern technology, such relationships would probably have been limited to an occasional wedding between a Chinese maiden and an itinerant sailor who had jumped ship in Taipei or some other port. A technological-determinist would say that social change is produced solely by the technospheric forces. The position taken in this book is that understanding the development of a technology provides a foundation of major importance as a determinant in some of the social changes that affect the mate selection process.

Without the products of science listed in the technosphere, the study of Chinese college students' attitudes toward intermarriage with American-Caucasians would not be possible, nor would it be necessary. Because of technological advances, the individual's reach has been extended across oceans, the voice can be heard around the world, and the eye can see into the outer reaches of the universe. The technological timetable will be briefly discussed in Chapter 10, focusing mainly on the Industrial Revolution.

There may be some question about classifying social mobility in the technosphere category. The reason for such an arrangement is that technological development has made all forms of social mobility possible. For instance, in the United States, technological development has expanded the economy, opening more opportunities for vertical mobility. It has made it possible to commute long distances to work or school. It has produced the mobile home enabling the retiree to live in the northern states during the mild seasons and the winter in Florida. The home on wheels has also enabled the migrant worker to ply his trade from site to site. These and other reasons justify the placement of social mobility in the technosphere.

No questions are framed to determine directly the influence of techno-logical development on the Chinese attitudes toward intermarriage with an American-Caucasian. The inquiry regarding the place of residence, how-ever, infers that technology affects the decision to some extent. Those indi-cating a preference for a post-marital residence in America, or other nations, would probably answer the question differently without the mod-ern methods of transportation, permitting them to return to the homeland overnight, and communication, enabling them to telephone to Taiwan as quickly as anywhere in the U.S. Other technological influences are revealed by the literature on the subject.

It should be recalled that the terms in Figure 4.1 were selected for three purposes. The first is to provide key concepts essential to an understanding of sociology. The application of the terms to sociological phenomena throughout the book should serve this purpose. The second objective is to provide linguistic pegs for a logically closed social system, which will be shown at the close of this chapter. The third goal is to choose concepts pertinent to the field study presented in the preceding chapter. The relationship between the major concepts in Figure 4.1 and the materials gathered through the questionnaire and readings in the study will be shown at this point.

A social system—or any other kind, kinship, electrical, or solar system—consists of interrelated parts. Without going into detail, a few illustrations will be helpful in showing the direct and indirect relationships within, between, and among selected cultural traits, listed in the five categories of Figure 4.1, as independent and dependent variables.

The first illustration treats the television program as an independent variable directly influencing other cultural traits. Within the technos-phere, the commercial breaks, or the interim between programs, regulates the use of the telephone, and the use of toilet facilities, for avid viewers.

Through televising the pageantry of inaugurations, political rallies, and patriotic celebrations, among other things, the "Three Principles of the Peo-ple" of the Republic of China, may draw more support from the patriots.

The television becomes a dependent variable when it is directly affected by cultural traits within its own and the other four spheres. For example, sometimes, because of the time factor, which may be a differential of as much as twelve hours, some television programs are taped and shown at a more convenient time. A direct telecast of a football game played at 2:00

P.M. Sunday is not going to have too many viewers at 2:00 o'clock Monday morning on the other side of the world—even if it is the Super Bowl. In these instances, sometimes the tape is shipped by air to distant places. Since professional football is a Sunday game, the television station program planner will delay the re-telecast until the following Sunday. In this way, the distant viewer is treated to the event at the same time, on the same day, a week later. In such cases, the timing of the television program relies on the air transportation system which makes it the dependent variable.

The television as a dependent variable being directly affected by a cultural trait in the psychosphere, such as the attitude toward public affairs, is seen if the patriotic fervor of the people prompts the television program producer to cover an inaugural event, rather than another program requesting the same time slot, even though the alternate programs would be more profitable monetarily. In these instances, the psychospheric trait is the independent variable.

Undoubtedly the home conditions, such as the working mother, nap time, and school dismissal time affect the scheduling of television's educational and other, programs designed for children. In other words, the family schedule in the instisphere wields an influence over the timing of television programs making the cultural trait in the technosphere, the television, a dependent variable.

Primary relationships especially between serious dating, or engaged, couples influence the manufacturers of wines, rings, and clothing, among other things, to sponsor television programs that appeal to couples enjoying such relationships. In such cases, the cultural trait in the statisphere, social relationships, influences the dependent variable, television in the technosphere.

Letters to the editors of news media, criticisms sent to the television producer, and protests of certain programs by religious, and other, groups are forms of interaction, a dynaspheric trait, which brings about changes in the dependent variable, television programs in the technosphere.

In addition to the direct relationships of the television as an independent variable, it has indirect relationships with other dependent or independent variables. Only one example will be given in each of these instances to illustrate this point. Suppose a viewer sees a commercial on the television advertising new cars at a reduced price, and rushes out to buy one. When all of the paper work is cleared and the car is brought home, a neighbor who does not own a TV, so did not see the commercial, goes over to inspect the car, and is convinced by the proud owner that it is a good buy, so he goes to the dealer and purchases one. The television is an independent variable that indirectly affects the sale of the automobile to the second buyer. The TV commercial is an independent variable exerting a direct influence on the first buyer, but an indirect influence on the second purchaser. The automobile sale is the dependent variable in both cases, because it resulted from the TV commercial.

The automobile sale can also serve as an independent variable indirectly influencing the purchase of a television set. This happens if the purchaser drives up to his home in the new car and the neighbor goes over to see, and talk about, it. When the neighbor, who does not have a television set, learns that the buyer bought the new car as a result of the commercial, he buys a TV because of the sales opportunities it offers. In this instance, the automobile is the independent variable indirectly influencing the sale of the television set.

This means that any single trait in any one of the five categories can influence, or be influenced by, either directly or indirectly, any one or all of the traits in any or all of the categories. These innumerable relationships are referred to as cultural relativity in sociological terminology. In essence, such a theory holds that because of these interrelationships, no cultural trait can be understood apart from its context. To illustrate, the tears of a couple coming out of church weeping can have many meanings. Perhaps the couple have made a confession and these are tears of relief. Possibly they have just witnessed a wedding and the tears are an expression of happiness, or maybe the couple have just attended a funeral and the tears are shed in sorrow. There is no way of interpreting the meaning of the tears without a context. If the couple is followed by pallbearers bearing a casket, the observer then knows that the tears are an expression of sorrow. If the couple is followed from the church by a bride in a wedding gown, and a number of persons throwing rice, then it is evidence that the tears are an expression of joy. The context provides meaning to the cultural trait.

Although the interrelationships between and among the concepts in Figure 4.1 have been shown, they have not been presented in any systematic arrangement. Since the fundamental concepts are all interrelated—each to the others, and to the whole—then these concepts in their proper relationships present the basic framework for a logically closed social system, providing a context in which each term can be better understood. Even though the terms have not been defined, by placing them in a systematic arrangement provides a context which reveals their function giving a better understanding of the term. At his point the logically closed social system can be considered a frame of reference for future use. In this respect, it represents a refinement of the classification system designed for present purposes.

All of the terms appearing in the classification system can be placed in the social system to be constructed, but the result would be so cumbersome that the purpose would not be accomplished. Consequently, a few significant cultural traits have been selected from Figure 4.1 to be systematically arranged. They are reproduced here for the reader's convenience. From the statisphere, culture, social structure, social groups, social status, and social roles have been selected. Society, social control, and social change represent the dynasphere. The instisphere is treated as a whole in the organizational structure. Socialization and social values are used from the psychosphere and the technosphere is included in its entirety. To make the various stages in the development of the ideal construct clearer, the key forms are underlined whenever it appears helpful.

The interrelationship of social *institutions* to other basic concepts is shown by the fact that they link social *groups* together and form the core of *social control*. Institutions are firmly embedded in the *social structure* of *society* and make social *change* difficult. They control the behavior of the individual, who is motivated through the process of *socialization* to acquire *status* and perform *roles*. Finally, institutions give permanency and continuity to *culture*.

The relationship between society and culture as presented in this chapter is the same as the relationship existing between a process and a product, when the latter is defined as the result of, and being constantly affected by, the former. In this sense, culture is the product of society that is being continuously retouched and reshaped through social processes. Culture, however, as a social heritage, had to precede society. The seeming contradiction of these two statements can be resolved by considering the relationship between society and interaction. For illustrative purposes, a simplified definition of society is a system of social and cultural relationships, involving more than interaction, which is actually social contacts. When social contacts become systematized, society exists. On the other hand, culture is produced with relative value, through even the most elementary forms of social contact. As soon as the first element of culture appears, progress has been made toward a system of such interactions. As this process continues, a system of social relationships is formed, and society results. As culture accumulates, it affects, and is affected by, future interactions of the new-born society.

Social interaction, then, gives birth to both society and culture. From the crudest and most primitive forms of interaction, the complex social systems of our present world have evolved. Likewise, from the first crude elements of culture, social interaction has produced a wealth of learned behavior.

In Chapter 1, the importance of language and the purpose of abstraction were considered briefly. At this point, the value of the process of abstraction can be seen. Through the process of abstraction, vast areas of knowledge have been narrowed to concise definitions. These definitions, that have been generally agreed upon, represent conceptions of perceived data and are labeled concepts. Now, those who agree in a large measure upon definitions and relationships of sociological concepts and agree upon which are basic to a theoretical social system will construct similar, but not identical, systems. The closer these agreements, the more identical the system, but because of communication failure, discussed in Chapter 1, no two systems can have identical meaning to different persons.

Through the process of abstractionism, those who accept the definitions of concepts in the following chapters, and who agree that these concepts in their proper relations compose a logically closed system, and when linked these concepts together in their functional positions will have a common basic framework for a logically closed social system.

The nucleus of such a system, then, is as follows: The individual through the process of *socialization* becomes a person, who through *interaction* acquires *status* and performs *roles* in *groups* that are linked together by *institutions* —the core of *social control* —protecting deeply embedded *values* in the *structure* of *society*, which undergoes *change* stimulated by *technology*. The processes and structure at any given moment represent *culture*, which provides the environment for the *socialization* of the individual. And the cycle is repeated.

The above statement is not to be interpreted as a prescription of the order which a chain of social reaction must follow. In fact, in many instances, social action affects all of these factors simultaneously. For example, when social contact is made between two or more persons, the social force set in motion can fan out in all directions simultaneously and even reach beyond a particular social system. Nor is it to be understood through the statement that the social chain of reaction must have its origin in the individual or person, it may be a group, community, or societal product. The statement is intended to reveal that social interaction establishes certain relationships among persons. These relationships develop patterns of behavior and controls that are woven into a social system.

A number of purposes have been served by this chapter. For one thing, the classification system, shown in Figure 4.1, provides an outline for the discussion of sociological concepts pertinent to an understanding of the process of mate selection. The second purpose is served by the construction of a theoretical social system, which clearly reveals the interrelationships of the basic concepts and provides a basis for the comparison of Chinese and American societies. In the third place, the relevance of the cultural traits shown in the classification system and the field study is shown. In all, a background is established for consideration of factors involved in intermarriage between Chinese and Americans.

# SECTION II

## COMPARISON OF KEY SOCIOLOGICAL CONCEPTS IN TRADITIONAL CHINESE AND AMERICAN SOCIAL SYSTEMS

The theoretical logically closed social system, presented in the preceding chapter, provides an ideal model with which to compare the actual social system of traditional China and that of the United States. The reason for considering both of these social systems is that the comparison of each of the concepts, as it functions in the two different social environments, provides a better understanding of the term. As mentioned earlier, by comparing two items, the qualities of each can be appreciated more fully than considering only one. Through comparison, a standard is set which enables the viewer to evaluate the object or idea more effectively.

For example, the previously considered concept "status" is more clearly understood when its meaning in the rural community is compared with its urban connotation. In rural areas, the successful farmer is held in high esteem, while in urban areas before the mechanization of agriculture and urbanization of rural areas, he is labeled a "clod hopper." With the change from subsistence to commercial farming, his status improved to that of a farm manager with a large business operation. The dwelling of the farmer is no longer a log cabin, a symbol of low status, but a respectable residence reflecting a higher status to the urban dweller. With improved residence, the inauguration of parity prices, crop quotas, and other measures, the status of the farmer has risen. Comparing the status of the farmer from the viewpoint of the "city slicker" in the past, who has become the suburbanite of the present, to that of the rural dweller, presently, reveals the importance of the concept "status" in ranking individuals in the social stratification system.

The procedure used in determining more clearly the meaning of each term is to first give a brief classical definition of the connotation assigned by one of the pioneers in European or American sociology. From this material, a definition is framed in keeping with the intent of the tone of the book *Conversational Sociology: An Intercultural Bridge Where East Meets West.* The gist of the concept is then embodied in a simplified form which cannot be dignified by the label "definition."

To further clarify the meaning of the concepts, the discussion of each cultural trait is summarized in outline form to reveal the interrelationships of the vital facets.

The second step in the procedure is to treat the concept in more detail at the beginning of the discussion, and then to apply it to the practical situation in describing the culture of traditional China and that of the United States. This is the reverse of the procedure used in the first stage. There, the term was narrowed from a broad field of meaning to a precise, scientific statement to a higher level of abstraction in the "conversational" definition and then to the less precise simplified identification. This second stage elaborates on the definition and delineates the meaning more clearly by relating each of its facets to a practical situation. A better understanding of the mate selection process is also provided as the operation of the mechanism is viewed in the traditional Chinese and American societies, and when it is, at times, applied to the social context of the Republic of China.

As a matter of convenience, the items appearing in the various spheres shown in Figure 4.1 of Chapter 4 are repeated at the beginning of each of the chapters dealing with that particular sphere. It would be helpful to have this figure readily available for reference as Chapters 5 to 9 are considered.

# 5

## The Chinese
## and American Statispheres

In this chapter dealing with the statisphere, the all-inclusive concept *culture* provides the context for comparing the Oriental way of life, as represented by traditional China, with the American life-style. The *social structure*, forming the framework in which the way of life is carried out in the two contrasting cultures, is also a major topic treated at this point. The treatment of *social group* focuses on the predominance of the primary relationships in traditional China as compared to the secondary society of America. The *social roles* enacted in the mainly acquired *status* of traditional China are differentiated from those played out in the achieved status stratification system of the United States. The degree of similarity in the concepts conditioned by the village way of life in traditional China is considered in respect to the industrial way of life in America.

### THE CONCEPT OF CULTURE

The use of the term culture in sociological literature varies from the inclusion of all products of the hand or the mind of human beings to the social practices common to a particular society. In the latter instance, as culture develops, it accumulates additional social material and is constantly changed through the interaction of the members of the society. Its value lies in the fact that it reflects the trials and errors of past social situations, furnishes a way of life for the present, and represents the social heritage of the future. Culture is the way of life within a society. It contains the patterns of behavior giving direction to the individuals in their pursuits of everyday life.

A classical definition by E. B. Tylor states that culture is "That complex whole which includes knowledge, belief, art, morals, way, custom, and any other capabilities and habits acquired by man as a member of society."

A composite definition formed by the terminology of various authorities forms a conversational definition. The concept culture designates the accumulated results of social interaction that has affected the modes of thought of human behavior, and which are socially (rather than biologically) acquired and transmitted, providing the factor of continuity to society.

A simplified definition of culture is "All products, both material and non-material, fashioned by the hand or mind of the members of a particular society."

In addition to the fivefold classification shown in Figure 4.1 of Chapter 4, culture has been classified in many different ways by sociological authorities. One essential dichotomy is the distinction between material and non-material culture. It must be remembered that these two segments of culture can be separated only for analytical purposes. In this classification, as well as all others, the traits are inextricably interwoven. In the dichotomy, for example, a table is an item of material culture, but the expertise required to assemble the table is non-material culture. The idea is essential before the product can take shape.

Another important classification system is offered by Ralph Linton's trifold categorization of traits according to the extent to which each trait is used in a culture. He distinguishes between and among universals, social alternatives, and specialties. Universals are those traits of society that are used by a vast majority of its members. In the U.S., eating with a fork, speaking English, and dress habits are examples. These are customs that a child internalizes as s/he grows older.

Social alternatives are various *acceptable* ways of doing the same thing. In an automat it makes very little difference to others if you have a sandwich, soup, or salad for lunch. All of these are acceptable ways of lunching. "Brown bagging" sandwiches in a country club house, however, would not be acceptable, and, hence, not a social alternative. Commuting to the office by automobile, taxi, car pool, or subway are all acceptable, and, therefore, social alternatives.

Specialties are those traits shared by a particular group in society such as plumbers, teachers, doctors, lawyers, etc. Within these groups, there are common characteristics which could be referred to as universals within this smaller segment of society.

By using Linton's classification (universals, alternatives, and specialties), an illustration of how a new cultural trait is introduced and accepted, or rejected, by society can be shown.

When a cultural innovation—which is defined as any new thought, practice, or material object—is introduced to society, it is pitted against an established cultural trait, either a specialty or a universal. The area of alternatives forms the battle ground where the innovation struggles with both universals and specialties for acceptance. If it gains a foothold, then the innovation is accepted as an alternative to either the universal or specialty trait and may eventually replace it. When an alternative is adopted by the whole society, it becomes a universal, or it may become a specialty when accepted by a particular group. Universals can, likewise, become specialties, or they may even be dropped completely from the culture.

The introduction and acceptance of the automobile as a means of local transportation illustrates this process clearly. When the automobile made its first appearance, it had the characteristics of a social problem. The noise from its backfires was responsible for many runaway horses. The manual starting instrument, the crank, broke many arms by its kickback, and the dust billowing from the contact of the wheels with the dirt road irritated everyone near enough to be affected by the "fallout."

The automobile was gradually accepted in the area of specialties as an instrument of recreation. The proud owner would don his duster to protect his clothing, his gloves to protect his hands, his goggles to protect his eyes from the flying particles, and his cap to protect his hair from the artificial dandruff. If the members of his family were rugged enough to join him, they would put on similar gear.

As the automobile became more and more accepted as a means of transportation, it posed a threat to the horses and buggy, which was the established mode of local travel. With the mass production of the Model "T" Ford, the price of the automobile became affordable. The conversion from the crank to the electrical starter made the automobile a bisexual, rather than a monosexual, vehicle. With these, and subsequent, improvements, the automobile won the battle of alternatives and became the universal practice in local travel. The horse and buggy retreated to the specialties area, and replaced the automobile there as a recreational resource, and a status symbol.

The selective process of culture determines the stability of a society. If the process is extremely discriminating, selecting very few of the alternatives, the universals in the society will predominate. This has been the pattern in traditional China.

> The evaluation of such practicality and realism to a dogma of social wisdom has dug the grave of Chinese reform. Some American skeptics are wont to say that yesterday's radical is today's conservative. That may be, but the fortunate fact is that today's conservative often has accomplished the radical task that he undertook yesterday. In China, for centuries the conservative has simply produced more conservatives for tomorrow, and the result has been a static society. (Hsu, 1981, p. 377)

From the foregoing, it can be seen that the stability of a society is affected by the proportions of universals to the total cultural traits, compared to the proportion of alternatives.

There is a positive relationship between stability and predictability. That is, the more stable the society, the higher the possibility of accurately predicting the behavior of its members. In an American restaurant, serving American food, the table will be set with silverware, because this is the universal practice. The waitress can accurately predict the type of tableware needed. It is difficult, however, to predict the customs of diners who select an American restaurant that serves only Chinese food. Some of the customers will prefer to eat with chopsticks rather than a fork. Consequently, such restaurants arrange the table with both types of utensils, affording the diner a choice.

In societies where tradition prevails, such as in pre-Communist China, stability is more evident, making predictability more accurate than in modern societies. If the traditional practice in mate selection is by arrangement of the parents, and tradition is an effective instrument of social control, then it can be predicted that the vast majority of marital mates will be selected in this way. In societies where the hand of tradition is not so heavy, then there is more individual choice in mate selection, and the prediction of marital mates is more difficult.

By using the classification system depicted in Figure 4.1, Chapter 4, as a point of reference, the function of cultural traits along with the selective process operating in the cultural system will become more evident. The term cultural trait is used advisedly. In the discussion of the classification of data, it was pointed out that cultural trait is a relative term. In this respect, socialization is a trait in the dynasphere, which is a trait in the cultural system or complex. Socialization, on the other hand, is a complex in which an agency, such as the family, is a trait.

Every cultural trait must serve a function in the society or it is doomed to extinction. The trait need not serve its original function to continue its existence in society, but it must serve some function. The tomahawk, for example, is of no value as a defensive weapon against a high powered rifle or a ballistics missile. However, as a museum relic, it serves an educational function. The tomahawk, and other relics, also function as a status symbol or a prestige item in the home of the owner. A cultural trait, then, that is outmoded must either change its function, continue as a status symbol, or die.

Archaeologists are continually unearthing remnants of primitive societies. The items recovered form somewhat of a cultural cycle. Some of them did not exist until they were ushered in through the cultural channel of innovation. For a while, they functioned in the primitive society as cultural traits and then they died with the extinction of the society. They were revised as cultural traits by the archaeologist when their function was changed from a utensil or tool to a museum item.

Because a cultural trait can be understood only in its context, according to the theory of cultural relativity, discussed in the preceding chapter, in order for a term to have a uniform meaning across a society, there must be a uniform context. This is more likely to be found in a traditional society, such as pre-Communist China, than in a modern society, such as the United States. In a complex society, a high degree of uniformity is not possible because the level of exposure to various segments of the culture differs among members of society. The skilled craftsman is mainly interested in the technospheric segment of culture. So, a garage repairman is much more likely to understand the operation of a diesel-powered electrical generator, which is in a field different from, but related to, automobile mechanics than a college professor in the field of literature. But the college professor in physics would understand the principle of operation of the generator better than the automobile mechanic would. The artist sees a different scene from a mountain highway overlook than an ordinary tourist. The difference in the degree of exposure to various cultural segments is greater in a complex society than in a simple one. Even in the most primitive societies, however, there is a difference in exposure to the culture, mainly based upon sex and age. In such societies, the cultural world of the female is different from that of the male. Also by crossing over the puberty line, the primitive novice is exposed to a different set of cultural practices than those experienced in childhood.

Inequitable exposure to culture has given birth to numerous types of subcultures in a society, which are defined as segments of society with distinctive lifestyles. Only to mention a few, there are male and female subcultures, teenage and elderly citizens subcultures, and professional athlete and construction worker subcultures. All of these categories or groupings have distinct characteristics which distinguish them from other social entities. The retirement centers of the elderly establish geographical boundaries in addition to the cultural differences. The jargon of the teenagers distinguish them linguistically in addition to their specialized interests. Many, many other examples could be given, but these should provide enough support to show that the American society is honeycombed with subcultures, some with more distinct characteristics than others.

From these illustrations, the difficulty in providing a uniform context in a single complex society is readily seen. When marriages cross over national boundaries, providing a uniform context is even more difficult. The degree of difference in such things as traditional practices, religious beliefs, and family structure construct cultural barriers which are difficult to overcome in intermarriage between Chinese and Americans.

Numerous ethnic pockets of population, which can be termed sub-cultures, are clearly distinguishable in the U.S. Chinatown, in New York, is a vivid example of a subculture. The restaurants specialize in Chinese food, the shops display Chinese products, and Chinese decor is everywhere in evidence. The spatial boundaries separating Chinatown from the rest of New York consist of nothing more than a narrow strip of asphalt, but the cultural boundaries extend across the North American Continent and the Pacific Ocean. There are also enclaves of Japanese and other nationalities. The European influence is strongly evidenced by the popular French Quarter in New Orleans, the Little Bohemia in New York City, and Little Italy in New York. There are numerous other communities scattered across the United States that are solidified by vestiges of an imported culture.

The rapid expansion of knowledge has made it impossible to master all facets of a highly specialized culture, resulting in an exposure centering mainly in one segment. The result is a division of labor and particularized interests. The school teacher's world revolves around education. In addition to the class hours, there are numerous teachers meetings, school activities requiring attendance, and those at which attendance is not required but expected. Seminars, special summer programs, including educational cruises, taking special courses to maintain standards, conferences and meeting with parents, and other teaching responsibilities leave little time for explorations into other fields of knowledge. Other careers are just as demanding, and some are even more so.

One of the main influences specialization has on personal relationships is in the development of different individual perspectives. For example, a number of persons with a variety of backgrounds witnessing an automobile accident would focus on different aspects of the unfortunate event. Although all would be concerned with the injuries sustained by the occupants, a doctor viewing the collision would calculate the possibilities of skull fracture or concussion, broken bones, or other bodily injuries. The mechanic would estimate the damages to the vehicle. The attorney would look at the possible grounds for a law suit. The insurance agent would wonder about possible claims. Still others would see the accident from other perspectives. Although different perspectives may provide stimuli for interesting conversations, lasting interpersonal relationships are, more often than not, developed between persons with similar perspectives.

Specialization splinters a society into distinctive segments. This has occurred to a much greater extent in the United States than in China. Consequently, the culture of America can be likened to a patchwork quilt compared to the solid-colored blanket of tradition characterizing Chinese culture. The differences in the two types of culture will become more evident as Chinese and American societies are contrasted throughout chapters five to nine. A contrast is drawn between the general type of culture in Taiwan, as well as other traits classified in the statisphere, with that of the United States in Chapter 10.

## SOCIAL STRUCTURE

Social structure, as used in a broad sociological sense, is the framework of society. It is a relatively fixed system of patterned social relationships with an appreciable degree of regularity. The degree of this regularity varies from that manifested by relationships of one individual to another, or to society, to that of the well-established social institutions. Just as structure is evident to the physicist in the single cell as well as in the astronomical system, social structure is evident in the most elementary, as well as in the most complex patterns of social relationships.

The use of the term social structure, then, in sociology is to provide culturally defined goals and the regulatory norms for the acceptable modes of achieving those goals. Both the goals and the norms are subject to constant redefinition. The rapidity and the extent of this re-definition varies with the degree of rigidity to which these goals and norms have been established in the social structure.

The expected patterns of behavior in every social situation are built into the social structure. A social situation is defined as a setting in which social interaction occurs. This may be in a flexibly structured group, in a rigidly established social institution, or in a casual association. In each of these situations, the persons involved refer to the segment of the social structure which sets forth the pattern of behavior expected of them in that particular social situation. Although proper conduct is prescribed by the social structure, circumstance may cause deviation from the normal pattern of behavior. Suppose, for example, the customs require a gentleman to tip his hat in greeting a lady. If the man with both arms loaded with bags of groceries meets a lady and follows the rules exactly, he must somehow free one arm, probably by putting the groceries on the walkway , and tip his hat. Since under such circumstances it is difficult, if not impossible, to conform to the expected pattern, the gentleman modifies the requirement. He may bow his head or lift a finger toward his hat or he may simply nod his head and smile. Such departure from the required behavior pattern is understandable and acceptable.

Social structure is not to be thought of as separate and distinct from the processes or functions of society, for these two are inextricably intertwined. They are the static and dynamic phases of the same reality—society. This can readily be seen by referring to the previously presented classification scheme. Although structural aspects of the social structure are distinguished from the functional aspects in the classification scheme, the differentiation is solely for analytical purposes. All social entities have structures and functions. The function is simply what the social unit does, and the structure determines the acceptable ways in which the function can be carried out. The linkage between social structure and social function, combined with the interrelationship between or among the various units within it, is termed social organization.

In addition, the static phase of society, social structure is not to be thought of as unchangeable. It is constantly acted upon by the processes which influence and reshape it. A change in the function of society causes a change in its structure, and vice versa.

A classical definition by Lester F. Ward states that a structure implies a certain orderly arrangement and harmonious adjustment of the materials, an adaptation of the parts and their subordination to the whole.

A composite definition formed by the terminology of various authorities forms a conversational definition. This definition states that the term social structure indicates a relatively fixed system of patterned social relationships, governed by culturally defined goals and regulatory norms that form the framework for any social group. Unless qualified by such terms as group structure, family structure, etc., it refers to the structure of society.

A simplified definition is "social structure is the framework of society."

A comparison of traditional Chinese and American social structures reveals the following differences. The focal point of the traditional Chinese social structure is group-centered compared to the individual-centered American social structure. In traditional China, the center of social activities is in the villages, compared to the urban centers in America. The cohesive force of the Chinese social structure is morale compared to interdependence in America.

The focal point represents the main difference in the social structure of traditional China and the United States.

[I]n the American way of life the emphasis is placed upon the predilections of the individual, a characteristic we shall call individual-centered. This is in contrast to the emphasis the Chinese put upon an individual's appropriate place and behavior among his fellowmen, a characteristic we shall term situation-centered. (Hsu, 1981, p. 11)

In a situation-centered social structure, such as traditional China, the individual is a vital link in a kinship system. In an individual-centered, social structure, such as that in the United States, he is nothing more than a dispensable number in a Social Security System. In the former, the individual is an end in a closely-knit, homogeneous social environment. In the latter, he is a means to an end in a heterogeneous social milieu. In the first instance, the individual is anchored to the solid foundation of tradition. In the latter instance, he is caught up in the whirl wind of urbanization. In the situation-centered society, the social control system operates efficiently, whereas in the individual-centered society social control has been undermined by anonymity.

The structural characteristics of societies or groups may influence behavior. Furthermore, certain types of social structure may promote conformity, while others do not. It is self-evident that in all of the above instances, the situation-centered society is more conducive to conformity than the individual-centered society. Therefore, the former type looks upon intercultural marriages less favorably than the latter type.

Life in traditional China revolved around the village. There are over half million villages in mainland China at the present time (Welty, 1984, p. 36). Villages and communities (the two terms are used synonymously) consist of neighborhoods, which are in turn a network of families. For the purposes of this discussion, the term community is used to identify a social phenomenon in the United States that the term village identifies in traditional China, which is a network of families. The degree to which the community spirit is evident in either society is dependent upon the degree of primary relationships demonstrated in its constituent parts. That is, if the "we" feeling which is paramount in families, is shared with the neighborhood, then this social unit radiates such a relationship. If the neighborhoods, constituting the village, all consist of families linked together by strong personal bonds, then the community spirit will be strong.

Morale is an important integrating force in the village way of life. Morale is a form of pride attached to membership in a particular social group. For example, the recruiting gimmick, "The U.S. Marine Corps needs a few more good men," reflects a high level of morale. If morale is high among the families, the neighborhood will serve as a medium through which such a characteristic is relayed to the village community. The importance of the morale factor in forming the community spirit in the U.S. can be seen in comparing suburban neighborhood with those in the ghettoes. The high level of morale is clearly evident in the neatly clipped lawns and the well-kept houses in the suburbs. On the other hand, the pornographic graffiti scrawled across the dimly lit corridors of tenements depicts the low level of morale existing in the ghettoes.

Although communities are usually thought of as locality groupings of population, it is difficult to establish clear-cut boundaries for such geographical entities in the United States. Boundaries delineating the political territory area are easily recognized, but communities usually spill over into areas beyond such demarcations. Services, such as repairs, utilities, and deliveries reach out from the community into the hinterland. The consolidation of schools has also blurred the community boundaries as children are bussed long distances from the outlying areas. Supermarkets establish shopping areas that fan out from the community center. In satisfying these various needs, the community encompasses neighborhoods in close spatial proximity, as well as those scattered across the nearby countryside.

The dispersed neighborhoods are incorporated into the community only to the degree of reciprocal interaction which takes place between them and the population center. For example, if the children in one of the outlying neighborhoods attended school in "Jonestown," most of the labor force of the neighborhood worked in Jonestown, and most of the families did their shopping there, the neighborhood would be much more fully integrated with the Jonestown community than a neighborhood in which only a few of the inhabitants used the center solely for shopping purposes.

The neighborhoods have more distinct geographical limits than the communities which they compose. Neighbors live in close spatial proximity to one another. A person can be neighborly to a friend who lives on the other side of a large city, but to become a neighbor one or the other has to change residence.

## THE CONCEPT OF SOCIAL GROUP

The concept group is of major importance in the field of sociology. Through its use, every type of human association is classified, all types of human collectivities, from a pair to a population, are designated. The group is an instrument of patterned relationships by which the individual is linked to the social structure.

Some authorities in sociology questionably hold that an adequate definition of a social group is two or more persons in reciprocal interaction. This means that every social situation is defined as a social group. Accordingly, two persons who have never seen each other before and speak to each other in passing provide the prerequisites for a social group. Such a definition is too broad to identify the special entity, social group. Even if the element of common interest is introduced, such as being pleasant in this illustration, the definition is still vague. It is essential for the interaction between the two persons to be structured before it can be defined as a group.

Structure, as indicated in the preceding discussion, involves patterned social relationships, which means behavior of individuals can be anticipated with some degree of accuracy. As an illustration, suppose a man waiting for a bus has an unlit cigarette between his finger and he asks an approaching passerby for a light. If the passerby responds, either positively or negatively, there is reciprocal interaction between the two persons. If the response of the passerby is favorable, the element of common interest is inserted into the interaction, which is to get the cigarette lit. The next morning the same man waiting on the same corner with an unlit cigarette makes the same request of the same passerby who responds in the same way. The third morning as the passerby approaches the same man waiting for a bus and sees an unlit cigarette dangling from his lips, s/he anticipates the request and produces his lighter before the request is made. In other words, he anticipated the behavior of the passerby on the corner because a pattern had been established. This forms the semblance of an informal group. If the relationship is perpetuated through a weekly luncheon meeting, or some other form of patterned interaction, an informal group is formed.

One classical definition of a group for sociology is a number of persons whose relations to each other are sufficiently impressive to demand attention.

A composite definition formed by the terminology of various authorities forms a conversational definition. According to this definition, a social group may be regarded as an entity of two or more persons united by a sense of emotional solidarity, of common purposes, or both, who enter into distinctive social relationships with one another.

A simplified definition of social group is that "a social group is two or more persons interacting with a common interest, forming a structured relationship."

There are various classifications of social groups. They can be categorized according to size, either large or small. Willingness is another basis for classifying groups. In this instance, they are either voluntary or involuntary. As the term suggests, voluntary groups involve a choice as far as membership is concerned, whereas identification with involuntary groups, such as conscripted units in the military, or prison relationships, or even the natural family, involves no choice. Social groups can also be sorted on the nature of their interests such as vested interest groups, which strive to maintain the status quo, or reform groups which seek to bring about changes, and thus unseat the vested interest groups.

The most significant classification of social groups has generally followed the example of Charles Horton Cooley in his distinction between small, intimate, groups and the large impersonal groups. These are usually designated "primary" and "secondary" groups respectively. Cooley makes the following distinction, without the use of the term secondary:

> By primary groups I mean those characterized by intimate face-to-face association and cooperation. They are primary in several senses, but chiefly in that they are fundamental in forming the social nature and deals of the individual. The result of intimate association...is a certain fusion of individualities in a common whole, so that one's very self, for many purposes at least, is the common life and purpose of the group. Perhaps the simplest way of describing this wholeness is by saying that it is a "We"; it involves the sort of sympathy and mutual identification for which "we" is the natural expression. (Cooley, 1902, p. 23)

As is seen throughout this work, a distinct line cannot be drawn between two types of social phenomena except for analytical purposes. Hence, there is no such thing as a pure form of primary or secondary group. In other words, the relationship in each such a social unit is not "either/or"; it is "both/and."

One of the characteristics of a primary group is intimacy, which means sharing the innermost feelings of an individual with another, while the secondary group is non-intimate. The impossibility of completely sharing our emotional experiences makes the primary group an analytical tool rather than a clear-cut delineation of relationships between two or more persons. It is an ideal type, as previously discussed, which does not exist in actuality. For example, suppose a friend expresses sympathy to a companion, who has recently lost his father through death, by saying, "I know exactly how you feel; I lost my father six months ago." No one knows "exactly" how another feels under such circumstances or in other experiences. Measured by this characteristic alone, then, a primary group is one that is more intimate than a secondary group, rather than being absolutely intimate.

The same can be said of a second distinction between a primary and a secondary group, which is the personal interests of the relationship. The primary group is more personal than the secondary group. A fine line separates personal feelings from intimate feelings. Again, the difference is a matter of degree and not of kind. An expression of intimacy may be considered a detailed account of a personal experience. The relationship may be likened to that between two friends as compared to that between two confidants. Two friends may discuss the sexual frigidity of one, which would be classified as a personal relationship, whereas a detailed description of the actual sexual experience would involve an intimate relation.

As with intimacy, the extremes of personal and impersonal relationships are not in evidence in normal associations. The qualifying term, normal, is used because there are historical instances in which the impersonal attitude is carried to extreme. There could not have been much personal interest on the part of the perpetrators of the "Death March" of Bataan, the concentration camps of Dachau and Buchenwald, and the atomic bombs of Nagasaki and Hiroshima. In all of these instances, the cause took precedence over personal feelings. This can also be said of present-day terrorism, criminal gang executions, and wanton homicides.

The third characteristic distinguishing primary group relationships from those of secondary groups is the degree of formality. Simply stated, form means structure. Hence, by definition of social group used in this work, structure is essential. There can be no such thing as a social group completely devoid of form. On the other hand, extreme formal relationships would be so rigidly regimented that they would be impractical. An exaggerated illustration of the "nth" degree of formality can be seen by two back-to-back introductory sociology classes given by the same professor in the same classroom. A student leaving one class, say at 8:27:321/2, can enter the next class an hour later at 9:27:321/2, and hear the professor speaking the same word the student heard in leaving the first class. About the only way this could be accomplished would be by using a tape recorder. Even then, if the instrument were started a split second later at the beginning of the second class than it was at the first class, the utterances would not be identical.

One way of determining whether a social group has a predominance of primary or secondary characteristics is through the use of titles. Formally called Doctor William Smith, the physician becomes "Bill" to his personal friends and is intimately called "Honey" by his wife.

Both primary and secondary groups have some advantages as well as some disadvantages. One advantage of the primary group is that it serves as an emotional outlet. An employee who has been reprimanded by his boss can purge himself emotionally through confiding in his wife or an intimate friend. Because of the compelling need for expressing emotions, the secondary society has provided some mechanisms, such as major athletic spectator sports, at which individuals can vent their frustrations, but such an arrangement only partly meets the need. The reprimanded employee goes to a football game, along with 85,000 others, and cloaked in this secondary robe of anonymity shouts, "Kill the bum." Little do the surrounding spectators know that the enthusiastic rooter has projected the image of his boss into the particular football uniformed individual to whom the threat is directed. Consequently, there is no sympathetic response on the part of others in this secondary setting as there is in the primary group.

A disadvantage of a primary group is that the emotional factor distorts objectivity in decision making. On the one hand, a military officer may select his son, rather than another equally qualified subordinate, for a preferential task, because of the emotional bonds. On the other hand, a military officer may select his son, rather than another equally qualified enlisted man, for a suicide mission in order to avoid being accused of showing parental favoritism.

One advantage of the secondary group is the greater opportunity it offers for achievement through ability rather than patronage, or lineage. For example, applications which do not indicate race, sex, or creed are screened on the basis of qualifications only. The employer, then, cannot be accused of favoritism or bias, and the applicants have an equal opportunity for employment.

A disadvantage of the secondary group, in this respect, is the dependence which must be placed upon the recommendations of others, especially former employers, regarding the character of the applicant. The superintendent of an applicant may write a glowing recommendation in order to rid his firm of an undesirable character. In this day when firing is fraught with difficulties, this may be the only means for the employer to cut occupational ties with the individual without the firm being sued.

In passing, it should be mentioned that size is an important factor in determining the type of relationship within a group. Primary groups are necessarily small because the number of interpersonal associations is limited. Although all primary groups are small, it does not follow that all secondary groups are large. A business relationship between a salesman and a regular customer, a secretary and an executive, a doctor and a patient may all very well be classified as secondary groups.

It should also be mentioned that the "face-to-face" condition in Cooley's definition is not necessarily a requirement of a primary group. The best example of a primary group is the family. To say that a primary group is dependent upon face-to-face contact is to say that the parental-child relationship ceases to exist when the child matures, marries, and leaves home for a lengthy period of time, if not permanently. The ordinary quality of the relationship may not be as intense but, normally, it is not terminated. In fact, the marriage of the son or daughter, which separate the offspring from the parents spatially may draw them closer together emotionally, strengthening the primary characteristics of the parent-child relationship.

Another example showing the lack of necessity for face-to-face contact in primary group relationships is shown by pen pals. Correspondents of this type may well use this channel of communication to express themselves more intimately than in face-to-face situations because it is less embarrassing. Some pen pal correspondence becomes so intimate that it leads to marriage and, possibly, the first face-to-face contact is made at the altar.

The social group serves two main functions in operating as an intermediary between the individual and society. One main function is to prepare the individual to become a responsible member of society, which will be discussed more fully later along with the topics of socialization in the dynasphere and family in the instisphere. The second important function is to act as a buffer to shield the individual from jolting experiences in society. Both primary and secondary groups serve these purposes.

In a traditional, or simple, society, where primary relationships prevail, the individual's contact with the social structure is direct. In a complex society, where secondary relationships are more predominant, the contact with the social structure is indirect. For example, suppose Joe's boy is having problems at a rural school. Joe meets the school superintendent at the market and says, "Jim, my son Johnny is having a problem with one of the teachers." Jim replies ,"I'll look into it." Whereas in a metropolitan center for Joe to go directly to the director of education, or to the principal for that matter, would be like a voice crying in the wilderness. Consequently, Joe goes to the PTA (Parent Teachers Association) with his son's problem. If the children of other parents have experienced similar problems, the PTA will probably take action. The concerted effort will yield far more effective results.

This example points out a difference between traditional China's social structure and that of the United States. Primary groups unite forces to shape secondary groups, which are merged to form associations, which combine to mold social institutions, which connect to form the social structure. In the above example, secondary groups resulting from the relationships of various families, and that consisting of teachers combine their resources to form the parent-teachers *association*, which is yoked to the other associations forming the social structure.

In the United States, the secondary groups and associations abound, while in traditional China, this in-between fabric is missing, which weakens the social structure. In both traditional Chinese and American societies

there are the nuclear organization of parents and children and the territorial organization, such as villages and towns. In both societies an overall national organization is headed by a central government. But while in China a near void exists between the two levels of organization, in America, an enormous number and variety of volunteer, nonkinship organizations mediate between them. A voluntary, nonkinship organization is used here to denote one that draws people together on some common interest for its promotion or prevention across territorial, communal, or kinship connections.

The primary importance of the kinship ties prevents the individual from wholehearted or even effective participation as a member of nonkinship groups or a citizen of the national state. The American individual is reared to leave the family and kinship base; he must find non-kinship groups in which he will find satisfaction of his social needs. Consequently the nonkinship groups proliferate, and the kinship group remains amorphous and permanently small. (Hsu, 1981, p. 396)

To contrast the search of nonkinship organizations in traditional China, and the proliferation of such groups in America, a study of "Participation in Organized Activities in a Kentucky Rural Community" is cited. The study is appropriate for showing the sharp difference between the secondary group structure in traditional China and the United States for two reasons. One is that the study was made in 1950, near the end of the period used in the book to distinguish between traditional Chinese and modern Chinese society. The other reason is that the study was made in a rural area, which provides a social environment more closely akin to the traditional Chinese milieu than that of the urban centers.

The community studied, numbering 1,900, incorporated the population within a geographical area radiating ten miles from the county seat. Approximately two-thirds of the adult population had membership in one or more of the 37 nonchurch, nonschool organizations. Eighty-four of the active members in the study spent an average of 381 hours a year, or over seven hours per week, in participating in the organizations. The ten most active members spent an average of 745 hours each per year, or more than 14 hours per week, in participation in the organization's program.

> The swift pace with which organized groups are appearing on the community horizon has given voice in many instances to "overorganization!" Such a criticism suggests that there are too many organizations in comparison with the amount of integrated community activity and perhaps that too few persons shoulder the responsibility for the programs. However, many individual organizations are concerned, in part at least, with the community as a whole and have as one of their objectives the integration of their membership into the total life of the community. (Richardson & Bauder, 1953, p. 3)

The functions of the family as a primary group will be discussed in the section on social institutions, but an adjunct to the family, the peer group, needs to be discussed at this point.

The peer group is a number of persons with similar backgrounds and are approximately the same age. They can have either a predominance of primary or secondary relationships in their associations. For the purposes of this book, the term peer group will be used to identify personal, intimate relationships. In this sense, it has a forceful effect on the process of mate selection in the United States. The first romantically-tinged associations with members of the opposite sex are usually experienced through group dating, which means that the peer opinion towards one of the members relations with a member of the opposite sex is influential. Even though the group member is strongly attracted to the particular person, in a romantic sense, the disapproval of the peer group during the early teen years will probably curtail the relationship, which could possibly have culminated in marriage. Even during the later dating period, the frequent practices of double dating requires compatibility of the four members in the limited circle.

The difference between the American and Chinese peer groups is that

> the American youth defends himself against the instability of his human relationships by making sure of his acceptance in some peer group. He furthers his needs for success by attaining some position of achievement in the group that accepts him. He also has to accomplish his efforts without consistent direction other than that of the dictates of this group.

The misconduct of the Chinese adolescent is more of an individual matter; his behavior is rarely dictated by his peer group. For the one group to which he is closely attached, and consequently the one group whose rules or commands have any real meaning, is the kinship group. If he gets into trouble, he not only incurs the displeasure of his parents and relatives, but he receives little moral support from most persons his own age. (Hsu, 1981, p. 350)

According to these two quotations, the American teenager is more dependent upon the peer group than the Chinese youngster, who is more dependent upon the kinship group. In both instances, the members are strongly interdependent.

The greater the interdependence of a group, that is, the more the members depend on one another and the more that rewards are given to the group rather than to the individual, the greater will be the conforming behavior. In independent groups, where rewards are given to individual members, there tends to be less conformity. conformity will probably be greater in team sports, such as football or soccer, than in an individual sport such as track or swimming. (Hsu, 1981, p. 39)

When the influence of the peer group is stronger than that of the family, then the behavior of the youth or young adult will be in the direction of the peer group, and vice versa. It follows that when the two groups are in accord regarding a particular issue an individual's position will either be strongly reinforced, if it is in agreement with that of the two groups, or heavy pressure will be exerted to alter the position if it is in disagreement.

There are three main differences between social groups in traditional China and the United States. One is that the first loyalty of the Chinese is always to their involuntary group, the family, whereas the American's principal loyalty is more than likely to be tied into a voluntary group. Many times the interests and values of the voluntary group differs from, or even conflicts with, those of the family. In traditional China, primary loyalty to the involuntary group prevents this from happening.

Another difference between the two societies is that in traditional China, the group relationships are predominantly of a primary nature, while in America the majority of relationships are in secondary group associations. As will be discussed later, even in business the emphasis is placed more upon the relationship between buyer and seller than it is upon the transaction.

The third dissimilarity between the social groups in traditional China and those in America is formed by the age factor. In the former instance, group relationships are more chronologically vertical than in America. Groups in China, both kinship and friendship types, include members of all ages. Children are constantly associated with parents, grandparents, uncles, aunts, and the friends of these relatives. In America, most groups consist of members in a similar age bracket. If the parents go to a party, a baby sitter usually takes care of the children. Adults are not welcome to children's or teenager's special events.

The importance of all three of these differences in mate selection will be discussed in Chapter 11.

## SOCIAL ROLE AND SOCIAL STATUS

Social role and social status are treated jointly because they are like two sides of a single coin. A social role is the basic trait of a society. In other words, it is the irreducible element in the complex of the social structure. A combination of social roles constitutes a social group which is the basic social unit of society. The social role defines the behavior required of an individual in a certain social position. The requirements of that particular position are determined by the social status. Much as a theatrical role portrays a particular character, the social role depicts a particular status or position. In other words, the status sets forth the expected behavior in a certain social position and the social role is the actual performance in that position. If the actor conforms closely to the expected pattern of behavior in the social—or theatrical—role, the individual is assigned a high status in that position.

For example, an individual occupying the status of college student is required to conform to certain standards assigned to that position. If the individual performs exceptionally well in all classes, he or she is placed on the Dean's List, and enjoys a high status as a student. Those who do not do so well are given a lower grade and occupy a lower status as a student.

In occupying the status of student, the individual plays a number of different roles simultaneously. Among these, in addition to the student role, the individual plays the role of classmate, a member of the student body, an ardent supporter of the university athletic teams, and as a representative of the university. Other possible roles are such as a fellow in a grant program, as a recipient in a student financial assistance program, as a dormitory roommate, and as student counselor. If all of these roles are played well, the student's name may appear in who is who in American colleges and universities.

In addition to ranking a role-player according to the performance, social status refers to an individual's total position in the stratification system of society. Social stratification provides a ranking system of individual members on the basis of their contributions to society. Since it is of vital importance to a society to maintain the health of its membership, doctors are ranked high on the stratification scale. Since culture, which is transmitted through educational channels, is essential to society, college professors also enjoy a high ranking social status.

A classical definition by Ralph Linton states that a status, as distinct from the individual who may occupy it, is simply a collection of rights and duties. A composite definition formed by the terminology of various authorities forms a conversational definition. The concept of social status indicates the relative position or standing of a person or group in the generalized institutional system that is recognized and supported by those with whom the individual or group interacts.

A simplified definition holds that status is an individual's ranking in the stratification system of society.

A classical definition by a modern sociologist, Talcott Parsons, says that a social role is the dynamic aspect of status, the behavior counterpart of the ideal or expected position defined by the concept status.

A composite definition formed by the terminology of various authorities forms a conversational definition. This definition describes a social role as the extent to which an individual conforms to expected patterns of behavior respecting the rights and duties associated with a particular status.

A simplified definition of social role is the "required behavior in a social position."

The two meanings of social status are distinguished by identifying the function of the term. When applied to a single status of an individual, the term is qualified by naming the positions occupied such as one's status as a student, parent, doctor, college professor, and others. In ordinary parlance, adjectives such as outstanding, good, average, below average, and poor are used to indicate the individual's ranking in a particular status. The other meaning of the term denotes the person's position in the stratification system.

The stratification system is usually classified according to two major categories—the social caste system and the social class system. The main difference between the two categories is the degree of freedom in moving up or down the social class scale, which is termed vertical mobility. President James Garfield might have exaggerated when he compared the rigidity of the European stratification system with the flexibility of that in the United States. The gist of his comparison was that the social status of an individual in the Old Country was firmly fixed like the strata of the earth, but in the New Country a person was like a drop of water which could be at the bottom of the deepest part of the ocean today and on the tip of the highest wave tomorrow.

The placement of individuals in a caste system is based mainly upon heredity. This is called ascribed status. That is, the position of the family in such a stratification system determines the social status of the offspring throughout life. Society assigns that position and the individual is yoked to it permanently. As distasteful as such a practice may seem, to one conditioned by a social class system, there are some advantages to it. For one thing, preparation for an occupation or career can begin in early childhood because the parents know what position the offspring is destined to occupy. In addition, pressure to improve one's social position is eliminated because the rigidity of the system prevents any upward movement on the social class scale. The tension of maintaining the social position is also relaxed because the person is fixed in the caste system. An important advantage is that the rigidity of the stratification system, which is the supporting framework of the social structure, stabilizes the society.

In a social class system, the social status is achieved. The position is determined by the family only as long as the individual is dependent upon that social unit. The flexibility of such a stratification framework makes it possible for a child, in the past at least, born and reared in a log cabin in Kentucky, with only the light reflected from the fireplace to study by, to become president of the United States. In the present day, however, the practice of giving the offspring of alumnae preferential treatment in the admission policies of prestigious schools makes vertical mobility a little more difficult by introducing another castelike characteristic into the social class system. One advantage of the social class system is the possibility of improving one's social position. This encourages initiative for individuals to produce, and this in turn contributes toward the progress of society. Another advantage of the stratification process in such a system is the selection of the best person for productive positions.

Although the stratification systems are separated through classification, some characteristics of each type are evident in the other type. Classlike practices encouraged by various events eventually caused the collapse of the four hundred year old Feudal caste system in England. The Black Plague that took a heavy toll of lives in England caused a reshuffling of the division of labor enabling competent serfs to advance themselves in the stratification system. The development of cities provided a haven for the underprivileged who advanced to the status of free men after one year of dwelling in the city. The church selected promising serfbound young men and improved their social status through the educational channel leading to priesthood. Other forces also undermined the rigid Feudalistic system causing its gradual conversion into a more flexible structure.

Likewise, in India the caste system has been weakened by social changes. The industrialization of the nation has caused changes in the division of labor, which is the basis of the caste system. One characteristic of an ideal caste system is the support of government and religion. The government in India withdrew its support in 1949 by outlawing the untouchable caste, which has weakened the caste structure significantly. Hinduism still supports the caste system, but education and urbanization have weakened its control over this type of stratification. Because social change cannot be legislated, caste is still evident in India. In order to survive, however, the caste system in India, has become more flexible by the infiltration of classlike characteristics.

Castelike characteristics are also strongly in evidence in social class systems such as that in the United States. The assignment of social positions on the basis of race, sex, religion, and nationality are traits of a caste system. Individuals placed by society in these categories at birth cannot rise above them regardless of their competency. Consequently, the stigma of caste is evident in social class systems which allow such inherited traits to influence that placement of individuals in positions of inferiority, or superiority, in the social stratification system.

The placement of an individual in the social class system is usually determined by three objective factors—wealth, education, and occupation—and several subjective ones. In addition to the subjective factors mentioned in the preceding paragraph, the attitude toward the objective factors is of extreme importance in identifying a person with a particular social class. A number of examples can be given to illustrate this point. A foundry worker is placed on a higher level in a steel center, such as Pittsburgh, Pennsylvania, than he would enjoy in an educational center. A college professor would be ranked higher in an educational center, such as Blacksburg, Virginia, where the school-term population by far outnumbers the resident population, than in a steel center. Wealth would be more important as a determining factor in ranking individuals in the stratification system in oil states, such as Texas and Oklahoma, where quick money is available, than in other states. Wealth also plays an important role in ranking individuals in resort centers, such as Miami Beach, Florida, Honolulu, Hawaii, and Reno, Nevada. As a result of these variations in ranking criteria in different geographical areas, it is difficult, if not impossible, to have a national social classification system in the U.S.

Before considering the concept of social role, it may be helpful to demonstrate the difference between the social caste and social class characteristics on the basis of choice. In ideal caste systems, there is no choice in occupational or marital selection, whereas in an ideal social class system there is. In the latter system, an individual may choose whether or not to marry. Marriage, then, is an achieved status. If the individual does marry, society assigns the male the role of husband and the female the role of wife. These are ascribed statuses.

As indicated earlier, numerous roles are attached to a particular status. Because these roles are enacted at the same time, they may very well come into conflict. Suppose a university is on the honor system as a result of student body action and an individual sees a classmate, who is also a friend, cheating on an examination. The question which social role should be given priority arises. The conflict between the student's role as a member of the student body, morally obligated to maintain the honor system, has come into conflict with the student's role as a classmate or friend.

In addition to occupying the status of college student, the individual may also be expected to conform to the requirements of the status of son or daughter, husband or wife, or mother or father. In the status of traditional motherhood, the student may also be expected to play the roles of wife, housekeeper, good neighbor, shopper, interior decorator, and other roles. These additional obligations make the possibility of role conflict more likely. If a child becomes ill on a day that a no-makeup examination is to be given in class, the individual must decide whether the mother or student role is to take precedence.

As a society becomes more complex, the possibility of role conflict becomes greater. For instance, the individual who occupies the status of father plays numerous roles. After he has made preparations for his workday, he plays the role of husband as he comes into the kitchen where his wife is preparing breakfast. In the role of customer, he goes out on the porch to get the morning paper. While there, the man who lives next door appears and the individual plays the role of a neighbor. As he goes back into the house, if the children have come downstairs he is thrust into the role of father. On the way to work, he plays the roles of a member of a car pool on the way to the station, a member of a commuter clique on the train, and a passenger on the elevator in his office building. Reaching the office he occupies different statuses as he goes from the outer office, where his position is superior to that of the receptionist and secretaries, through his office where his status is equal with that of his colleagues, and to his boss's office where his status is subordinate. Upon returning to his desk, the telephone rings and the individual wonders which among these and many other roles will he have to play. When the receptionist informs him who the caller is, he is given an instant in which to mentally muster the behavior patterns required in this particular role. So, when the receptionist asks, "May I say who's calling?" the purpose is not usually to decide whether or not the executive will receive the call, but to give him a second or two to adjust to the role he must play.

Because social roles involve required patterns of behavior, conditioning periods are needed to prepare an individual to perform as expected in a particular social position. Anticipatory roles serve this function in many, if not all, cases. Children play house in anticipation of the roles they will play as husband or wife, or mother or father. The engagement period is a time when the couple anticipates the roles they will play after the wedding ceremony. Orientation week for entering freshmen is a period in which they are introduced to the roles they will play later as college students. If the training is adequate, the transition into the new role will be smooth. If the preparation is not adequate, maladjustment occurs, resulting in conflict with roles of others. In marriage, the husband's expectations of the wife's role may differ from the conception the wife has of her role. The husband's image of the wife's role is more often than not patterned according to the behavior of his mother's role as wife. Likewise, the bride has conceived her idea of the wife's role from the association with her mother. Consequently, if the two mothers have different ideas as to how the wife's role should be played, the husband's and wife's ideas concerning the role will conflict.

The different role conceptions develop even though the cultural context is relatively homogeneous. It follows that conflict is much more likely to occur when intercultural marriages take place, especially between Chinese and Americans.

When a Chinese woman married in traditional China, her adjustment to the wife's role was difficult.

When she entered her new home, she was obliged to adjust to a new environment and a new set of relationships. Usually, she had not seen any of the family members before, including her husband. The sudden and sharp change from a secluded, familiar life to this rather public unfamiliar life frightened and confused her. Her most difficult adjustment was to her mother-in-law. Chinese mothers-in-law . . . were the rulers in the home, especially with regard to the daughter-in-law's training, discipline, and duties. (Welty, 1984, pp. 202–203)

How much more difficult it would be for an American woman marrying a Chinese to make the adjustment. She is reared in a social environment that condemns in-law meddling. To marry into a situation in which both she and her husband will be completely dominated by the mother-in-law would be entering into a role which would be constantly in conflict with that of her mother-in-law. The wide variation in the marital role concepts in the two societies discourages intermarriage between Chinese and American-Caucasians.

Chapter 5 has shown the variations in the statisphere of the traditional Chinese type of culture with that of the modern United States. Although many changes have occurred during the past half century lessening the obstacles of intermarriage between these two cultures, it is essential to bridge other gaps before such marriages are fully acceptable.

# 6

## The Chinese
## and American Dynaspheres

The functional aspects of society are treated in this chapter. Because society is a constantly changing phenomenon, it is treated in the dynasphere as a cultural concept. Social interaction, discussed in this chapter, is the basic process by which society is shaped, maintained, and improved. Social control is another of the dynaspheric traits which is essential to maintain order in society by regulating the behavior of its members. One of the functions of socialization, which is to be treated in this chapter also, is to prepare individuals for their roles in society and to develop the concept of self.

### THE CONCEPT SOCIETY

A very thin nomenclatorial line separates the term society from community, discussed previously. The use of the concept society, like that of community, sometimes is confusing because it, too, is an all-inclusive concept on the one hand, and is assigned a limited meaning on the other. There are societies with geographical boundaries, like the American society, and there are societies that are universal, such as professional societies.

The countless types of societies make it mandatory to define the term at a high level of abstraction. The small roaming band of food gatherers, forming a primitive society, must be included in the definition, as well as the sprawling, technologically oriented, modern societies. The sociological use of the concept society is to define the geographical territory recognized as an exclusive social unit involving a self-sufficient group on a national, or designated, level. In primitive societies, the application of the concept is limited to the territorial, rather than the national, scale. Although the types of societies vary widely, there are some common elements. These will be discussed later, along with social institutions.

The difficulty in giving a single clear-cut definition of society is evidenced by the numerous definitions appearing in the English language dictionaries. The term came into English usage in the sixteenth century and was derived from the Old French "Societe," and the Latin "Socius," meaning companion. Most of the definitions list it as a "corporate body of persons having a definite place of residence," or as a reference to cultured or fashionable society.

## COOLEY'S CLASSICAL DEFINITION OF SOCIETY

A classical definition by Charles Horton Cooley (1902) states that society is a complex of forms or processes each of which is living and growing by interaction with the others, the whole being so unified that what takes place in one part affects all the rest. It is a vast tissue of reciprocal activity, differentiated into innumerable systems, some of them quite distinct, others not readily traceable, and all interwoven to such a degree that you see different systems according to the point of view you take.

## COMPOSITE DEFINITION OF SOCIETY

A composite definition in the terminology of various authorities forms a conversational definition of society. The term society designates an everchanging complex system of sociocultural relationships, differentiated into innumerable systems with varying degrees of distinctness, so unified through reciprocal activity that the whole is affected by any one of its parts.

## SIMPLIFIED DEFINITION OF SOCIETY

A simplified definition of society is "society is culture in action in a particular geographic locality." Traditional China can be considered an agrarian, primary, traditional, or rural society. These types can be compared to American classifications such as industrial, secondary, modern, or urban society.

Because the term society is used in an all-inclusive sense, it is essential to place the concept in a classification scheme in order to gain a clearer understanding of its sociological meaning. Various criteria are used in classifying societies. Since society was defined as culture in action, the basis for classification is the predominant cultural characteristics. A rather detailed comparison of various aspects of traditional Chinese and American societies is given throughout Section II. At the risk of repetition, a general view of the differences between these two societies will be briefly discussed in relation to a few of the many classifications.

The classification of societies on the basis of technology results in distinguishing between pre-industrial and industrial societies. Traditional China, at least in the first part of the present century, cannot be labeled pre-industrial. Although the proportion of the labor force was insignificant in industry, there were some industrial plants.

Up to World War II the largest plants, the most up-to-date machinery, and the majority of China's industrial laborers were employed in the textile industry. Yet as late as 1930, hand looms consumed about 78.5 percent of the cotton yarn on the Chinese market. In 1933 the best reliable estimates showed that China had less than two million industrial workers and of this number, less than one-tenth of them were employed in plants hiring ten or more workers and utilizing some form of mechanical power. (Hsu, 1981, p. 312)

A more appropriate term for identifying traditional China is as an agrarian society, because the vast majority of the workers were involved in agriculture, which is the criterion used to distinguish between agrarian and industrial societies. When a predominance of the labor force is employed in manufacturing and service occupations it is termed an industrial society. In traditional China "at least 75 percent of the population had their roots in the villages or existed as absentee land lords" (Hsu, 1981, p. 299).

Another classification scheme based on the type of human relationships was developed by an early German sociologist, Ferdinand Toennies who labeled the two types Gemeinschaft and Gesellschaft societies. There is no exact translation of the German terminology, but the former type is similar to societies characterized by primary relationships while the predominant type of relationships in the latter are of a secondary nature.

In traditional China, primary relationships prevail. The members are held together by a set of common practices. Their behavior can be predicted, their interests are focused on another's needs, because the individual's concerns are group centered. These factors form a basis for primary relationships, which characterize traditional China. In America, secondary relationships permeate the social structure. Many forces are at work causing members of such a society to focus on individual interests. Business and friendship normally do not mix. Legality supersedes morality as a controlling device. The philosophy is live and let live, as contrasted to the Chinese viewpoint live and help live. Charitable institutions and social welfare programs have taken the tenderness out of helping others. Their needs are ignored because there are specialized agencies and programs designed to meet these needs at the secondary, rather than at the primary, level. Familism, a major influence in maintaining the primary relationships in traditional China, will be discussed later. It would be helpful at this point to consider two major types of societies classified by prominent sociologists and the reasons they had for designating them with distinguishing terms.

Emile Durkheim distinguished between mechanical solidarity and organic solidarity, based upon the nature of the cohesive forces in a society. The former refers to rural society unified mainly by tradition, and the latter term designates interdependence, through a division of labor, as the cohesive forces. The two terms seem to be reversed. The term mechanical solidarity, as Durkheim applies it, refers to the cohesiveness of a traditional society in which behavior is mechanical or automatic, based upon tradition which cements the community together. No thought is given to possible alternatives to the traditional method. This is the way it has always been done, and this is the way the individual was taught to carry out the practice. It is prescribed behavior and to deviate from the pattern is unthinkable. The term organic solidarity is applied to the urban type of society because the highly specialized division of labor necessitates a complex organization. The basis of cohesion in the urban society is interdependence, according to Durkheim.

Agrarian and industrial societies are terms used to classify societies on the basis of the predominance of occupation. These two types are similar to, if not identical with, classification of rural and urban societies on the basis of population distribution. Industrialization leads to urbanization. It follows that the difference in the two classification systems, rural/urban, exists because each is designed to satisfy the purpose of a particular study. The industrial arrangement emphasizes the impact of industrialization on the way of life, compared to agrarian societies. The rural/urban dichotomy emphasizes the effect of urbanization on the way of life, compared to rural societies.

As indicated earlier, this chapter compares rural and urban characteristics within Taiwan. To foreshadow any premature impressions that this portion of the chapter is a duplication of Section II, in which traditional China was compared to modern America, a distinction needs to be made between traditional and rural societies. Tradition is, without question, a characteristic of rural society, but it pinpoints only one difference. On the other hand, the rural characteristics to be used in the comparison with urban society are also found in traditional societies. In other words, these characteristics are constants, and as revealed in Chapter 2, cannot explain the differences between rural and traditional societies.

The variable that accounts for the distinction between rural and traditional societies, for the purposes of this chapter, is vulnerability to social change. There are two main factors that determine the penetration of the traditional armor of a society, converting it from a traditional into a rural type. One is the exposure to social innovations. A primitive society is an ideal example of this point. The adoption of new practices is slow and infinitesimal in such social units. Consequently, they represent the extreme type of a traditional society. The other factor is the acceptance of social innovations by members of a society. Earlier social alternatives were referred to as the battleground for social innovations. If the new cultural traits, over a long period of time of course, are adopted by the society, then they become social universals as a result of social change.

China, as dealt with in Section II, represents this type of traditional society. The cultural borders of the Great Wall are extended to coincide with the national boundaries. The traditional barriers of mainland China can be termed the Confucian curtain, rather than the bamboo curtain of the present-day. Although China was exposed to a significant degree of Western commerce for a century before the establishment of the Nationalist government on Taiwan, it did not yield to the pressure to industrialize. As a result, it was a traditional society, exposed to, but not penetrated by, Western influences and, therefore, was culturally invulnerable until the middle of the twentieth century. The Communists drastically, and abruptly, perforated the traditional social fabric of mainland China, and by force converted it into a rural society. Taiwan was also transformed into a rural society at that time through the necessity to rehabilitate the island and to gain recognition as the Republic of China.

Although there is a minor distinction between the two types, for the purposes of this book, the terms rural and traditional society will be used synonymously, as will urban and industrial or modern society. It should be noted that the reference here is to society and not to culture. Since traditional China has a predominance of rural characteristics, it is referred to as a rural society. Because of the predominance of urban characteristics, America is classified as an urban society. The rural sectors within the United States, however, are referred to as rural cultural areas, not as rural society. Likewise, the urban areas are designated urban cultural areas. Urbanization and industrialization will be discussed more fully later.

Societies are also classified according to the types of economy prevalent in the social structure. The earliest form of economy is referred to as the food gathering economy or societies. These are represented by small roaming bands, with an estimated population of fifty to two hundred. Such societies were constantly on the move, because the limited food supply of a particular geographical area was rapidly exhausted.

The hunting economy enabled society to become slightly more sedentary. The hunters ranged out into an extended area and supplemented the food supply by bringing back the game to the camp site. The fishing economy provided the stability that contributed toward the establishment of the first semi-permanent villages along rivers and lakes. The food gathered, and that resulting from hunting expeditions, was augmented by the supply of fish floating by the door. The agrarian economy provided the basis for a much more sedentary type of society through the cultivation of crops and the domestication of animals. The food was now available not only by chance, but the supply could be carefully planned and the harvest rather accurately predicted. The industrial economy has produced a highly complex modern society. The food problem in an industrial society is not so much how to produce it, but how to control the production, so that the market is not glutted. The food production problem has been solved, the major problem in modern society is its distribution.

Among other classifications, are those based upon literacy—preliterate, nonliterate, illiterate, and literate; those based upon political structure—monarchy, oligarchy, democracy, communistic, and theocratic; and those based upon modern economic types—capitalistic, communistic, and socialistic.

## THE CONCEPT SOCIAL INTERACTION

Social interaction is the irreducible trait in the process by which various aspects of society are formed and maintained. It is one of the primary bases of human behavior and social organization. The social structure provides the framework in which social interaction takes place and it is also a product of social interaction. For example, two persons meet and decide to form a group relationship. The agreement to create the group evolves from interaction between the two and the structure of the groups is developed through the same process. After the group is established, it provides the mechanism by which other social interaction is carried out.

Social interaction involves meaningful, reciprocal relations between or among two or more persons. Whether or not meaning is essential for social interaction is not a question. The meaning of social interaction ranges all the way from being barely discernible to a position of paramount significance. On a crowded elevator, it is almost impossible to avoid unintentionally touching another passenger. Whether or not this physical contact, especially between members of the opposite sex, represents social interaction, depends upon the degree of meaning attached to it. Usually such a physical brush with another is ignored. If the contact is unintentional on the part of the male, and the female determines that by looking at the unintentional offender, then there is some degree of meaning attached to it. If the act is intentional, and the female recognizes it as such, then the meaning may become of paramount significance, leading to a lawsuit or trip to the altar. Regardless of the direction, the result may lead to in the future, social interaction has taken place.

A composite definition based on the terminology of various authorities forms a conversational definition of social interaction. Social interaction may be defined as meaningful reciprocal relations between or among individuals.

A simplified definition of social interaction is "reciprocal relations between or among individuals."

Since all human behavior is the result of social interaction, the different types operate directly or indirectly, at different levels of society, and to varying degrees of intensity. Direct interaction is a meaningful exchange through interpersonal relationship with one or more individuals. Indirect interaction takes place when the exchange is culminated through an intermediary, which can be either a person or a thing. To illustrate this point, consider three different situations involving a lovelorn young boy. On Valentine's Day, the lad takes a heart-shape box of candy to a young lady he has been admiring secretly as a means of informing her of his affection, which he has been too shy to reveal verbally. Whether the girl accepts the candy and rejects the overtures, or accepts or rejects both, this is a form of direct social interaction. If the teenager sends the symbolic message by a messenger, and the girl responds in one of the three ways mentioned, this represents indirect social interaction through another person.

Perhaps the teenager is not old enough to deliver the message by either of these methods, but rather expresses his emotions by carving his initials and those of his girl friend, enclosed in a heart-shape, on a tree. An act such as this represents the interaction of an individual with the physical environment, but it is not at this point, social interaction. If the lad's friend says to him, "I didn't know you cared," then the act becomes meaningful. The carving on the tree, a thing, becomes the instrument through which indirect social interaction takes place.

In addition to the person-to-person level, social interaction takes place between an individual and a group, or between groups, on a societal level or intersocietal level. The intensity ranges from a casual comment to a casualty as a result of violent protests, from the explosion of a firecracker on Independence Day, to the explosion of an atomic bomb over Nagasaki and Hiroshima. This is saying that social interaction occurs in every imaginable social situation.

Some forms of interaction cause discord within groups, while other forms promote harmony. Although both competition and conflict are usually classified as disruptive interaction patterns, competition is not detrimental to congenial relationships unless it develops into conflict. For example, in a football game, where good sportsmanship prevails, the two teams are in competition with one another. International interaction of this type is used at times to create good will between nations, if the ball carrier gets what he thinks is an unnecessarily rough tackle from a linesman on the other team and says, "I'll get that guy," the competition turns into conflict for that particular player. In a lighter vein, if the player is only upset physically he continues to compete, but if he is upset emotionally, as well, the game becomes a conflict for him.

Competition is a much milder form of opposition than conflict. Competition attacks the issue, while conflict attacks the person. The channel of communication in competition is discussion, while in conflict it takes the form of an argument.

The heavy emphasis upon major athletic events, especially in professional sports, and to a significant extent at the college level, and even in major high schools, has shifted the form of interaction in these events from competition to conflict. Some high schools deny a major portion of the students an adequate physical educational program in order to field an eleven-man football team. Some coaches direct the team on the expedient philosophy, that the end justifies the means. Contradicting this position, Grantland Rice writes, "For when the one Great Scorer comes to write against your name, He marks—not that you won or lost—but how you played the game." This has been paraphrased by some coaches to read "It isn't how you played the game, but if you won or lost."

Such attitudes in sports, and the reversal of the Golden Rule in business "Do it unto others, before they do it unto you" has mace competition more divisive in America than it was in traditional China.

> Instead of being divisive, Chinese competitiveness tends to bring men together. Chinese families strive to pass their equals in ceremonial activities" bigger and better funerals, weddings and birthday celebrations, and larger and finer residence, clan temples and genealogical records. All of this is directly related to obligations to parents, relatives, and even the community at large. The initiators gain face and the participants share the glory. Competitive victories of this order do not depend on the success of one person being based on the failure of another. . . .
>
> American competitiveness, in spite of many rules and attitudes concerning sportsmanship and chivalry, never brings men together because its basis is "each for himself." One individual's gain invariably means some degree of loss to others. (Hsu, 1981, pp. 320, 322)

Conflict, as a form of social interaction, is in evidence in America in many different social areas. The race problem, the generation gap, inequitable distribution of goods and services, the struggle for women's rights, labor/management disputes, and many other social conditions are all examples of discontent. These result in protest marches, sit-ins, demonstrations, and many times, violence. In a word, conflict is evidenced in America through the interaction of reform groups and the vested interest groups.

Although conditions were much more conducive to such movements than in the United States, reform groups did not exist in traditional China.

> For many centuries China has been overpopulated, land has been scarce, agriculture has been arduous, and malnutrition and even starvation have been the lot of untold millions. But instead of producing an inventive or even commercially aggressive spirit, these facts induced in the people who inhabited the villages an even greater desire to stay where they were

in spite of the fact that it meant a further reduction of their already low standard of living.

Further, the relationship between the gentry, representative of the vested interest group, and the peasantry, a source of potential reformers, was "characterized as personal, paternal, and, therefore, often cordial" (Hsu, 1981, pp. 300, 321).

There are three patterns of social interaction that tend to solidify members of groups, or societies. In two of these types, cooperation and accommodation, the individuals retain their identify, while in the other, the dominance and submission pattern, the identity of the subordinate one is merged with that of the superordinate individual.

Cooperation is simply the act of pooling resources. Although this type of interaction is a characteristic of the dynasphere in both traditional Chinese and American societies, it serves different purposes. Americans cooperate with one another because their individual efforts are not adequate to meet the demands of the undertaking. Swapping labor in rural areas is an example of this type of interaction. In traditional China, cooperation was an inherent element in the social structure. The difference between the two societies is in the perspectives. The American looks at the task and determines whether or not he needs to seek cooperation. The Chinese, as an integral member of a cooperative group, looks at the tasks which can be accomplished through this pattern of interaction.

As the term suggests, accommodation is adjusting to an unwanted minor condition in order to attain a desirable major goal. A husband and wife will ignore their minor differences for the sake of the children. A developing nation, whose citizens are irritated by the ethnocentric American will minimize this attitude of superiority in order to receive assistance from the United States. As soon as the aid comes to an end, they express their actual feeling with, "Yankee go home." Accommodation is a pressured cooperation which, nevertheless, serves as a combining influence. Accommodation is an important type of social interaction for the purposes of this book, because intercultural marriages require that minor cultural interests be subordinated to major marital interests. Whether to eat with a fork or chopsticks should not be a major stumbling block to marital success.

The dominance-submission type of social interaction considered is of significance in the study of Chinese/American-Caucasians marriages. It is a trait of traditional China's patriarchal family. The personality of the submissive one is completely submerged into the interests of the dominant one. The questioning term, "why?" is deleted from the vocabulary of the submissive wife and children. When the patriarch gives a command, the only question the submissive ones can ask are those dealing with instructions needed to carry out the order. So when the husband/father says, "jump!", the wife/children ask, "how high?"

To summarize, five types have been listed in the discussion of social interaction. The first of these is competition in which the relationship is impersonal. The second, conflict, is a type of interaction in which the relationship is personal. The third type, cooperation, is the pooling of resources. The fourth type can be simply described as an agreement to disagree. Finally, the fifth type is dominance and submission and is the submergence of the subordinate personality into that of the dominant person.

## THE CONCEPT SOCIAL CONTROL

Social control was not born full-grown as a set of restrictive measures, but it evolved parallel with and as part of society. Both social control and society as known today are twin-born products of stimulus and response. Since stimulus and response are impossible without association, the sources of social control are the desires and attitudes of the individual as these have been shaped by his association with others. The very root of social control, then, is self-control, as the individual endeavors to order his life in a pattern acceptable to his associates. Because the majority of human beings are responsive, and conform to the patterns of expected behavior, cohesion and stability are provided the social order.

All forms of social interaction, discussed previously, are governed by the process of social control. This regulative capacity of social control standardizes human behavior. The patterns of culture, discussed also earlier, establish the ideal, or the normative, level of behavior. The effectiveness of social control is measured by the degree to which the actual pattern of behavior conforms to the ideal. The actual, or statistical, level of behavior, however, does not always conform to the expected practices. The wider the gap existing between these two levels, the smaller the measure of stability within the society. Social control narrows the gulf between the statistical and the normative levels of behavior, thereby stabilizing the society. An ideal stable society—which does not exist—is one in which no change occurs.

Stability makes human behavior more predictable. The normative order, for example, requires a Chinese to marry a Chinese. If this endogamous ideal, which is to marry within one's own social group, is adhered to in every instance, prediction that a particular Chinese woman is going to marry a Chinese man would be highly accurate. Changes in the mate selection patterns widens the gap between the statistical level, the actual number of intermarriages, and the normative level, the expected number of intermarriages, making predictions less reliable.

A composite definition based on a combination of terminology of various authorities forms a conversational definition. Social controls are those particular processes and instrumentalities whereby the behavior or feeling of any person or group is influenced in such a way that some restoration of regularity, uniformity, and predictability of their behavior is assured.

A simplified definition of social control is "social control is the process by which human behavior is regulated, standardized, and is made predictable.

The core of social control consists of social norms which are required behavior patterns in certain social situations. The main function of social control is to make human behavior more orderly. This is done by applying social pressure to bring the actual behavior patterns into conformity with the ideal model. Social controls are designed to protect the values of society. The degree of pressure applied to protect those values vital to the existence of society is greater than that exerted to protect less important values. If a practice is of no consequence to society, such as whether the shoe is put on the left or the right foot first, then no pressure is applied to make the practice uniform. In practices involving social values, however, the social pressure ranges all the way from the use of gossip to the use of the death chamber to penalize offenders.

Folkways include such customary practices as etiquette, courtesy, proper dress, and the show of respect, among other things. The least of the normative pressures is applied to assure conformity to these mundane behavior codes. Nonconformity to the folkways results in ridicule, gossip, or some other light penalty that causes embarrassment.

Mores are must behavior patterns such as those required by religious groups and prestigious organizations. They are deeply entrenched in the culture. They are more obligatory than the folkways and form the basis of religious laws. The penalty invoked for violating the mores is ostracism, or banishment from the group. Since the practices protected by the mores are of more value to society than those protected by the folkways, the penalty for violations is much more severe.

Laws range in authority from regulatory laws, such as building codes and traffic regulations, to customary laws, which are established by precedent. Laws apply the ultimate pressure to bring the behavior of individuals into conformity with the required pattern. Violators are punished by the threat of, or actual, physical punishment. Deviations from all three norm types result in varying degrees of emotional punishment, but only violators of the law are threatened with, or actually endure, physical punishment. Occasionally, a judge will deem the emotional suffering of a first-time offender as sufficient to assure proper conduct in the future, and will waive the prison sentence or will put the offender on probation.

The degree of effectiveness at these different levels of social control varies from society to society and even from subculture to subculture, or situation to situation. In a society where reputability or face-saving, is of high value, such as traditional China, the folkways exert stronger control than in societies in which it is of little consequence. This is also true of tradition-bound small communities where an individual's actions reflect on the whole family. Folkways do not control behavior, however, in a situation where anonymity prevails, such as in metropolitan areas of the United States. A person slurping soup in a New York automat is not overly concerned about the negative comments of those at the next table. The soup will soon be slurped, the diners will be dispersed, the echoes of the critical remarks will remain at the table where they were uttered, and the soup slurper will be lost in the crowd. In contrast, noisily consuming food in traditional China conformed to the folkways. Slurping soup, chewing with the mouth open, and belching were forms of compliments to the chef.

In the same way, the degree of effectiveness of mores as instruments of social control varies according to the circumstances. In primitive societies, mores are much more effective in controlling behavior than in modern societies. The severity of the penalty, ostracism, is tantamount to the death penalty in primitive societies because survival is contingent upon societal cooperation. Whereas in modern society if an individual is ostracized from one group, it is easy for him to unite with another group, serving the same purpose. There are some organizations in modern society, however, in which the mores operate effectively in controlling behavior. Being excommunicated from certain religious orders, for some, means eternal damnation, so these conform to the group requirements rather than run the risk of such punishment. Conformity to the ethical codes of the American Medical Association, and the American Bar Association, can be expected because ostracism usually means the destruction of a career. The mores of prestigious groups, or close-knit families, exercise similar control.

Even though the mores are very effective in some instances in regulating behavior in American society, they were much more effective in traditional China. A good example of this difference is the unbelievable power filial piety wielded over the individual. Financial support for the parents was a primary responsibility for the son, even if it meant depriving his own children of essential food. The obligation did not end with a satisfactory performance in this respect because economic support is not the only way in which Chinese children are obligated to their parents. The son not only has to follow the Confucian dictum that "parents are always right," but at all times and in all circumstances he must try to satisfy their wishes

and look after their safety. If the parents are indisposed, the son should spare no trouble in obtaining a cure for them. Formerly, if a parent was sentenced to prison, the son might arrange to take that parent's place.

If the parents were displeased with their daughter-in-law, the good son did not hesitate to think about divorce. In the service of the elders, no effort was too extraordinary or too great. (Hsu, 1981, p. 81)

It was not uncommon for a son to voluntarily enter into economic bondage for the rest of his life to express his loyalty to his parents by arranging an extravagant funeral for them at their deaths.

Filial piety was not limited to the sons. Daughters also had responsibilities in this respect. "In a 1966 autobiographical article, Mr. Keng-sheng Hao, the most important figure in Chinese Olympic affairs in China before 1949," gives the following description of this mother:

Mother was well known as a woman of charity and piety (shan jen). She was also filial to the point of foolishness as well as superstitious. Before marriage, she sliced flesh from one of her arms for my maternal grandmother's illness. After marriage, she once did the same for my paternal grandmother's recovery. Even today I still find it hard to imagine how she could do it in her rural conditions of life, with a pair of scissors but no anesthetic and no sterilizing agent. (Hsu, 1981, p. 82)

Law applies the strongest social pressure to implement conformity, and through authorized agents it protects the highest values of any society. In primitive societies, a council formed by village chiefs or the patriarchs constitutes the legislative, interpretative, and enforcement agents of the laws. In modern society, those responsibilities are delegated through elections or by appointments. The individuals selected are given the authority to act in these various capacities. In fact, in modern society, the legal machinery has become so complicated and the knowledge so specialized that it is almost necessary to consult an attorney to determine which attorney to retain for a particular legal problem.

In spite of all the laws ground out by the wheels of justice, many turning on a full time basis, at the national, state, and local levels, social problems abound in modern society. Whereas in primitive society with no written, and few customary, laws, there are few social problems. From this, the conclusion can at least be inferred that mores are more effective instruments of social control in primitive society than laws are in modern society. From the example of filial piety, it appears that the same inference can be made in regard to social controls in the traditional Chinese society.

On the levels of the folkways and mores, group pressure is the most influential behavioral control. Whereas laws wield the strongest force at the societal level. The strongest form of social control is evidenced when the mores and laws support one another. This occurs where the value protected, such as human life, is of supreme importance to the society. Laws that do not have the support of the norms are difficult to enforce and are usually repealed, witness the Volstead Act. Mores, without the support of the law, such as prohibitions of interreligious marriages are even more difficult to enforce.

The norms not only vary from situation to situation. They also change over a period of time. Prior to the prohibition era, consumption of alcoholic beverages by men in the United States did not violate the norms in some segments of society, such as that of the construction workers. In fact, in this category, the ability of a man to hold his liquor was a prestige symbol. In some social circles, such as among athletes, drinking alcoholic beverages was a violation of the folkways. Most churches considered it a violation of the mores resulting in excommunication. In all of these instances, the consumption of alcoholic beverages was controlled by group pressure through the folkways or mores, if controlled at all. What this says is that the control of alcoholic beverages changed in some instances from no pressure to the pressure of the law, by putting probationary measures into law in 1919 through the Volstead Act.

Since this Eighteenth Amendment to the Constitution of the United States did not have the full support of the mores, it was an ineffective measure which was repealed in 1933. In other instances, it changed from the slight pressure of the folkways, or heavy pressure of the mores, to the full pressure of the law. Then the social pressure was relaxed and the control reverted from the law to the group enforcement of folkways and mores.

## THE CONCEPT NORMS OF DEVIATION

Deviation from the norms in a complex society is inevitable because for one thing, the norms come into conflict with one another at times. Suppose, for example, a husband's wife becomes suddenly and critically ill and he is driving her to the hospital early in the morning with very little traffic on the streets. In this emergency situation, he could get his wife to the hospital sooner if he exceeded the speed limit discreetly. He has the choice of conforming to the norm included in his marriage vow to "protect" his wife or obeying the speed law. The norms have come into conflict so the husband cannot conform to both completely.

Further, as a result of the diagnosis of his wife's illness, the doctors inform the husband that the disease is terminal, but that the wife should not be made aware of the fact at this time. When the wife asks her husband, "what did the doctor say?" the man faces another norm conflict. He must either conform to the norm of truthfulness, or conform to the norm that requires him to "protect" his wife from the knowledge that would put her in further jeopardy.

Habitual deviation from the norms, because of conflict or other reasons, by a significant number of people establishes norms of deviation. It is doubtful if any police officer would stop a motorist traveling 46 mph in a 45 mile zone. Although slight, this is a deviation from the norm. There is a tolerance limit on each side of the norm that allows for some deviation. When the behavior stays within these limits, it is considered normal, but when it exceeds these limits to a significant degree the individual is classified as a social deviant. An educated guess would be that the vast majority of drivers exceed the 45 mph speed limit, at times at least, by approximately five miles, and are seldom stopped by a traffic officer even in a radar zone. When this deviation becomes standard speed, then the norm which *requires* the speed to be limited to 45 mph becomes a norm of deviation which *expects* the speed to exceed the norm by a bout five miles.

These norms of deviation result in evolutionary, rather than revolutionary, social change. Although social change will be discussed more fully later, the above example offers an opportunity to illustrate gradual social change. Suppose the legislators recognizing that a significant number of motorists are driving 50 mph, instead of adhering to the speed limit, decide to enact a law changing the speed limit to 50 mph and strictly enforce it, rather than leave it at 45 mph with lax enforcement. For awhile, this new law would be adhered to but gradually the norm of deviation would be established at 55 mph. The legislators again would yield to the actual behavior and change the required limit to 55 mph and gradually the expected pattern becomes 60 mph, and on and on. Through norms of deviation, evolutionary social change occurs.

In summary, the application of social norms to present-day American, and traditional Chinese, marriages will illustrate the different levels of social pressure applied in each society and the differences between the marital practices. In the United States, rice throwing serves as an example of the folkways, intrareligious marriages are required by the mores, and the marriage license is required by law. In traditional China the fixing of the marriage date was a folkway, the arrangement of the marriage by the parents, through the middle-man, was required by the mores, and signing the marriage contract fulfilled the legal requirement. Many other examples could be given on each pressure level. It should be noted that the degree of pressure varies according to the importance placed upon the practice in various segments of society. Rice throwing, for example, in some marriages may be considered more essential than in others, and could well be classified among the mores rather than the folkways.

Figure 6.1 depicts in tabular form the description of the norms and the penalty for violating them.

FIGURE 6.1:  Penalties for Breaking Norms

| Norm | Description | Penalty for violation |
|---|---|---|
| Folkways | Least pressure: customs | Ridicule, gossip, embarrassment |
| Mores | More pressure: religious laws | Ostracism: exclusion from the social group |
| Laws | Most pressure: legal authority | Actual or threat of physical punishment |

# 7

## The Chinese
## and American Psychospheres

The materials in this chapter provide the key to understanding the attitudes toward intercultural marriage because they are concerned with the mental aspects of culture. Without becoming involved in psychological theory, framed with the precision of scientific terminology, the factors involved in forming attitudes toward intercultural marriages are briefly discussed. *Socialization* produces the *personality* of the *individual*, by framing the *attitudes* toward *values*, and prepares the person at various *stages* and through certain *agencies* for a responsible position in *society*. The underlined terms are to be treated in this chapter in respect to their importance in intercultural marriage between Chinese and American-Caucasians.

The terms selected to represent the contents of the psychospheres are considered pertinent to the classification system especially designed to serve the purposes of this study, and are not by any means all-inclusive. For example, a treatise on the impact of industrialization on mate selection in America would more than likely include materialism as a major factor in the psychospheres. Neither should an exhaustive discussion of the key terms, which are listed, be expected. A listing of values, to name only one of the key terms in the psychospheres, would be limitless. Only those values considered of major importance to the attitudes of Chinese college students toward intermarriage with an American-Caucasian are considered.

### SOCIALIZATION

One of the effects of social interaction, discussed earlier, is the socialization of the interacting individuals. From the moment of birth, physical and social environmental factors begin to have their effect on the infant. Socialization is a two-pronged process. It involves more than simply conformity to the practices of the group. This is the beginning point in the process, but as the individual becomes aware of the expectations others hold regarding his behavior, the concept of self emerges. As this occurs, he becomes more and more governed by the attitudes and wishes of others, which he has internalized, and less and less regulated by external forces. This phase is carried out mainly during the periods of infancy, childhood, and adolescence. The second prong of socialization acquaints the individual with, and prepares him for, roles to be enacted as a member of society. This process begins early in childhood and continues on into adulthood and even into senility. It is effective in every instance where the individual is willing to, and capable of, redefining a social situation. In other words, the individual is never completely socialized. The twofold function of socialization, then, is to shape and develop the person through the individual's absorption of group ideals, among other things, and through the external forces of social control.

One classical definition states that socialization is the process by which individuals are taught to function in the group in which their wishes are created and realized.

A composite definition resulting from the terminology of various authorities forms a conversational definition of socialization. According to this definition, socialization is the process by which the person is developed through interaction, by the internalization of group ideals, attitudes, and wishes, and by the influence of external sanctions, all of which make the individual member a functional unit in his group.

A simplified definition would describe socialization as being the process by which the individual develops into a responsible member of society.

## THE INDIVIDUAL, THE SELF, AND THE PERSON

The individual, in the strictest sense of the word, is the biological self. It is the sum total of the single human being's biologically inherited traits and characteristics. Each biological organism at birth is an individual, the raw material from which society is formed, and a subject of socialization. For this reason, the original nature of the individual is important to sociology. Before the individual is an hour old, the process of socialization begins, which develops the self-concept. As the individual denotes traits, characteristics, and potentialities that are inherited, the self denotes traits, characteristics, and potentialities that are acquired through social contact. In the process, the personality, which is an expression of the self, takes shape. The person does not participate as a total entity in all social relationships. Hence, there are many selves that are evident in a single person, each differing according to the situation. These various selves are reflected through personality traits.

The family plays an extremely important role in the earliest stages of development of the self. The family provides the first significant social environment during the most impressionable years of the child's life. It is in this social context that the first measures of social control are applied to modify the biological drives of the infant, and give direction to the emerging self. Because of this virtually singular social influence, the individual's self will be closely similar to the family pattern, at least during the early years of childhood.

The development of the self goes through a selective process. In modern society, family members select those traits which they deem desirable and establish them as a guide for the developing child. At first, these are accepted without question. But as the child is exposed to different ways of doing things, especially in the peer group, questions are raised about the recommendations of the family. As a child gets older, s/he initiates a selective process of their own, as far as parental tolerance limits will allow. If the deviation from the recommendations are not condoned by the parents, the child compartmentalizes the self. One aspect of the self is displayed in behavior in associations with the parents, while the other aspect is presented to the peer group. In traditional society, there is no need for a screening process on the part of the parents because the practices are universal and are transmitted intact from one generation to the next.

Compartmentalization of the self is not as prevalent in traditional societies as it is in a modern one, but it does occur. As the father disciplines the son, for example, he is stern. As he teaches the son hunting skills, he is tolerant. And as he consoles the sick child, he is understanding. There is no pretense as these roles are expressed in the form of personality traits. In other words, the personality traits and the various aspects of the self are practically identical in traditional society.

Such is not the case in modern society. The congenial salesman may actually be a cantankerous individual. In making a sale, he may converse with the customer in a cordial manner. At home, he grumbles with his wife. He may respond graciously to questions of the buyer. In answering his child's inquiries, he may respond gruffly with "Don't plague me with your questions, go ask your mother." He may listen sympathetically to the difficulties of the purchaser, but when the wife seeks an attentive ear to air her frustrations, he shuts her off abruptly by saying, "Don't tell me about your problems. I have enough of my own at work." In other words, the radiant personality of the salesman is a pretense that differs widely from the self, or the true personality traits, of the husband and father.

At home, the salesman "lets his hair down." He acts himself. For some, this is also one of the functions served by a vacation. The employee is relieved of the pressure of conforming to an artificial behavior pattern. A businessman's convention in a distant city also frees some husbands and fathers who fit themselves into a pretentious mold of family relationships. In this respect, a traveling salesman, as well as his wife and children, may derive benefits from his work away from home that are not available to the home-based agent. Some marriages succeed because of extended absences, of this nature, while others are weakened for the same reason.

For the most part, even in modern societies, personality traits at least approximate genuine reflections of the self. This means that persons are straightforward, or as Popeye would say, "I yam what I yam." Even though persons attempt to be their real selves, certain social situations cause them to apply controls that alter their expressions. Such alterations are acceptable and even sometimes admired. For example, if a person with an abrasive personality is leveling a barrage of barbs at an individual, the target's self may want to cry out, "Shut up!", but the individual being mild-mannered will control that urge. S/he will either ignore the remarks or will respond in an even tone that draws a conspicuous contrast between the two types of communication.

The dominant personality traits are usually evident in all areas of an individual's activities. That is, an industrious university student will be ambitious in a chosen career after graduation, and will be aggressive in pursuing other goals. On the other hand, a timid person will be reticent at work, in social gatherings, or in the home.

A society reflects the general personality types of its members. The image can be seen more clearly in traditional societies, than in those that are modern, because the personalities are cast in a uniform mold. Various sectors of a modern society, however, reveal distinctly different personality types. In the United States, for example, the north-eastern area reflects a more aggressive type of personality than in other areas. The rural area personality types are more conservative, and more reserved than the urban personality types.

Since personality traits are the products of culture, intermarriage between a Chinese and an American-Caucasian will, in most instances, bring together two different personality types. The general characteristics in traditional and modern society, discussed above, reveal some of the differences between the types of personalities prevalent in traditional China and in the United States. As the agencies and stages of socialization are discussed later in this chapter, the effect of the cultural variations on the personality will be dealt with more specifically.

## ATTITUDES AND PERSONALITY DEVELOPMENT

The personality is a composite of the attitudes of an individual. If a person has a wholesome attitude toward life in general, then the personality will reflect such a disposition. The attitudes of the parents and others are of paramount importance in the developing child. The family provides an emotional environment in which attitudes are nurtured. These, in some instances, are imposed by the parents. At other times, the attitudes are developed through psychological osmosis. No deliberate attempts are made in such instances. The attitudes evolve as a product of the emotional environment. A sensitive child can detect tension between parents even if it is not overtly expressed. Emotional vibrations convey messages between two individuals in intimate relationships that need not be communicated orally. A parents pat on the hand of a child may serve as an expression of affection, assurance, or may even be interpreted as a form of censure, even though it is exerted with the same pressure in each instance. The emotional context distinguishes between the meanings.

However conveyed, the attitudes of others are instrumental in shaping the personality as they are incorporated by the child, or individual, and become an integral part of the self. Not only do the attitudes *of* others influence personality development, but the child's attitude *toward* others, and their attitudes *toward* him, are important in this respect. If the attitude toward another is one of respect, then the child will modify its behavior in such a way that the action will be favorably received by that person. The response, in other words, depends upon the child's attitude toward the individual providing the stimulus.

The Chinese culture affords the child a much broader field of associations in which to form attitudes toward others than the cultural context in the U.S.

> The Chinese child grows up amid continuing or frequent contacts with a number of related individuals besides his own parents and siblings, but his American counterpart grows up in much greater physical isolation. Thus very early in life the former is conditioned to getting along with a wide circle of relatives while the latter is not. (Hsu, 1981, p. 86)

The Chinese child's attitude toward his parents then is conditioned by intimate associations with numerous other members of the kinship group. The American child's attitudes toward his parents is limited to his interaction with them only, especially during the earlier years.

This conditioning of the Chinese child by extensive, intimate associations with other members of the kinship group provides a different emotional context in which attitudes toward others develop than is found in the American family.

> The mutual affection of Chinese parents and children is toned down compared to that of their American counterparts. Since parental authority varies with circumstances, the parental image in the mind of the growing child must necessarily share the spot-light with men and women held in much higher esteem, such as grandparents and with those regarded as the equals of the parents, such as uncles and aunts.

The feeling toward parents and other adult authority figures being divided and diluted, the child does not develop a paralyzing attachment to, or strong repulsion against, the elders. . . .

The inevitable result of the omnipresent and exclusive control of American parents over their children is greater and there is a deeper emotional involvement. The American parent-child relationship is close and exclusive. To the extent that they are the only objects of worship, they also are liable to become the only oppressors. Accordingly, when an American child likes his parents, they are his idols. When he dislikes them, they are his enemies. (Hsu, 1981, pp. 87, 86)

Just as important in shaping the personality, and probably more so, are the attitudes of the parents and others toward the child. In traditional China, children are exposed to the adult world at an earlier age. They participate in birthday celebrations of the elders and in other social events. Likewise, the parents and other older relatives participate in the children's special occasions.

The American social scene is quite different. The child's world and that of adults are distinctly and purposely separated. Elaborate plans are made by the mother for the child's birthday, but she and the father do not intrude upon the special occasions of their youngster.

The separation of the children's and the parents' worlds marks a significant difference in their attitudes toward the child. The attitude of the American parents is that they are provider, protectors, and agents to serve the child's needs. On the other hand, the Chinese parents consider the relationships they have with the child of secondary importance compared to the relationships they have with other relatives, especially their own parents. They do not shield the child from the real world, as American parents do. Actually, they place the child in a definite role, and encourage him to assume a responsible position in society as ability permits. In other words, Americans "glorify their children's behavior," while the Chinese "take their children for granted" and "minimize their importance." "The important thing to Americans is what parents should do for their children. While to the Chinese, it is what children should do for their parents" (Hsu, 1981, p. 80).

## PERSONAL AND SOCIAL VALUES

The attitudes of persons center in personal or social values. If an attitude is to develop, there must be an object toward which the attitude is directed. This means that an attitude is actually a value judgment. An individual has the most favorable attitude toward whatever may be of greatest importance in his scheme of things.

Values, both personal and social, are prioritized according to their importance, forming a set of personal values on the one hand and a social value system on the other. When a significant number of persons agree on the importance of certain principles, these become social values, which, for one thing, form the foundation for religion. In other words, values are central to a religious faith. For example, top priority is given to filial piety in the personal values scheme of all traditional Chinese, which makes it a social value. Filial piety, in traditional China, was elevated to the status of religion through ancestor worship.

Socialization perpetuates the values of a society. The process is carried out more effectively in a traditional society than in a modern one, resulting in a more uniform value system. This is because the major social institutions are intermeshed through a strain of consistency. In traditional China, for example, belief in Confucianism permeated the social structure in a dominating capacity for 2,000 years. The core of Confucianism is "right action" defined in five basic social relationships. Three of these relationships deal with the family-filial piety, older brother and younger brother, and husband-wife relationships. The foundation of the educational system is Confucianism. Government leaders were selected on the basis of their knowledge of Confucianism. Proper conduct in economic endeavors is required in the social relationships between neighbor and neighbor.

In modern society, such as the United States, because of the widely varying interests, the social values within, between and among the major social institutions often come into conflict. Different political philosophies are expressed through the liberal Democratic Party and the conservative Republican Party. There are also liberal and conservative forces that oppose one another in the religious realm. A major division is in evidence between labor and management in the economic institution. There are no uniform procedures in the socialization of the child in either the home or at school. Consequently, the value system of America is much more diverse than that of traditional China.

Lack of concerted effort in promoting social values offers the opportunity for personal values to become of primary importance to the individual. Simply stated, the focus determines the difference between personal and social values. Personal values are those interests of importance to the individual, while social values are principles considered of major importance to society. As pointed out in the discussion of social control in the dynasphere, the norms protect social values. When conformity to the norms prevails, as in traditional society, the social values take precedence over personal values. If more emphasis is placed on personal values, as in modern society, value-conflicts occur and social problems develop.

Personal values form the core of an individual's life. These are the things that make life worthwhile for the person, and actually form the basis for an individual religion. A personal value is a driving force that gives purpose to life, which is a function of religion. Individual religion can be simply defined as "belief in a supreme value." For some, this supreme value is wealth. In order to gain it, these individuals sacrifice family, friends, and even health. If this core disintegrates for some reason, the worshipper has nothing to live for so, in many instances, he takes his own life. Some live for Friday night and payday, when they can look forward to a weekend of revelry and squandering. Individual religion serves functions similar to those of established religions. The difference is in the object of worship and the fact that individual religions are not based on a system of beliefs.

Personal values conflict frequently even in an intracultural marriage. The husband may place a high priority on business and consider his home more as a convenience. In this instance, the home is a means of attaining his goal in business. The wife may have the opposite view. To her, the business is a means of providing a home. Such a situation does not mean, necessarily, that the marriage is doomed to failure. One set of personal values may complement the other. A division of labor is established in which matters of business are the responsibility of the husband, and homemaking, and social relationships, are the primary concerns of the wife. Or, the interaction pattern may be one of accommodation, discussed earlier, in which the husband or wife, or both, adopt an attitudes of tolerance toward the other's set of values in order to pursue their own interest.

## SOCIALIZATION AGENCIES

There are numerous socialization agencies and other social influences that contribute toward the preparation of individuals for their roles in society. In the first primitive societies, the family was the only agency necessary to perform this function. The complexity of society today, however, has made it impossible for the family to completely satisfy all of the needs of its members to enable them to function efficiently in society. Consequently, additional agencies have developed to perform specialized functions in socializing the members of society.

### THE FAMILY

The family is the primary agency of socialization even in contemporary society. It is in this emotionally charged social unit that the small package of squirming original nature begins its development into a social being. Many and varied factors determine the nature of the socialization process. The order of birth (first, second, or third child), the sex, the state of health (frail or hardy), the social class of the parents, and many other external conditions influence the shaping of the infant as it develops into childhood and the later stages of biological development.

Parent-child relationships also influence the socialization process. The order of birth is of importance in this respect. The first child is the center of attention of the parents for the first year or two. If a second child becomes a part of the family unit, then the attention of the parents has to be shared. Unless calculated preparations are made, the first child may resent the intrusion of the second child. Whatever the attitude of the first born, the socialization process changes. The process also varies in accordance with the size of the family. In large families, such as found in traditional China, siblings are given more responsibility in child training and care than in small families found in the United States.

The degree of companionship with each parent is likewise of importance in the socialization of a child. If the father's occupation keeps him around the home much of the time, as is the case in an agrarian society, the socialization process is different from one in which the father travels most of the time, or even when he commutes long distances to work.

In some of the large cities in America, the father has to leave home for work before the child arises and returns home after the child has been put to bed, which leaves only the weekends for companionship with the child. In these cases, the early socialization is mostly the responsibility of the mother. If the father is home most of the time, the social distance between him and the infant or child determines the degree of companionship of the two.

In cases where the mother has work in addition to her home responsibilities, the child is deprived of her companionship much of the time. This does not necessarily mean that the mother who spends all of her time in the home does a better job of socializing the child than one with a second career. Many full-time mothers are less of a companion than one who spends only two or three hours a day with the child. The measure of a good mother, as far as the socialization process is concerned, is not how much time she is with the child, but how she spends that time. In this day of push button appliances, the main function of the mother is making a home rather than keeping a house. As Edgar Guest says, "It takes a heap o' livin' to make a home . . ." This statement refers to the development of a satisfying emotional family unit with bonds strengthened through companionship. A mother with a second career sometimes can heap more livin' into the life of a child in a few hours than one who is with it all day.

Regardless of the conditions, the primary responsibility of the family as a socialization agency is to serve as a link between the child and the general society. The family selects behavior patterns it wants the child to follow. It sifts out the values it wants the child to adopt, and it interprets for the child the role it is to play as a responsible member of society. In other words, as an agent of socialization, the family endows the child with behavior patterns that will serve as a guide, a set of values that will provide motivation, and emotional maturity that will provide fortitude in preparing the child for a responsible position in the society.

## THE PEER GROUP

The peer group, which is composed of members with similar backgrounds and who are near the same age, is another important socialization agency. A main contribution of the peer group is that it exposes the child to a social unit that does not exercise the same degree of authority over its members as the family does. The child may even play a role in which he, himself, exercises authority. In younger peer groups anticipatory roles are played that acquaint the actors, through an imaginary world, with the positions they may well occupy in adulthood. Friendships are formed and the child's horizons are widened as the number of associations increases.

The peer group is of much more importance in American society in this respect than it is in traditional China.

When the American child, driven by independence training, wants to make it on his own, he must seek another group to substitute for the group at hand. This means that the American youngster, at school age, must learn to transfer his allegiance from the kinship (and kinship-connected) group to a group composed of his unrelated peers, the gang. (Hsu, 1981, p. 111)

On the other hand, the compulsion to seek satisfaction of social needs outside the family is not felt by the Chinese children or youth.

[T]he Chinese child not only finds satisfaction of all his social needs in the kinship group where he begins life, but he is under no compulsion to leave it as he grows up. ... If the child has a few friends among unrelated peers it is condoned. But if he has too many of them and their common activities interfere with his studies or family duties, his friends will be branded "fox friends and dog cronies" and he a wastrel. On the other hand, he will be much admired as an example of a good son and a good man if he has few outside associations and devotes his entire energy toward working and pleasing his parents. Popularity among peers is a condition which some Chinese youngsters may enjoy, but it is not an objective toward which they must strive. (Hsu, 1981, p. 115)

Possibly, if not probably, the values of the peer group will differ among various members. Because of this, the parents have the responsibility of determining whether or not the values of the peer group members are in accord with those of their child, especially when the child reaches the teenage bracket. This is not necessarily for the purpose of having the child avoid all playmates with differing values, but it is to acquaint him with the variations in order to prevent the child from being confused by other values.

American peer groups are much more likely to counteract the socialization process of the family than those in China which usually reinforce the family training.

The American adolescent's misconduct is likely to be the price of his belonging to his own age group. Trouble with the law merely hurts his parents, whom he often intentionally disregards, but it may earn him a firmer place among his own, and it is their rejection he fears. Under this compulsion, he is likely to do anything dictated by his peers.

The misconduct of the Chinese adolescent is more of an individual matter; his behavior is rarely dictated by his peer group. For the one group to which he is closely attached, and consequently the one group whose rules or commands have real meaning, is the kinship group. If he gets into trouble, he not only incurs the displeasure of his parents and relatives, but he receives little moral support form most persons his own age (Hsu, 1981, p. 350).

During the teenage period, the peer group's importance and influence increases in the United States. The needs of an adolescent are different from those of a child, and the peer group is designed to meet these needs. One function of the peer group is to implement an association between the sexes. The first stage of this development is usually carried out through mixed parties. In this heterosexual setting, the teenager normally has the support of his or her counterparts of the same sex. The peer group after, or even during, the party can give guidance to the teenager by constructively criticizing his or her actions.

In traditional Chinese society, such guidance is unnecessary, because marriages are arranged by the parents. In many instances, the bride and groom do not even see each other until the wedding.

The teenage subculture is a prominent part of modern society. This fact extends the influence of direct contact with teenage peers to the broad scope of the national teenage image. In order to conform to the mores of such a sub-unit of society, and conform to the image, teenagers will often compromise their own values. They will, many times, listen to music that grates on their nerves, and pretend to like it. They will wear distasteful clothing in a matter-of-fact way. And they will endure the discomfort of long, scraggly hair all in order to be recognized as a conforming teenager by their peers.

THE SCHOOL

In teen age, the American school is indispensable as an agency of socialization. The explosion of knowledge has made it necessary to have specialized education at the high school and the university levels. Usually the high school has a basic core of required courses which serve the fundamental socialization needs. With the aid of these courses, the student is able to develop into a well-rounded individual as he approaches biological maturity. Through the behavioral sciences, the student matures socially developing tact in his relationship with others. Through this field, he also develops emotional maturity, enabling him to accept defeat or failure without becoming unduly disturbed. Courses in English and literature sharpen his communication skills. Such courses as logic and philosophy enable him to mature intellectually, and courses in specialized fields contribute to his vocational maturity. All of these forces, as well as many others, supplement the family efforts in the socialization process.

School organizations also open opportunities on both the higher and lower academic levels for the process of socialization to work more effectively in developing necessary skills which prepare the student in a practical way for society. Debating teams, and civic organizations expose the students to the democratic process. Interest in the arts is cultivated through music, art, and drama clubs. Experience in exercising authority is gained through leadership in various organizations. All of these activities along with peer group associations in an ever increasing sphere of influence are vital parts of the socialization process.

The school does not function in the same way in traditional China in socializing the child. "Practically all Americans go to school until they are sixteen, while even in 1945 (upgrade to recent times) less than 30 percent of Chinese children received any formal education at all" (Hsu, 1981, p. 117).

THE MASS MEDIA

The various forms of mass media wield a heavy influence in the socialization of the individual. The television and other forms of communication media, through fact and fiction, through cartoons and travelogues, and even through commercials, parade socialization forces before the viewer. The TV serves as baby sitter for the child; it transports a rock music concert to the teenager's living room; it provides insights into family problems for the adult; and it exposes senior citizens to profitable retirement experiences. Needless to say, mass media have been much more important in America in these respects than in traditional China.

In closing this part on socialization, it should be said that the patterns used by all of these agencies, as well as other social forces, in the socialization process include the social norms on all levels of pressure. If the socialization agencies operate efficiently, proper conduct on the part of the individual will be assured, meaning that social control will be operating at a high level of efficiency.

## STAGES OF SOCIALIZATION

The socialization process can be thought of as a series of unique experiences. Uniqueness, like many other sociological phenomena, is a matter of degree. For the person, who has never flown before, taking a jetliner from San Francisco to Honolulu is a unique experience. For the pilot and crew, the flight is routine. There are various stages of socialization and each new stage represents a unique experience for the entrant. The process continues from the moment of birth until death.

Within a few days after birth, the infant is introduced to the distinction between the sexes by the decor of the nursery in the home. The color of the bed linen, and clothing, if not the nursery walls, the pictures, celluloid rattles, and crib gadgets surround the new comer with symbols of one sex or the other.

The early childhood stage of socialization is spent in preparation for school. This is an extremely critical period in the training of the child for it is the stage in which norm internalization should occur. Norm internalization means that a social norm has been accepted and integrated within an individual's own value system.

When norms are internalized, behavior becomes automatic. There will be a strong tendency for the person who has deeply internalized the norms of politeness to say "Thank you" to the mechanical voice that gives the time of day over the telephone. A person is not naturally polite or naturally kind, as is sometimes said. The person internalizes the norms to such an extent that the resulting behavior becomes second in nature. There will be no indecision regarding proper conduct in areas in which the person has been trained, because he or she will "naturally" do the right thing.

The next level in the socialization process is geared to meet the demands as the child is prepared for adolescence. The American family faces more of a challenge during this period of development, than in infancy, for two reasons. One is that the child's time is divided between the home and the school for most of the year. This mean that the socializing efforts of the family are limited timewise, making it essential for the family to carry out the task in a more concentrated manner. The second reason is that the child is exposed to values that differ from those of the family. If the norms and values have been internalized during early childhood, the association of the child with others who have been trained differently will be more problem-free than if the norms have not been internalized.

These two problems are not as evident in traditional China as they are in the United States. Because of the constant association with relatives, old and young alike, the relatively few Chinese children who are able to attend school have more than likely internalized the norms. In addition, in attending school, they are in the company of children who have been exposed to the same traditional training as they have received. Hence, value-conflict very seldom occurs.

Adolescence is a transitional period which has become established to meet the needs peculiar to a complex society, such as the American society. In primitive societies, the child is ushered directly into adulthood by observing ritualistic practices as the puberty line is crossed. Likewise, there is no need for the transitional period in pre-Communist China, because tradition has mapped out step by step procedures in the development of the child, so adulthood is merely the expansion of practices which the child has already mastered.

> Until the time of extensive contact with the West, the Chinese did not recognize adolescence as a specific period of human development, had no exact term to designate it, and had no literature on the subject. (Hsu, 1981, p. 117)

In modern society, the adolescent period provides the teenagers with experimental opportunities in preparing for adulthood. The childhood interest in becoming president of the United States or some other ambitious undertaking, is reconsidered in the light of the realistic preparation necessary to achieve these goals. The teenagers search for opportunities to launch satisfactory career and checks these out with the feasibility of success in such a career.

This is the period, also, when the teenager begins preparing for marriage. The group dating of childhood and early adolescence changes into casual dating on a paired basis. Such a practice enables the teenager to become acquainted with members of the opposite sex and to catalog the appealing and unappealing characteristics of the various partners. Serious dating, limited to one partner, may begin late in this period, but it is not unusual for such a practice to be delayed until later.

Preparation for marriage in the United States continues into the early part of the young adult stage of socialization. The serious dating stage is followed by the engagement period. The engagement period allows the couple privileges in discussing personal interests that are not available in earlier stages of preparation. Properly used, the engagement period enables the couple to determine the degree of compatibility, except sexually, existing between them. It allows the couple to make whatever adjustments are necessary to make the future marriage a success. If these adjustments are not made during the engagement period, it is doubtful that they will be made after the ceremony. If either or both parties are unwilling to make necessary adjustments prior to marriage, the engagement should be broken. Far too often the engagement announcement is tantamount to the marriage vows for many young couples. The engagement parties, bridal showers, and public announcements create situations which make it embarrassing to break an engagement. Consequently, numerous couples proceed with the plan hoping that the problems can be worked out after marriage. If there were more broken engagements, there would be fewer broken marriages, or homes.

No such preparatory measures for marriages by the teenager in traditional China were necessary. More elaborate procedures on the part of the parents, however, were involved. Because mate selection is the core of this study, a rather lengthy description of the customary practices in China will be of value at this point.

Arranging marriages for their children was one of the primary obligations of the parents. The boys must be married in order that the family line might be continued and descendants created to perpetuate the ancestral rites. Girls must be married so that they might fulfill themselves as women and strengthen the family fortunes. Gentry families were interested in making a strategic family alliance. Peasant families desired money for their daughters and were reluctant to marry them to families who owned or rented little or no land. Marriages were arranged by the families concerned. The prospective bride and groom had little to say about either the choice of their mate or the marriage arrangements. In fact, they rarely see each other before the marriage. A meeting of the two before marriage was sufficient reason for calling off the ceremony, because it violated the custom of separating the sexes and compromised the girl. Marriages were contracted between families on the basis of convenience. The social and financial position of the families concerned was carefully scrutinized before the marriage contract was signed.

A middle-man always negotiated the marriage. He or she—the middle-man could be either male or female-did the talking and bargaining, carried messages, and conducted all the many delicate but necessary negotiations required to bring the marriage preliminaries to a successful conclusion.

When the bride's parents agreed to the proposed match, they sent, via the middle-man, a card bearing the girl's eight characters to the boy's family. These eight characters, which represented her name, and the hour, day, month, and year of her birth, were then compared with the boy's personal data by one skilled in such matters. If the comparison indicated future harmony and happiness for the two individuals, negotiations to connect the families through marriage began in earnest. One of the most important questions to be settled, especially for the poor peasant families, was the size of the dowry to be paid by the family of the bridegroom to the family of the bride. The girl's family used part of the dowry money to purchase the bridal outfit and, if there were unmarried sons in the family, often used the rest as dowry money again, to obtain wives for them. The wealthier gentry families used all the dowry and much more besides to outfit the bride. The more furniture, chests, household equipment, clothes, and other articles that were carried in the bridal procession when she was escorted to the home of the bridegroom, the greater the prestige that devolved upon her family.

Marriage preliminaries were concluded with the fixing of the date of marriage and the signing of the betrothal contract by the family heads. The marriage day was selected by an individual skilled in the choosing of lucky days for important events. On that day the bride was carried in a long procession, together with her personal property and bedroom equipment, to the home of the bride-groom. She usually stayed there for the rest of her life. (Welty, 1984, p. 201)

Also, in the early phase of the young adult American socialization process, preparation is made for establishing a career in a professional or vocational field, a home in the community, and a civic role in the society. This is a period for sinking roots, establishing a reputation, converting the uncertainly of youth into mature judgment, and laying the foundation for a stable life.

Such preparations are not essential in traditional Chinese society. The son, with few exceptions, followed in the vocational footsteps of the father on the farm, in the guild, or in the small shop. The daughter mimicked her mother in house-hold duties, and in peasant families by doing work in the fields. The home was already established for the son. In traditional China, a son is never lost through marriage, although the daughters are. Also, the son's reputation is already established through the father.

The social tie between Chinese parents and sons is equally automatic, inviolable, and life-long. This proverb expresses the essence of the pattern: "First Thirty years, one looks at the father and respects the son; second thirty years, one looks at the son and respects the father." That is to say, while the son is young the father's social status determines that of the son; but later the son's social status determines that of the father. (Hsu, 1981, p. 114)

The next stage of socialization prepares mature adults for one of two major adjustments. One is made by the mother in American society, when the children have all married and established homes of their own. When the life-expectancy was fifty years of age, as it was in the United States at the beginning of this century, the prayer of the parents was to live long enough to take care of their children until they were old enough to take care of themselves. By the time the children were "on their own," the parents had just about lived out their allotted years. So there were very few years of loneliness to be endured by the mother when all of the children had established homes of their own. In addition, the newly established homes were usually in close proximity to that of the homeplace.

With the present-day life expectancy of seventy-five years for the females, she can be expected to live about twenty-five years from the time the children leave home. Unless preparations have been made for this period, when it is no longer necessary for her to play the role of mother on a full-time basis, the experience could well be traumatic. Many women in modern society fill this void by starting a second career during the latter part of the children's presence in the home, or soon after they leave. Rendering voluntary community service and other activities, are among the ways this adjustment can be made.

The Chinese mother, traditionally, does not have to make such an adjustment. Her family nest is never empty. Although upon marriage the daughters move out, they are replaced by the daughters-in-law. The strict supervision of the son's wife keeps the mother busier than when she was caring for her own daughters. Even if the life expectancy of the Chinese should reach one hundred years, the daughters who married and left home would be replaced by a continuous procession of brides at each generational level.

The major adjustment for the mature, adult American male is made at the time of retirement. Men, especially at the executive level, are married to their careers. When retirement time arrives, unless preparations have been made, the severance of relations with the firm is similar to the difficult experience of divorce. With the retirement age remaining stable, and the life expectancy of the male increasing, life is far from over when the person's career has ended because of age. Many males also launch second careers, particularly the military retirees, or take up hobbies to occupy their time.

The elder citizen needs socialization in the aging process. That is, persons in this category need to learn how to grow old with dignity. An "old crab" has not been adequately socialized to play the role of a senior citizen. Persons who feel that they have been "put out to pasture" at retirement have not been prepared for this occasion through socialization. A properly socialized person will see the valuable services which can be rendered in various ways. One important role the oldster can play is in keying her or his generation to the age level of their grandchildren or great grandchildren, and in this way contributing somewhat to the stability of society.

The Chinese attitude toward aging is quite different. "The Chinese lived in anticipation of old age, or growing old as pleasant. Age was respected. It was a time of leisure and of little responsibility" (Welty, 1984, p. 204). The Chinese male does not live a lonely life in old age. He is surrounded by members of the extended family. The family ties during his productive years are much stronger than those which attached him to his career. So when the secondary bonds to his work are severed, his familial bonds are strengthened as his children are given an opportunity to express their filial piety by meeting the needs of their aged parent.

Socialization is also essential at the early age level as a means of preparing for the last earthly experience—death. The hospitals have decreased the influence of socialization in this respect. At one time, lingering patients died in the home. All family members could see the gradual deterioration of the body of the loved one. Although this is not a desirable experience, it does prepare one for death better than popping into the hospital for a fifteen minute daily visit. Very little thought is given to the preparation for death in the United States. It is usually limited to the short hospital visits mentioned and to the attendance of wakes and funerals. A minor form of socialization is provided through news telecasts of deaths or occasionally funerals of celebrities. In addition, the fabricated portrayals of deaths in dramas, or in mysteries and westerns, serve a similar purpose.

Ancestor worship is a form of socialization that prepares the Chinese for death. Respect for the aged in traditional China becomes reverence for the departed ancestors. The interaction with the ancestors is just as intense and just as real to the Chinese as it was while the ancestors were still on earth. One reason for the respect for the elderly is the thought that they are not too far away from being ancestors who will be in a position to wield power on behalf of the living in the spirit world. So, death to the Chinese is not like crossing over a wide gulf which suspends relationships until some future meeting. Death for them is extending the boundaries of interaction to three, or four, or more preceding generations.

As can be seen from the foregoing discussion, the traditional Chinese family is much more fully involved in the socialization process at every stage than the American family.

Parents were obliged to train their children to assume their proper stations in Chinese society. For each generation, for each age, for each sex, there was an accepted pattern of behavior which each Chinese individual had to be taught. Thus, from about four to fifteen or sixteen years of age, the children were taught their future duties. (Welty, 1984, p. 201)

In addition, the marriages of the children are arranged, the socializing influence of the home remains the same for the son even after marriage, and the latter stages of life are directly linked to the family through filial piety and ancestor worship.

Regardless of the agencies involved in performing the functions, effective socialization at each of these levels makes possible a smooth adjustment to the ensuing stage. Satisfactory socialization at all of these levels provides a foundation for a highly successful life.

# 8

## The Chinese and American Instispheres

The various forms of social control, or regulatory norms, discussed in Chapter 6, are interwoven about certain basic needs of human beings to form the most articulate element of social structure—institutions. The institutions of a society, both major and minor, are structured as connecting links between groups. They are instruments of cultural heritage.

Social institutions form the bulwark of society. All basic needs of members of society are met by one or the other, or a combination, of these social institutions. The need for membership replacement and child care are met by the family. The economic institution satisfies the need for sustenance. Whereas training and preparation of individuals for a responsible position in society is carried out by the educational institution, the political institution establishes a system of authority to control the behavior of the members—which is a prerequisite of society. Finally, the value system is reinforced and rationalized by religious institutions.

As a society becomes more complex, the social institutions become more specialized. Said scientifically, there is a positive relationship between the complexity of society and the specialized services of its social institutions. Because of this development, some sociologists classify social institutions in modern society on the basis of eight or ten major areas of need. In addition to the five basic institutions already listed, they include social welfare, the military, and recreation as major social institutions. Their reasoning is that a major social institution is one which involves a significant number of society members, spending a significant amount of time in satisfying needs at a significant financial expense. Certainly, on this basis, welfare, military, and recreational services, among others, deserve recognition as major social institutions in the United States. In this book, however, they are considered as minor social institutions. Social welfare and the military are classified as minor institutions within the major political structure, while recreation is treated as a part of the economic institution, since it has become so highly commercialized.

127

A network of folkways, mores, and laws provides a network of rules and regulations by which the above functions must be carried out. The institutional structure is shaped by the social, as well as physical, forces within a society, and by intersocietal interaction. Consequently, the structure varies widely from society to society. Whereas, since the fundamental needs of individuals across the world are similar, the functions of various social institutions are virtually the same universally. The purpose of this chapter is to compare each of the five major social institutions in traditional China to those in the United States. In this way, a background is prepared for the discussion of the impact of social change on the social institutions of these two countries.

A classical definition by Cooley states that "an institution is a complex, integrated organization of collective behavior, established in the social heritage and meeting some persistent need or want."

A composite definition produced by combining the terminology used by notable sociologists forms a conversational definition. According to this definition, a social institution is a complex and integrated system of norms interrelated with and dependent upon other institutions. This system is interwoven with moral sentiments, built around one or more functions, and standardizes and regulates human behavior toward the values considered essential to welfare and survival.

A simplified definition is "a social institution is a network of norms centered in a particular need of society."

The following partially imaginary account is designed to illustrate the development of social institutions. It is not intended to establish a scientific theory explaining their evolution. It could, however, be considered a quasi-historical account, but no claim is made to its authenticity in this respect.

Social institutions developed in response to increased needs of society. In the food gathering society, the needs were simple. There was no need for vocational training in order to provide a livelihood for individual members of the primitive society. Even a toddler could master some of the food gathering techniques. Engineering schools were not essential, because there is nothing mechanical about a dibble stick, which is a piece of wood tapered on one end, thought to be the first crude manmade all-purpose implement. It was used mainly to grub in the earth for worms and insects. It could also be used as a weapon or a tool providing leverage. There was no need for the girls to take a home economics course because the food was eaten raw, making cooking knowledge unnecessary. The first shelters were nothing more than lean-tos constructed of whatever materials nature provided such as fallen limbs or tall weeds, so housekeeping was not a responsibility of the wife or mother. When the members of the primitive society got hungry, they just scrounged around for food until their appetites were satisfied. They would then lounge around until hunger struck again, at which time they would scrounge around for more food. As can be seen, in each primitive society, social institutions other than the family, or kinship group, were unnecessary because all of the members' needs were met within the small group.

As society developed, the needs expanded beyond the ability of the family to satisfy them all. As a result, other institutions came into existence to supplement the family efforts. The innovation of hunting expanded the economy of the society. Not all of the families included skilled hunters in their number, so a crude form of barter was ushered in supplying the foundation, which is exchange, for the economic institution. Since the patriarch, or leader, of the nomadic band could not go on the hunting expedition and at the same time exercise control over those remaining at the camp site authority had to be delegated, sowing the seeds of the political institution. Additional skills needed in hunting, that were at times beyond the father's ability, inaugurated the educational institution as the son received instructions from some one other than the father. Natural phenomena, such as storms, floods, and lighting needed explanations beyond the knowledge of the family. Consequently, the religious institutions, heavily saturated with magic at this point, took shape ushering in authorities who not only explained the mysteries but appeared to have the power to manipulate and control the supernatural.

As societies developed, the family shifted more and more of its functions over to other institutions, and non-family institutions became more and more specialized. The main focus of this book spotlights the institutions of traditional China during the early part of this century. Also, treated are the changes that have occurred in those institutions in Taiwan during the past four decades, and the contemporary social institutions in the United States. The concept of each of the social institutions is treated in this chapter, along with a comparison of traditional Chinese, and contemporary American, institutions. The reason for using traditional China as a basis of comparison is twofold. First, the assumption is that clearly discernible elements of traditional Chinese culture are evident in China today. For this reason references to traditional China, in the discussion which follows, are in the present tense. The second reason is to magnify the social power of social change as it weakens the strongly entrenched structures of social institutions. This will be discussed in Section III.

Each of the social institutions in modern society has gone through various stages of development. Continuing with the semi-fictive technique, these various stages are shown in the following it-could-have-been account, using the political institution as an example.

As previously mentioned, when the economy expanded to include hunting expeditions, the need for delegating authority arose. There were no democratic or totalitarian patterns available for guidance in the selection process. So, the first stage in the development of an institution is a thrashing around period in which the trial and error method is used in the search for a workable plan.

Suppose the leader appoints his son as the leader of the hunting group instead of the most skilled hunter. Out in the field, the skilled hunter recommends that the band go in one direction in the search for game, but the son, exercising his authority, takes them on a fruitless search in another direction. When they return to the camp site empty-handed, the leader decides to try another method. He appoints the skilled hunter as a co-leader of the group. Out in the field, the son and the skilled hunter again differ on the direction to take in search of game. As a result, half of the group goes in one direction with the skilled hunter and the other half goes with the son in a different direction. The skilled hunter's group finds some game but, because the hunting force is divided, they'd not have the manpower to corral and slay it. Again, they return to the camp site empty-handed.

The leader tries another method in which every member has a voice in the direction to be taken on the hunting trip, with the decision resting in the hands of the majority. This method works, so it is adopted as a regular procedure. When the hunters return to the camp site with the meat, however, there is a distribution problem. Each hunter takes the meat he has bagged and gives it to whomever he wants. This causes a ruckus in the camp site, so the leader appoints a distributor from the non-hunting contingent of the primitive band. Some of the members complain to the leader that the distributor is showing partiality in the apportionment of the meat. So, the leader appoints an arbiter who hears these complaints and works out a settlement.

Finally, all of the wrinkles are ironed out and the plan is operating efficiently. One of the hunters, at the time, recognizes the strategic position the hunting band is in to benefit themselves. He convinces the band to trade some of the game for favors from another primitive group near the hunting site. This appeals to the hunters so much that they ignore the purpose for which the group came into existence, i.e., to provide meat for their own society. In promoting their own interest, the neglect results in an inadequate supply of meat for the camp site group. The leader starts experimenting again to meet his members' need for food and the cycle starts again.

Applying this illustration to the institutional structures of traditional China and that of the United States, the Chinese model is functioning far more efficiently than the United States institutions. Without going into detail, the following comments by Francis Hsu should illustrate this point.

Social institutions functioning efficiently should meet the needs of society at all ages. The needs of the elderly are more fully satisfied in traditional Chinese society than they are in America.

For the average American, the approach of old age means the end of almost everything that gives life meaning. To the average Chinese, however, it marks the beginning of a loftier and more respected status. . . .

At the threshold of old age, the self-reliant American faces problems rarely known to his Chinese brethren. (Hsu, 1981, p. 335)

Perhaps the main reasons for social problems in the United States is the shift of the functions of the family to other social institutions. This has not been done in China as much as it has been done in America. The social welfare program is a case in point. When America was a rural society up until the beginning of the present century, the family carried its own social welfare and insurance programs. The home place was retained as a haven for the children who had problems in establishing their own homes. If the mate died, for example, the son (or daughter) would move back to the home place taking his (or her) children with him. As old age incapacitated the parents, arrangements would be worked out to take care of them, usually in the home place. If an unmarried child were living there, many times s/he would forgo her or his own marriage to care for the parents. The homes were large and could accommodate two or three families. So it was not unusual for one of the children to move back into the home place, with the spouse and children, to take care of the parents, or the parents would move into one of the children's homes. Since the children usually established their own homes in close proximity to their parents, many times on land that was part of the home place estate, they could take care of their parents without anyone changing residences.

As urbanism spread throughout the United States, the way of life changed. Children moved long distances away from the home place because of better job opportunities and better school opportunities for their children. Not anticipating the necessity of caring for their aged parents, and because space was at a premium, they moved into smaller houses or apartments. The family function of providing a haven for the elderly, as well as orphaned children, was shifted over to charitable institutions. Since these institutions were dependent upon the voluntary contributions of the altruistic, they did not fare so well. Insurance companies and pension plans then made an appearance in order to meet these needs. Some workers could not afford insurance, and not everyone was able to get into a retirement plan. Consequently, the federal and state governments assumed the responsibility of providing for the elderly and other needs through social welfare programs such as Social Security, Medicare, Medicaid, aid to dependent children, and unemployment insurance. As can be seen from this illustration, the responsibility of caring for the aged, orphans, and needy in the United States was transferred from the home to religious institutions, then to the economic institutions, and finally to the political institutions. In China, these functions are retained by the family and are being carried out more efficiently.

There are two possible reasons why the American social institutions are not adequately meeting the demands made upon them. One is that these needs are changing so rapidly that the slow-changing institutions cannot make the necessary adjustments fast enough to cope with the new situations, resulting in cultural lag discussed earlier. The other possible reason is that the American institutions are functioning on the self-interest stage. These malfunctions will be considered as each of the major social institutions is discussed in the remainder of this chapter.

## THE FAMILY

Most families are united through the bonds of marriage, blood, adoption, or a combination of the three. Legally, families can be formed through marriage only, such as a husband and wife. They can also be united through blood only, such as brother and sister, or parent and offspring. Also, through legal adoption, a family can be formed. A family including children is normally united through a combination of marriage, husband and wife, and blood parents and children. This means that a childless married couple constitutes a family, which differs from the popular opinion that children are essential in defining family. It also means that an unwed parent, usually the mother, living with an illegitimate child constitutes a family, which is contrary to the usual assumption that marriage, as well as children, is essential to identify a family unit.

Further, marriages exist in the United States without the sanctions of the clergy, or a duly appointed official. When a couple cohabit as husband and wife, without going through legal channels, after a period of time which differs by states, they become legally bound through common-law marriage. Usually, after the couple have lived together illegally for a while and decide to separate, there are no problems. If they have cohabited beyond the state limit, however, and one member objects, the separation does not go quite so smoothly. In the event that the objector can establish the relationship as that of husband and wife, the union has to be dissolved through the same divorce procedures as though the marriage had been consummated through normal procedures.

In addition to blood and marriage, adoption serves as a bond forming a family relationship. When a childless couple adopts an infant, for example, there is no blood relationship in the family unit. The couple is linked through marriage and the child by adoption. When a couple marry and both have children from a former marriage, then the wife's offspring become the step-children of the husband, and vice versa. The children's relationship is that of step-brother or step-sister. Any offspring from the marital union would be recognized as half-brother or half-sister to the children from the previous marriage.

The sociological and legal definitions of family are identical in all of the aforementioned instances. One difference in these definitions is that, in addition to the relationships described, interaction between or among the members of the unit is a characteristic of the sociological definition of the family, but is not essential in the legal sense. A couple may live separately for any number of years, without any communication, but until their relationship is dissolved through official channels, they are still regarded legally as husband and wife.

Sociologically, however, interaction is essential for a married couple, with or without children, to exist as a family. Two persons united through marriage can live in the same household for any amount of time, say twenty years, but if they do not interact, there is no family according to the sociological definition. Both legal and sociological definitions require that a family be united through marriage, blood, or adoption, but only the sociological definition requires interaction.

The family is the basic social unit of a society. For the infant, the family is society. As the infant becomes a child, its society is broadened. The horizons are further extended in adolescence and more so in adulthood. This means that society exists for the individual only so far as it is incorporated into that person's experience. Cooley held this position.

In this sense, the family is fundamental in shaping the child's conception of society. It sifts out those values, goals, and behavior patterns it wants the child to adopt. From these selected features, the foundation of the child's society is laid, which is instrumental in the development of its concept of society through the period of adolescence and into adulthood.

In a homogeneous society, such as traditional China, the couple's concepts of society will be more similar than in a heterogeneous society such as the United States. Mate selection is more critical in the latter case than in the former. Although the couple may not realize it, their marriage involves the merging of two conceptions of society that may differ widely. When the selection of a mate crosses over national, race, or cultural boundaries, the process becomes even more critical.

Mate selection is an essential process in forming families through marriage. Its function is to sort out potential marital partners who will satisfy his or her needs in establishing a family. The needs to be satisfied in the family of procreation have been determined by the family of orientation. A simple distinction between these two types of families is that the family of procreation is one in which an individual, or Ego, is a potential parent, whereas in the family of orientation, Ego is a child. In traditional China, the family of procreation follows very closely the pattern of the family of orientation. In the United States, however, the newly established family may or may not follow the pattern of the family in which Ego was oriented to society. If Ego is a product of a family that enforced strict discipline and attributes success in life to such a practice, he probably will use this as a model and structure his family of procreation accordingly. On the other hand, if Ego feels that the discipline in the family of orientation was too rigid, and prevented the development of his full potential, the pattern of the family of procreation may be just the opposite, resulting in a much more flexible disciplinary system.

Since mate selection is to satisfy the needs of two different individuals in establishing a family, it is necessary to determine the needs to be satisfied in order to fully understand the selection process. The needs are determined in this chapter by first comparing the function of the traditional Chinese family with those of the American family. The same procedure is used in discussing family structure. The comparison of traditional Chinese and American mate selection practices will be given in Section III in which the impact of social change on mate selection in China is discussed.

Practically all of the needs of the infant, with the possible exception of medical attention and religious rituals are met by the family in both types of societies. In addition to procreation, the family functions to satisfy the needs for protection, providing economic necessities, education, socialization, and the development of the emotional bonds.

The major differences between the two types is that the American family has transferred many of its functions over to specialized institutions, at a very early age of the child, while the traditional Chinese family has not. In the case of a mother working outside of the home, the American infant is cared for by a baby sitter. At the age of two or three, the child is often placed in a nursery or day-care center. The Chinese infant or child, when the mother works outside of the home, is placed in the hands of a relative. Since the family patterns are similar in a traditional society, the child makes very little adjustment because the substitute mother's role is almost identical to the actual mother, except for the direct blood relationship.

The traditional Chinese family is almost solely responsible for the protection of the child. It is able to satisfy the needs in this respect because, for one thing, child molestation is practically unknown in a traditional society. It is difficult to distinguish between the two societies on the basis of child abuse because of the difference in interpretation of such treatment.

An acceptable degree of physical discipline in traditional China may be considered child abuse in the United States. When this abuse appears to be excessive in China, the grandparents, or some other family authority, exercise control over the disciplinarian. In America, legal authorities control it. In other words, the U. S. government not only provides protection of the child for the family, it also protects the child from the family.

In traditional China, the economic responsibility is shouldered completely by family members. If the parents are not able to satisfy this need, then their brothers or sisters, or some other family member assumes the obligation. If the parents of the American child are not able to assume the economic responsibility, the political institution provides for the child as well as other members of the family through the food stamp program, aid to dependent children, or some other agency. If the parents cannot provide proper care for the child, or mistreats the child, the court will order a social worker to place the child in a foster home.

Even though the mother is not working outside the home, more and more American children are being put into pre-school facilities. One of the reasons for this is the specialized training in child education that is available in the better pre-school centers. Another reason is to allow the mother more time to function in the homemaking career. Her responsibilities extend far beyond cooking and housekeeping, as is the case among the peasantry class in traditional China. There was time for little else, in this situation, as the wife and mother assisted in eking out an existence for the family. This is also true in the lower class of American society. But in the middle and upper social classes, the wife and mother function in many roles, such as executive, social secretary, dietitian, interior decorator, child psychologist, companion to both husband and children, as well as many other roles. Of course, she is assisted in these various areas by specialists when the demand is beyond her ability.

The American mother has much assistance in the socialization of the child. Her efforts are supplemented by the television, various school groups and classes, scouting organizations, the peer group, and various child-centered civic and commercial programs. In traditional China, the socialization process focuses on the development of the child's loyalty to the family through filial piety, and thus becoming a good citizen of the state, which is considered an extension of the family. This can best be done by parental example which renders supplemental efforts less necessary.

The most important differences between the functions of the two family types lies in the nurture of the emotional bonds between parents and children. The previously cited examples of filial piety illustrate clearly the strong emotional bonds existing between the Chinese parents and children. These bonds are not weakened when the child matures into adulthood. In fact, they are strengthened because the adult is better able to express his or her concern for the parents than the child is. Whereas in American society, some children can hardly wait until they reach the age of majority so they can escape the authority of the parents, and free themselves of the pressure of the pretense of emotional bonds that never existed. When emotional bonds are strong, the parent-child relationships are little effected by the youngster crossing the arbitrary age line separating adolescence from adulthood.

In traditional society, both American and Chinese, socialization was simply a matter of observing the parents in their work roles and in their associations with others, with some guidance through advice. In this way, emotional bonds developed without paying particular attention to them. Many American parents cling to the traditional role conception that providing food, shelter, and clothing for the children is all that is required of them in carrying out their responsibilities. The measure of successful parents, according to this idea, is evaluated on the basis of the size of the house, type of TV, and the style of the clothes. In this day of push-button economy, the housekeeping chores are carried out easily. All that is needed is to set the automatic washer at the right cycle, the laundry dryer at the right temperature, and the microwave oven at the right time, and these tasks are accomplished simultaneously.

Instead of spending the time that is saved in strengthening the emotional bonds, a number of mothers spend it in gossipy coffee clutches, or in watching soap operas on the television. For instance, the son who usually brings home a "D" grade on math exams, burst into the house to tell his mother that he got an "A" on one. As he elatedly attempts to tell his mother of this achievement, she interrupts with, "Wait until the commercial to tell me." Needless to say, the child's enthusiasm is squashed as his mother's interest in him is subordinated to her interest in the television program. The youngster turns to outside sources, such as a peer, or a peer's parent, or others to satisfy this desire for recognition and the emotional bond between parent and child is weakened.

These are some of the differences in parent or spouse roles that have to be taken into account when a Chinese selects an American-Caucasian as a mate. The adjustment will not be as great in a marriage between a native born American-Chinese and an American-Caucasian as it will be if the latter marries a native Chinese.

Various types of family structure have been established to meet the needs of societies across the world. Two forms of polygamy are designed to carry out various functions. Polygyny, defined as one husband with two or more wives, serves to some extent as a social welfare program. A wealthy man can support a number of wives who otherwise would have to eke out an existence in some menial task that would not even provide her with an adequate diet. Polygyny also serves as a prestige symbol for the husband. A man that can afford more than one wife is recognized as being in a higher social class than one who cannot. A quasi-polygynist marriage was carried out in traditional China, by those who could afford it, through the practice of concubinage. This was not a pure form of polygyny because the concubines were secondary wives.

Polyandry, the practice of one wife having two or more husbands, is another form of polygamy. This practice was established through economic necessity. In geographical areas where it is difficult to produce enough to satisfy one's own needs, the individual could not provide for himself and a wife. Consequently, he and another person, usually a brother, would pool their resources and take unto themselves a wife in partnership. In this way, they could produce enough for themselves and one additional person.

Another purpose served by various forms of family structures is to strengthen the family by extending its base. This is done in a variety of ways. One practice is referred to as the levirate. By such an arrangement, a form of insurance is provided for the wife and children. If the husband dies, he is replaced by his younger brother. In some societies, the younger brother, the uncle of the children, is also called father. The adjustment to the father's death is much less traumatic for the children in such instances. Also, because it is expected that the younger brother will replace the husband in the future, the practice of anticipatory levirate has been established. Instead of waiting until death necessitates the replacement of the husband by the younger brother, the wife is shared by the two.

Another means of extending the family base is by interlocking families by the means of the susu. In this type of family structure, the child has a biological father and a sociological father. The only function of the husband in this arrangement is procreation. After the children are brought into existence, the brother of the wife assumes the responsibility of providing for and training the children. The biological father of the children assumes the same responsibilities of his sister's children. So, every man in this society who has sisters is a biological father in one family and a sociological father in another.

The means of strengthening the familial bonds in a traditional society is through the extended family, which is defined as more than two generations living in a single household. A structure of this type enables the family members to absorb the shock of any adverse developments. For example, if there are ten persons involved in providing a livelihood for the extended family and one of them is incapacitated, or dies, the other nine are still able to meet the needs. Another advantage of the extended family is of an emotional nature. If a husband dies, the widow is surrounded by sympathizers in the future daily life. The void is filled much more completely in this way than in modern society when friends and relatives gather for a few days and then the widow has to face the future alone in surroundings constantly reminding her of the deceased mate.

In contrast, the nuclear family, defined as the parents and their children, which constitutes the principle type in the United States, is much weaker for a number of reasons. For one thing, it has a short life. To illustrate this, suppose a couple marries and has three children, with the oldest being six years of age when the youngest is born completing the nuclear family unit. If the oldest one marries and leaves home at the age of eighteen, the nuclear family as a complete unit would have lived together for only twelve years. On the other hand, the extended family continues on throughout generations. Also, the nuclear family is fragile, being easily broken through death, divorce, or desertion. The extended family may be ruptured by the death of one of its members, but it is not broken.

The base of the extended family in traditional China is not limited to those who are living, but it includes those who have died as well. "The ties of blood and kinship were strengthened by ancestral ceremonies, common property, and a common interest in preserving and increasing the prestige of the clan and the welfare of its members" (Welty, 1984, p. 192). Ancestral worship contributes toward respect for the elderly. "Memorial service was one of the reasons why the Chinese paid such great respect to the aged. Since they were only a step away from becoming ancestors themselves, the aged were felt to be entitled to great honor and homage" (Welty, 1984, p. 193). The respect for the parents of a married man superseded the importance of, and loyalty to, his own children. "Greatly prized and respected, the aged in traditional China were valued even over children. Children could be had again, but the aged could not be duplicated, and they soon would become powerful ancestors who could be of great aid to the family" (Welty, 1984, p. 203).

The priorities of loyalty in the traditional Chinese family are far different from those in the American family. In the Chinese family, the primary loyalty is always to the parents, the secondary loyalty is to the brothers and sisters, and loyalty to the mate and children is third. In American society, the primary loyalty is to the wife and children, the secondary loyalty is to the parents, and tertiary loyalty is to the brothers and sisters. This means that an intermarriage between a Chinese and an American necessitates an adjustment in priorities as far as loyalty is concerned on the part of both persons.

## THE RELIGIOUS INSTITUTION

Religion means many things to many people. To some, it is the essence of life; to others, it is a veneer of piety. To some it is a mystical means of salvation; to others it is a myth. To some it is a divine revelation of human existence on earth; to others it is a concocted account explaining such a development. Whatever religion means to various persons, all religions have a twofold function. First is to satisfy the needs of the individual, and the second is to meet the needs of society.

Religion is helpful in enabling the individual to accept inalterable circumstances such as death, terminal diseases, and other tragedies. It offers stability to the insecure, recognition for the ordinary person, and companionship for the lonely. Its function in society is to provide a moral code enforced by the threat of eternal punishment for the violator. In this way, it serves as a measure of social control, regulating the behavior of individual members of society.

All religions have a belief, but that is the extent of their similarity. Even within a single religion, a definition that goes beyond this limit raises questions. In Christianity, for example, followers who adopt the name of the founder differ in their interpretation of religion. Some believe in Jesus as the savior of mankind. Some believe in him as a prophet, as a teacher, as a savior, as a philosopher, or in many other ways. But most of them believe.

In ordinary usage, and as a social institution, these beliefs are from a system that is shared by a group. There are eleven major religious systems across the world, all of which provide the members with an object of devotion having a divine nature. The divinity is revealed by the supernatural in some of the beliefs, such as Christianity, in others, such as Confucianism, the divine nature has been assigned to the founder by the devotees, converting a philosophy into a religion after the founder's death. These major religions are divided into denominations or a myriad of sects, all claiming to provide the proper guide to life and a key to the understanding of its mysteries. In addition, mystical cults have developed offering a magical formula for the present life and an insurance policy for a blessed life to come.

A definition of religion must be broad enough to include all of these branches of established religions, in addition to many other forms, and specific enough to distinguish it from other phenomena such as the closely related field of philosophy. It must include monotheism, the belief in one God; deism, a belief that God created the world and then withdrew; polytheism, a belief in many gods; pantheism, the worship of nature; animism, the embodiment of spirit in inanimate objects; and many other types.

There is one common prerequisite in all religions, and that is belief. That is about as far as a definition can go without raising questions. When the object of belief is pinpointed, controversy begins. To take Christianity, a small segment of established religions, beyond that point divides opinions. Some accept, without question, the founder of Christianity, Jesus, as a savior. What is the object? Some of us need to be saved from boredom, some from ignorance, others from fear, etc. The bulk of Christians believe that Jesus saves us from sin and its consequences, which is a life of eternal condemnation.

Writing the myriad of meanings attached to religion, it seems that the definition of institutionalized religion can be reduced no further that to say it is a system of beliefs centered in a supreme value and adjustment to that value. That supreme value can be natural or supernatural.

An individual's religion is not a system of beliefs. It is simply belief centered in a supreme value. That supreme value can be anything that takes priority in the life of an individual, such as an automobile, a fortune, a philosophy, or any other such things.

The function of religion differs to some extent from society to society, because the needs differ. In societies where the masses are uneducated, there is a need to explain the mysterious natural phenomena. For instance, why do the floods come, tornadoes strike, or droughts occur? For the unenlightened, God is displeased with the behavior of one, some, or all members of society, so he is wreaking vengeance. For those who are scientifically enlightened, meteorology explains these phenomena. Since religion is no longer necessary to carry out this function, it loses its appeal for some. As a result, its influence over the lives of individuals has been weakened.

In modern society, a fundamental need has developed which the religious institution is designed to meet. Present-day society is besieged by splintering forces. The magnification of differences in social classes, races, vested interests and reform groups, the generation gap, and the credibility gap in the political structure have segmented society. The desperate need in modern society is for an integrating force that will solidify it. This cannot be done by the political institution because social change cannot be legislated. As previously mentioned, the law desegregating schools did not result in integration. A power above the law is needed that prompts individuals to do things because they want to, not because they have to according to the law.

The religious institution can do this by reinforcing society's moral code. Morality can be defined as person to person relationships, while religion is a person's relationship to God. The purpose of religion is to insure proper relationship between and among fellowmen. It uses two different approaches in improving society. One is to develop moral individuals. If all members of society conduct themselves according to the moral code, then the society will be moral. The second approach is to right the wrongs of society. If the society is a moral entity, then it will produce moral individuals.

One main reason religious institutions in the United States are not functioning efficiently in this respect is that there is no united effort. Instead of working together, religious groups are pitted against one another. Major denominations have been divided over insignificant differences of opinion. One such division resulted over whether the preposition "in" or "into" should be used in the baptismal ritual, for instance. One held that the individual should be baptized "in the name of Jesus," whereas the other held that the phrase should be "into the name of Jesus." Another major denomination split over whether or not instrumental music should be allowed in the church worship services.

RELIGIOUS STRUCTURES

Religious structure varies all the way from the barely discernible organization of cults to the rigid hierarchy of some denominations. The cult thrives on the charisma of its leader. Charisma is the assignment of divine characteristics to an individual. Charismatic leadership is found in political, as well as, religious circles. The Emperor of Japan, Adolf Hitler, and to a lesser extent, Franklin Roosevelt, possessed this quality during and just prior to World War II. The mass suicide in Jonestown was under the direction of a charismatic leader. The cult wields a powerful influence, based entirely upon mysticism over its members.

American sects are fundamentalist religious groups that cling tenaciously to a literal interpretation of the sacred writing. It makes little difference that the words of Christ were recorded years after they were spoken, or that his sayings have undergone a number of translations, and through several revisions, before appearing in their present form, whether it is the King James Version of the Bible or not. One New Testament verse should serve to illustrate this point. According to the King James Version, Jesus said to one of the thieves hanging on a cross beside him, "Verily I say unto thee, Today thou shalt be with me in paradise" (Mk. 23:43). Jesus was writhing in pain on the cross. The statement was not written down at the moment, and perhaps the punctuation mark was misplaced. It is quite possible that Jesus said, "Verily I say unto you today, Thou shalt be with me in paradise." This is not pointed out to contradict the biblical scholars, but simply to indicate the difficulty in establishing a literal translation of the Scriptures.

Confucianism was the intellectual aspect of Chinese religion. Confucius had no intention of founding a new religion. His purpose was to establish a philosophy assisting individuals to derive benefits from living as members of society. Around 100 B.C., approximately 400 years after the death of

Confucius, his teachings were "adopted as the orthodox Chinese Philosophy" (Welty, 1984, p. 146). "When Confucianism became the orthodox doctrine of the empire, religious functions were incorporated into it. Confucius, along with his ancestors and his famous followers, became objects of worship and veneration. Confucian temples were erected all over the empire, tablets to Confucius and his followers were placed within these temples, and sacrifices and rituals were performed before these tablets and elsewhere" (Welty, 1984, p. 154).

Confucianism served as the basic core of the Chinese educational system and continued in this position for two thousand years until it was weakened through a mixture with "Western liberal thought as propounded by Sun Yet-sen, the father of modern China, and became the official political theory of the state" (Welty, 1984, p. 148).

> Confucianism teaches that man is compelled by his nature to live in the company of other men, that is to say, in society. Only unnatural and abnormal people live outside the communities. This social way of life is the best way to live, because it is only in society that men reach their fullest development and realize their potentialities. (Welty, 1984, p. 149)

Jesus, in the Sermon on the Mount, advises a similar practice.

> Ye are the light of the world. A city that is set on an hill cannot be hid.

> Neither do men light a candle, and put it under a bushel, but on a candlestick; and it giveth light unto all that are in the house.

> Let your light so shine before men, that they may see your good works, and glorify your Father which is in heaven. (Matt. 5:14-16)

The gist of Confucianism is found in this ethical code of living.

> "The right action" is defined by Confucians in terms of the duties and obligations implicit in five basic social relationships. These five relationships are: ruler and subject, father and son, elder brother and younger brother, husband and wife, friend and friend. All of them except the last involve the authority of one person over the other. (Welty, 1984, p. 151)

The Christian religion requires similar relationships in all instances except the submission of the younger brother to the elder brother. In regard to civil obedience, Jesus says, "Render therefore unto Caesar the things that are Caesar's; and unto God the things that are God's" (Matt. 23:21). As for obedience to one's parents, Jesus says, "For God commanded, saying, Honour thy father and mother . . ." (Matt. 15:4). In referring to the dominance of the husband over the wife, Paul says, "Wives submit yourselves unto your own husbands, as unto the Lord" (Eph. 5:22). Finally, we should "love our neighbors as ourselves."

And thou shalt love the Lord thy God with all thy heart, and with all thy soul, and with all thy mind, and with all thy strength: this is the first commandment.

And the second is like unto it, namely this, Thou shalt love thy neighbor as thyself. . . . (Mk. 12:30-31)

The main difference between the two sets of requirements is obedience to God. Confucianism makes no reference to this because at the time of writing his teachings were not considered religious.

Another element in the Chinese religious structure, Taoism, differs form Christianity in two important ways. One is the vagueness of defining Taoism as compared with the belabored precision of defining Christianity. Although Taoism is in essence a philosophy, its incorporation into the Chinese ideology has given it a religious character.

It is barely possible to suggest what the Tao is. The early Taoists never directly defined it because they believed language incapable of adequately determining its precise meaning. "Those who know the Tao do not speak of it; those who speak of it do not know it." Chuang Tzu stated that he should not seek precision in trying to understand the Tao. . . . The Tao lies beyond shape and feature like an uncarved block and is eternally nameless. Taoists spoke of it as "a shape without shape, a form without form." (Welty, 1984, p. 159)

On the other hand, the New Testament is filled with sayings depicting the characteristics of Christianity. Jesus described the Christian life in the Sermon on the Mount in three chapters of the Gospel of Matthew (chapters 5 through 7), as well as in other passages. He even gave the listeners the words of prayer, which are repeated as they are recorded in the Lord's Prayer, in various religious services. The Acts of the Apostles gives direction to church members, as do the Pauline Epistles. Many Christian creeds, including the Apostles' Creed, spell out the meaning of Christianity. In addition, numerous doctrines have been articulated defining precisely the meaning of Christianity.

The second difference between Taoism and Christianity is the way to be followed.

Taoism advised men that the best way to live is the natural way. He is happiest who lives in accordance with his nature. Man's fears, man's sufferings, man's problems, are the result of man's unnatural life. Man can be truly free only when he liberates himself from all artificial restraints. Taoism, which is also described as "The way of the Uninhibited," stresses such words as "naturalness," "spontaneity," and "simplicity." (Welty, 1984, p. 159)

The way of the Christian is quite different. Jesus has provided a pattern for his followers. "For I have given you an example, that ye should do as I have done to you" (Jn. 13:15). Further,

And whither I go ye know, and the way ye know.

Thomas saith unto him, Lord, we know not whither thou goest; and how can we know the way?

Jesus saith unto him, I am the way, the truth, and the life; no man cometh unto the Father, but by me.

If ye had known me, ye should have known my Father also: and from hence forth ye know him, and have seen him. (Jn. 14:4-7)

The third element in Chinese religion, Buddhism, offers a good example of how religion compromises to meet the needs of a society.

Buddhism in China played down its foreign elements and made itself as Chinese as possible.

It built on the foundations of the other ideologies popular during the early part of the Christian era. Since Taoism was popular among the commoners and intellectuals alike, Buddhists used Taoism as an instrument of conversion by taking over Taoist terms, writing commentaries on Taoist books, and identifying Buddhism with Taoist teaching and practice. The common elements in Taoist and Buddhist doctrine were deliberately stressed over and over again. At times, indeed, the truth was stretched in order to make Taoism and Buddhism agree. They honored Confucianism by speaking of a Bodhisattva as being an incarnation of Confucius, by naming a temple after Confucius, and by stressing the virtue of filial piety as an aspect of Buddhist teaching. (Welty, 1984, p. 176)

Buddhism supplemented the two previously discussed elements of Chinese religion by providing hope for the future.

Confucianists and Taoists did not regard this life as preliminary or probationary to another life in some hereafter. They were primarily interested in bettering human society and handling human problems.

Mahayana Buddhism, on the other hand, painted a graphic picture of the heaven and hell that awaited the good and bad people of the world. In this sense it possessed a more comprehensive doctrine than Taoism and a more spiritual character than the ethical code of Confucianism. Buddhism provided the Chinese...with a hope of material and spiritual benefits which attracted great numbers of them to the Buddhist faith. (Welty, 1984, p. 147)

The last book of the Bible, Revelations, pictures the eternal dwelling place of the righteous in the Christian faith. In next to the final chapter of the book, John writes:

And I saw a new heaven and a new earth: for the first heaven and the first earth were passed away; and there was no more sea. (21:1)

And God shall wipe away all tears from their eyes; and there shall be no more death, neither sorrow, nor crying, neither shall there be any more pain: for the former things are passed away. (21:4)

The whole book of Revelation is devoted to giving a picture of the life to come on earth as well as in heaven.

As can be seen from the foregoing comparison, American religion is much more exclusive than that of the Chinese. This reflects the general attitudes of the two societies mentioned earlier, that American interaction is individually centered, whereas the Chinese interaction is situation-centered. An exclusive religion supports the monotheistic conception of the divine being, and fosters less religious tolerance than an inclusive religion, which is more likely to promote polytheism.

## THE EDUCATIONAL INSTITUTION

Education is the foundation of society. It is the means by which the way of life, or culture, is perpetuated. Every society must have a communication system to survive, and education is the means by which this basic prerequisite is provided.

Popularly, education is limited to the established formal institutions of various types, such as primary and secondary schools and educational institutions of higher learning. The informal component is many times overlooked. Through the informal education in the home, through mass media, and by members of the peer group, the attitude toward education is shaped. If these influences are of a positive nature, then the child will approach the educational opportunity with a different frame of mind than that formed when the influences are negative. The difference can be illustrated by comparing a youngster in an elite private high school, from a family in the upper social class, with one in a public schools from a lower class family. The informal parental pressure on the upper class youth may force him into a career, such as that of medicine, which has been a family profession for many generations. Conformity to the parental pressure may not provide the necessary motivation to cause the student to exert the necessary effort to perform well. On the other hand, the undesirable physical environment may prod the lower social class youth into a determined effort to excel as a student in order to rise above the slum conditions.

The value of informal education is expressed in the cliché "Experience is the best teacher." Experience is, in actuality, the only teacher. Education materials are recordings of experiences of experiments of the past.

Education serves a twofold function—to perpetuate culture and to improve it. In a traditional society, the emphasis is upon the preservation of culture. In modern society, the emphasis is upon improving culture.

Informal education plays a more important role in the perpetuation of culture than formal education. When this is the main function of education, much training is carried out in the home by the parents and siblings before the child reaches school age. In a traditional agrarian, society, the way of life is simple. All the male child needs to know, as far as occupation is concerned, is how to handle a few animals and tend crops. This he learns at an early age. The schooling is limited to a few basics such as reading, writing, and arithmetic. Prior to the United States compulsory education law, a person who was acquainted with the three "Rs" was considered educated above the average. In the same vein, the girls had only to learn how to cook and keep house.

As knowledge became more specialized, formal education became more necessary. In the early part of this century, a "normal school" education, which consisted of two years in a "finishing school," was all the education an average school teacher needed. Now a masters degree, or the equivalent, is essential to teach in the better high schools.

As formal education becomes more necessary, the social boundaries of the child are extended. The youngster can make more associations outside of the home and learn new and different ways of life. Each one of these new experiences weakens the family ties and strengthens the individual interests.

The American society is far advanced in this respect. As the emphasis in Chinese education moves in this direction, Taiwan is changing from a group-centered society to an individual-centered one. Such a change has weakened the bonds of tradition in Taiwan. However, this change develops a greater similarity in the backgrounds of the members of the two societies.

Education carried to the specialized level, as is occurring in Taiwan, places heavier demand on marital ties. In addition to satisfying the ordinary prerequisites for a successful marriage, the highly educated individual must work a third party, a career, into the plans. Much thought must be given to arranging priorities such as career, children, and companionship with the mate in such a marriage.

In spite of the educational problem of weaving a career into the relationship, a higher education promotes tolerance and understanding which contribute toward a more conducive attitude toward inter-cultural marriages.

## THE POLITICAL INSTITUTION

Distinctions should be made between the terms political institution, political state, and government, which are sometimes used interchangeably. All

societies, whether modern or primitive, have some form of political institution. A society requires organization which is provided by the political
institution resulting in order. Political state is used synonymously with
nation or nation-state, which is a political entity with geographical boundaries. The government is the administrative unit of the political state. It is
the national and international voice and agent of the nation.

The main distinguishing characteristic between government and political state is sovereignty. Sovereignty is ultimate political power. The political state has it, the government does not. The various states within the
United States have government, but ultimate political authority is exercised
at the national level. A good example of this is the confrontation of the
governor of Alabama with the federal government in the enforcement of
the ruling of the Supreme Court to desegregate schools. When a politician
orates on "the great sovereign state of Virginia," or any other state, he is
using the term figuratively. One reason why the United Nations has not
been more successful in controlling the actions of its member nations is
because it lacks sovereignty.

The political institution has both internal and external functions. Internally, it regulates the behavior of the societal members and provides an arbi-
trative mechanism for settling disputes between or among them. Externally,
it protects the society and develops intersocietal relationships. These functions are similar in all societies whether primitive, modern, or traditional.

The complexity of the needs to be satisfied in the various types of societies vary widely. The simpler the society, such as the small, roaming food
gathering bands, the simpler the internal and external functions. There is
no need for an arbitrating group to settle questions regarding property
rights, because there was no land boundaries drawn by ownership. Internal control was exercised mainly through brute strength. There was no
need for an elaborate defense system in carrying out its external functions
because such a society had nothing to protect, except its women and possibly a productive area of wild growth. No conference tables were needed,
with many days being spent in discussing proper seating arrangements.
Their only decision was to either defend or run. The criterion on which
the decision was based was the size of the attacking band. If it were larger
or had more fighting power than the defending group, the strategy was to
flee. If not, the site was defended. There were no homes to defend, no
boundaries to protect, or ideologies to preserve. There were only a few
scant food resources to be safeguarded, and these could be had by simply
moving to another location.

As society developed, the political needs expanded. Additional internal
and external measures were necessary to carry out the functions of the
political institution. In a society such as traditional China, the needs are

more easily satisfied than in a modern society, such as the United States. The internal function of regulating the behavior of individuals in a traditional society is carried out to a large extent by the family and by the religious institutions. The main function of the political institution is to arbitrate and to take action necessary to keep the country united. Externally, the function of the political institution in a traditional society is mainly to protect its members. A traditional society is usually isolationist, so there is very little need for developing international relationships.

In a modern complex society, all four functions of the political institution become involved processes. Internally, the problem of unifying a society splintered by divisive interests of management and labor, political factions, crime syndicates, racial differences, social class contrasts, and many others is complicated. As an arbitrator, the political institution has to provide the means of handling problems preventing the exploitation of the weaker members by the stronger, and to settle disputes between the various interests listed above, to name only a few. At the international level, the political institution in modern society develops an intricate defense system geared to push-button missile warfare. It attempts to promote harmony with other nations through a diplomatic network. All of the functions of the modern political institutions are becoming more and more complex as the development of technology accelerates.

The political structure of traditional China and the present-day United States differs widely. The emphasis of Confucius on the dominance and submission pattern of interaction carried over into the political arena establishing what is widely recognized as the two classes of people in China—the ruler and the ruled.

> From about the third century B.C., to the early years of the twentieth century, rule by an emperor was the Chinese mode of government. His rule was absolute, and there was no pretense of popular representation or majority rule. The emperor "owned" the empire and his subjects were his "children." It was technically possible for the emperor to change unilaterally any point of law he wished, and death was often the punishment that awaited any person—court minister or peasant—who opposed his will. (Hsu, 1981, p. 190)

Throughout the reign of imperial dynasties, efforts were made with a marked degree of success, to centralize power in the hands of the emperor. Although Western influences made some inroads during the last 300 years of imperial rule, centralized power continued until the birth of the Republic of China in 1912.

The Chinese, proud of their old culture and civilization, struggled long to resist this cultural penetration by the West, but internal weakness coupled with strong pressure from the West broke down their defenses and permitted Western science and philosophy to spread throughout the land. Their rapid sweep left the Chinese confused, upset, bitter, and desperately groping for a synthesis that would tie the old and the new together in some effective but understandable form.

The establishment in 1912 of the Republic of China marked the beginning of almost fifty years of political confusion and discord as the Chinese struggled to formulate a political philosophy and establish political institutions which would combine both Western and Chinese elements. (Welty, 1984, p. 212)

Accordingly, the Republic of China was not an effective form of government until its center of authority was transferred to Taiwan. The influence of this political change on intermarriage will be discussed in Section III.

## THE ECONOMIC INSTITUTION

Property is the basic element of the economic institution. Property involves an object and a set of relationships surrounding the object. The air we breathe is not property, but if someone puts the air in a cylinder and compresses it, then it becomes property. There are air rights, however, that go with the purchase of land. When a person purchases a lot, the mineral rights below the surface and the air rights above the surface usually go with the land. No one can build a bridge across the lot, ten feet off the ground, because they are infringing upon the rights of the owner.

One characteristic of property is its transferability. Only that which can be transferred from owner to owner is considered property. A wife in modern society is not property. A husband can say, "Meet my wife," but the pronoun does not place her in the category of property. Human beings become property when they can be bought and sold as slaves, or in societies where bride-purchase is practiced. Skill in itself is not property, because it cannot be transferred. When a skilled person formulates the knowledge of how to develop a skill, that is property. The individual had better copyright the material or else it becomes anyone's property, not exclusively his own.

The functions of the economic institution are the production and distribution of goods and services to meet the needs of society. Here, again, there is a positive relationship between the complexity of a society and its economic needs. For example, the automobile in American society was at one time a luxury, but with the development of industrialization and urbanization it has become a necessity. There are no daily deliveries of ice anymore, so the electric refrigerator becomes a necessity replacing the ice box or the cellar. The increased needs of modern society have resulted in an elaborate division of labor. To meet the demands for goods and services in the United States, thousands of professions and vocations have emerged, which are related through a complex system of interdependence.

The various types of societies, listed in Chapter 6, illustrate the differences in the functions of the economic institution. In the food gathering society, the method of production of goods was simply foraging and grubbing in the earth. The method of exchange was by confiscation. Those that were big and strong enough took what they wanted. In the hunting and fishing societies, production was through the application of skills in these two types of endeavors. As societies developed to these more advanced stages, a division of labor was established, which gave birth to bartering as a means of exchange.

In the agrarian society, production was by cultivation of crops and domestication of animals. This more sedentary way of life required a medium of exchange. Unusual or rare items were exchanged for various commodities. Such items as rare stones, furs, shells, and many others were used. Gold and silver were used as items of exchange long before they were shaped into coins and assigned a value. Paper money came into existence as a medium of exchange about 400 years ago. The method of exchange in an agrarian society is a combination of barter, money, and credit. When the United States was predominantly rural, farm products such as meat, eggs, grain, vegetables, and others would be taken to the general merchandise store and traded for those things not produced on the farm. This is still practiced in some rural areas. The strict inspection standards set up by the U.S. Department of Agriculture have limited the number of items which can be exchanged in this way to such things as fruit, vegetables, and eggs. Since the farmer's payday came only once a year, at harvest time, some trading was done on a credit basis. The settlement time coincided with the harvest.

In industrial society, money and credit are used as media of exchanges. Credit by far exceeds the use of money in this respect. The installment plan is a long-term credit arrangement, while the personal check is a short-term form of credit. Many merchants will not accept personal checks because it is a form of credit that is often abused.

In addition to transactions through the two forms of trade, barter or sale, property is also exchanged through gifts. In trade, the emphasis is upon the object, while gift exchange emphasizes the relationships surrounding the object. "Business is business" is the position of the trader. If he can take advantage of another's desperate need stemming from some emergency and buy a car for example, at $100 less than it is worth, then that is business. On the other hand, the real value of a gift is its sentiment. A birthday card consisting of a crude drawing of a Coca Cola bottle with the scrawled words "To the best Pop in the world" is priceless to the father; on the market, it is valueless.

In traditional China, trading places more emphasis on the relationship than it does in the United States.

All important customers are known personally to the management. In these firms a typical business transaction takes place as follows: upon entering the customer is received by the manager who sits on a long bench near the entrance. The two of them sit down and, while drinking tea served by an apprentice, they chat about the weather, the market, and local affairs. Eventually the customer may say that he wishes to look at a certain kind of cloth, and the manager asks one of the clerks to show him the goods. . . . The customer examines the goods, and, if satisfied, the transaction is completed.

This manner of doing business may be described as friendship before trade. (Hsu, 1981, p. 296)

The Chinese, who retains his primary ties to which he relates all subsequent bonds, finds his security in human relationships. The American, who regards all human relationships as subject to severance or to being repatterned when personally convenient, must seek security outside the human fold. An since God helps him who helps himself, the one remaining source of security is the acquisition of material possessions or the conquest of the physical environment in other ways. (Hsu, 1981, p. 306)

In this chapter, the various social institutions have been compared in traditional China and the United States. The purpose has been to show the types of adjustments which need to be made in order for an intermarriage between members of two types of society to be successful.

# 9

## The Chinese
## and American Technospheres

Some examples of the reciprocal relationships between technospheric traits and other cultural traits were shown in Chapter 4. When technology develops gradually, the resulting social change is manageable because social control measures adjust to meet the new demands. When technology mushrooms, as it did during the Industrial Revolution and is continuing today, problems develop because the control mechanisms are not able to adapt rapidly enough to establish new patterns governing behavior associated with the technospheric innovations. Industrialization is the process by which large scale changes occur in the technosphere at a rapid rate. This did not occur in China until the middle of the twentieth century. This chapter considers the effect of industrialization on American society and the lack of it in traditional China until approximately forty years ago.

It should be noted here that social mobility and industrialization, to be discussed in this chapter, are intricately interwoven with urbanization, which will be treated in Chapter 10. On the one hand, social mobility and urbanization are products of industrialization. In this sense, industrialization stimulates urbanization, which accelerates social mobility. On the other hand, social mobility contributes toward the development of the urbanization process, which adds fuel to the fires of industrialization. In other words, each of the three processes is a dependent variable in one instance and an independent variable in another instance.

Social mobility, simply defined, is exposure to a different way of life. Its role became more and more important as technology advanced. Vertical mobility, by which a change is made from one social class level to another, is one type of social mobility. The way of life differs from one social position to another. A second type is personal mobility, which occurs when the individual is exposed to a different way of life by travel, or commuting to work. In the latter instance, the worker lives in one social environment and works in another. The third type, residential mobility, as the term suggests, is changing the living quarters from one locality to another, such as from rural to urban areas. The operation of all three of these forms of social mobility are evident in every stage of the Industrial Revolution, and even before. A fourth type, which can be referred to as ideational mobility, reached a significant stage of development in the early part of the twentieth century, with the development of mass media through the use of electronics and the printing press. Such technological instruments as the radio, television, periodicals, and others, made it possible to view other ways of life without leaving one's own living room. The effects of social mobility will be discussed at appropriate levels of the technological development, where it makes a major social impact.

The discussion of the concept social change and its relationship to technology provides a framework in which to consider the influence of industrialization in the Republic of China, which will be dealt with in the next chapter. The major portion of this chapter is concerned with the influence of technological advancement on society generally. The influences are shown briefly by surveying the various stages of technology from its crudest stages in primitive society to its mind-boggling accomplishments of modern society. The reason for starting with primitive technology is because the effects of innovations are more easily traced in a simple society than in a complex one. Another emphasis in the chapter involves the accelerating pace of the Industrial Revolution from its assigned beginning date in the eighteenth century to the present. The purpose in glimpsing these two stages in the development of technology is not to give a detailed account of the rapid expansion of technical knowledge, but to pinpoint a few major technological strides and indicate the impact these have made on society. Social mobility is discussed throughout the chapter as one of the most significant developments of the Industrial Revolution.

The placement of the cultural trait social change in the technosphere needs further explanation before considering its effects on society. To begin with, any classification system is arbitrary. A line has been struck designating persons with a particular set of characteristics as constituting one social class, and all others are placed in a different category. When a significant number of authorities, in whatever specialized field the distinction is made, agrees, then the classification of these two types is established. In other words, the predominance of one characteristic will determine the category in which the item will be placed. Since social change is predominantly the result of changes in technology, it is placed in the technosphere.

In the second place, when a cause and effect relationship exists between technology and social change, they cannot be separated, except for analytical purposes. Since the interest in technology in this study is as an instigator of social change, both concepts are placed in the technosphere.

As technology breeds both cultural and social changes, a distinction between these two types of change needs to be made. Society can be considered culture in action. It can be thought of as a set of human relationships that prescribes the means by which culture is enacted. It follows, then, that any and every alteration in culture affects society. But all societal changes are not necessarily social change. Only those involving social relationships to a significant degree are considered social change. There are some society-wide cultural changes that do not necessarily evoke social changes. Among these, are changing modes of dress, changes in eating habits, changes in greeting customs, and other such cultural variations which may or may not evoke social change.

In other words, social change affects human relationships directly, whereas cultural change influences them indirectly. For example, the use of the bus to transport children from rural areas to a consolidated school results in a social change because it significantly affects the process of the educational agency of socialization by bringing about change in social relationships through social interaction among students which could not otherwise exist. On the other hand, when the bus is used as a public transportation vehicle for commuters or travelers, it simply provides another alternative to travel by train, streetcar, or subway. Since this use does not involve a change in human relationships, necessarily, it is classified as a cultural—not social—change. Likewise, a law that desegregates schools inaugurates social change by causing major adjustments in race relations, while a law regulating international trade does not significantly affect social relationships.

Social change stems from both technological and nontechnological cultural changes. The former source can be illustrated by the automobile. In the early stages of production, as previously discussed, the automobile was a luxury item. Very few people could afford one, so its effect on social relationships was limited to a very small portion of society's members. With the introduction of the assembly line in the early part of this century by Henry Ford, mass production lowered the cost per unit, enabling more individuals to own a car. With the increase in the number of owners, social relationships became more and more affected until the impact became significant, at which time the development could be classified as social change. The Protestant Reformation, and other revolutionary ideological movements, illustrate social change of the nontechnological nature.

Social change can be thought of as a midwife functioning in the process which brings into existence innovative social relationships struggling to be born. Social change is inevitable because society is a process, not a state. Society exists only for the moment in certain patterned relationships produced by social change of the past, and will be altered by social changes in the future.

A classical definition describes social change as variations or modifications in any aspect of social process pattern or form.

A composite or sociological definition forms the conversational definition. Based on this definition, social change is any significant alteration of a pre-existing social or cultural element or complex that results in a significant variation or modification of the structure or function of society.

A simplified definition states that social change is a societal alteration that significantly affects human relationships.

As a result of technological development, the rate of social change varies from one type of society, such as industrial, to another type, such as agrarian. The industrial society stimulates change, whereas the agrarian society retards it. The previously discussed norms of deviation, which are conducive to social change, are more prevalent in industrialized societies than in those characterized by agriculture. Likewise, the prevalence of cultural alternatives in industrial societies, encourages the recognition and acceptance of various practices which stimulate social change. On the other hand, emphasis on traditional practices, as well as commemorative events such as national holidays, religious holidays and all observances recalling the past, serve to retard social change.

The rate of social change also varies within a society. A difference in the rate of social change between societies causes no social problems. For example, changes in the United States are much more rapid than in some remote Pacific Island, but this difference has little effect on the society in either of these geographical areas. But when the rate of change varies widely between one aspect and another, or others, within a society, malfunctions occur. William Chase Ogburn calls this imbalance in the rate of change "cultural lag," which means that one phase of culture is lagging behind another in the society's development.

Although the concept is usually applied to the difference in the rates of change in material culture, as compared with nonmaterial culture, it can likewise be applied to different rates of change within each category. Relating this concept to the above distinction between social and cultural change, it can be said that cultural lag occurs when social change takes place at a different rate from cultural change. It can also be said that if social changes happen at different rates in a society and, similarly, cultural changes occur at different rates, cultural lag results in both instances. The following illustrations will help to explain the application of the concept cultural lag to both social and cultural changes.

The technospheric changes are occurring much more rapidly in present-day society, in both Taiwan and America, than changes in social control, listed in the dynasphere. The acceleration in the development of ballistics missiles without concomitant progress in international controls present a frightening illustration of cultural lag between material and nonmaterial culture. The threat posed by such a military monster is the result of a cultural change because it does not significantly affect the relationships within society, although it does create tensions between societies.

Cultural lag within material culture can be illustrated by considering air travel. The improvement from the propeller driven plane to the jetliner has made longer nonstop flights possible at much higher speeds. But the improvements in the transportation vehicle have not been matched by similar changes of the airport and local transportation facilities. A cross-country flight takes about five hours. It takes the same amount time, or more, to get to the airport and check in for departure, and get through the destination airport and to a downtown hotel. Again, even though the flight time from New York to Washington is only twenty percent of the time it takes to go by train, it is quicker to go from a downtown hotel in Manhattan to a downtown hotel in Washington by Amtrak. Although the development of air travel offers an opportunity for more frequent social exchanges, it is predominantly a cultural change, illustrating cultural lag within the technosphere.

Some fundamentalist religious beliefs are in conflict with a number of acceptable social practices. This causes a malfunctioning of the social mechanism, resulting in cultural lag within nonmaterial culture. For example, residents in a small county in Kentucky rebelled against adjusting the clock on the county courthouse to the daylight saving time schedule. The county officials were willing, but the residents proclaimed so loudly that they wanted to operate on "God's time" that the clock was not changed. With the county political unit operating on one time schedule and the business segment of the community operating on another, caused some confusion. The determination to schedule events according to "God's time" is further illustrated by the parents who went to court to change the birthdate of an infant born in a Louisville, Kentucky hospital at 12:45 A.M. Central Daylight Time, on June 3rd, to 11:45 P.M., Central Standard Time, June 2nd (the time and dates are examples, but the account is actual).

The sectarian belief that Saturday, the seventh day of the week, is the Sabbath and is therefore the proper day of worship, in a society which considers Saturday a regular business day, disrupts the smooth operation of society. Again, the fundamentalist's tenacity in holding to the biblical theory of creation has deprived many young people of a college education because the parents consider state colleges instruments of the devil for teaching the evolutionary theory. Both of these are examples of cultural lag within nonmaterial culture.

The interrelationships within, between, and among the five major categories in the classification systems especially devised for this book are so intricately interwoven that a change in one cultural trait affects, either directly or indirectly, each of the others. The discussion on social change supports such a statement. Although alterations in individual cultural traits exert an influence upon one another and upon the whole, it is only as these cultural changes become of significant proportions that they are identified as social changes.

Two types of social change have shaken the foundations of the social structure of traditional China. In 1949, after four years of civil war, Communists assumed control of the mainland and ushered in revolutionary changes. The main concern of this book is the second type of change which is taking place in the Republic of China:

> In Nationalist China, and among the Chinese living elsewhere in the world . . . change . . . is more gradual, evolutionary rather than revolutionary, and more of the traditional practices are honored and retained. (Welty, 1984, p. 179)

The important point here is that Chinese society, prior to 1949, was more saturated with tradition. The infiltration of Western influence was almost imperceptible. This means that at the middle of the twentieth century both mainland Chinese and those in Taiwan were the products of the same traditional mold, and that the practices and beliefs that were established centuries earlier were still in vogue. Both societies have changed-one through proscription of Communistic leaders, and the other through voluntary adjustments to meet the demands of a drastically different societal context.

Up to this point, an effort has been made to give the reader a basic understanding of sociology by defining and classifying the key concepts. A better understanding of the terms is given by applying them to the traditional Chinese and modern American societies. The remainder of the book places an emphasis upon understanding human relationships, rather than understanding the study of human relationships.

Three levels of scientific certainty are evident in this effort. In Chapter 10, industrialization and urbanization in Taiwan—and some of the materials in other chapters—are supported by authoritative sources which can be classified as scientific documentation. The intermediate level of certainty, theory, is based upon information drawn from the field study presented in Chapter 3. That means that Section III consists more of a set of hypothetical statements rather than of scientific conclusions.

Although the more sedentary way of life made possible by the various types of economies was mentioned briefly in Chapter 6 on the dynasphere, it is discussed at this point in more detail.

Technology seems to create a cycle consisting of the sedentary and the mobile way of life. Its developing crude forms in primitive society enabled the members to settle more permanently, while advanced technology makes the society more mobile. Even the dibble stick made it possible to provide more food in a limited geographical locality than was available before it came into existence. This enabled the primitives to remain a little longer in one area. Prior to its use, only food on the earth's surface was available. After it was discovered that the piece of wood could be converted into a tool by sharpening one end, the food gatherers could tap the food supply readily accessible slightly below the earth's surface.

The dibble stick is referred to as discovery, advisedly, because it represents new knowledge. How it originated can only be theorized. Possibly a limb was splintered by lightning and it was found that the pointed end penetrated the earth more easily than the blunt end. However it came into use as a tool, its utility probably was an accidental discovery.

The first durable tool was a stone rounded on one end, called an eolith. The term means "dawn stone." It is not known whether the instrument was shaped by hand or by nature. If man-made, it would be more properly termed "artifact." The utilitarian value of the eolith probably was also accidentally discovered.

Both the dibble stick and eolith represent new knowledge. A combination of these two bits of knowledge occurred later, when it was found that by lashing the stone to the stick a more efficient tool would result. Through this process, the hefted stone ax was invented. In other words, a discovery is new knowledge, while a combination of existing knowledge is an invention.

Invention may also result from happenstance, as suggested in the above examples of discovery, or it may be a deliberate attempt to improve an object. For example, suppose a native is walking in a lane with a fagot of wood on his shoulder. As he passes beneath a tree limb, a wild animal leaps at him and lands on the shoulder covered with the bundle of wood rather than on the bare shoulder. The native gets the idea that by weaving a heavy mat he can protect the upper part of his body from animal or enemy attacks. This represents an accidental invention. In combat with foes using stones and clubs, the woven mat serves as an effective protective garment. Later, however, as more effective means of warfare are developed, such as the bow and arrow, the fiber mat does not prevent the penetration of the arrow. The warrior, equipped with the protective principle of the garment sets about to improve materials to prevent the arrow from penetrating the covering. This represents an intentional invention.

Since invention is a new combination of old knowledge, it follows that the broader the technological base, the more rapid the rate of invention. Consequently, as knowledge accumulates, the number of inventions accelerates. Since the development of atomic energy in the early 1940s, the rapidity of inventions has resulted in a technological explosion.

There was not much opportunity for broadening the technological base in the food gathering societies, which constantly shifted their temporary bases of operation in their search for food. Any invention at that time involved various uses of stones as tools or weapons. To lug a half-completed stone object from one camp site to another was cumbersome, especially with no method of conveyance except the back of the migrant. The hunting economy enables the societies to settle down a little more permanently. Even then there was not much incentive to combine existing knowledge into new ways of doing things. The methods provided by tradition, although far from adequate in present-day society, satisfied the needs at that time. In addition to providing additional food, the hunting society members were able to fashion bone tools which made their technology a little more versatile. The animal hides provided warmer clothing for the body and were also used to cover the lean-to protecting the occupants more fully from the elements. In other words, every part of the animal was used. All that was not edible was converted into some kind of tool, utensil, or cover.

The recession of the last glacier, which occurred between 15,000 B.C. and 10,000 B.C., resulted in an over-abundant supply of water creating new streams and large lakes. Such a development provided an additional source of natural food. In addition to the food available through grubbing and hunting, the supply was supplemented through fishing. This additional resource not only made possible a more sedimentary way of life, it introduced a new type of tool. The fish bones served as needle-like instruments for piercing pelts and for fastening materials together.

The most significant impact resulting from increasing natural resources was the establishment of the first semi-permanent villages. These social units consisted of shelters clustered around the lakes and along the river banks. They were built up on stilts which made the crude living quarters functional in a number of ways. The distance off of the ground served as a barrier against wild animals. It also provided storage space and a work area protected from the sun. The air flowed over, through the thatched siding, and under the structure serving as a natural air conditioner. Some of the dwellings partially protruded over the water serving two additional purposes. For one thing, fishing was convenient. The food supply was delivered fresh to the door as the baited barb dangling in the water lured the main course for the next meal. Another purpose served by part of the crude dwelling being over the water was that a natural garbage and waste disposal service was provided.

Village life required an entirely different type of social structure. Property rights began to emerge, so it became necessary to establish guidelines regarding its usage and possible transfer. As ownership emerged in the village, it became necessary to develop some sort of a defense system. A more detailed division of labor had to be developed. The patterns regulating social relationships became more sophisticated. Kinship bonds were drawn more tightly and became more distinct. Many other adjustments had to be made to accommodate village living.

Technology expanded much more rapidly during the Neolithic Period, or the New Stone Age, than in the Mesolithic Period, or Middle Stone Age. The Mesolithic Period lasted for approximately 7,000 years, ending about 8,000 B.C., at which time the Neolithic Period began, and continued for approximately 3,000 years. Both of these ages, as well as the Paleolithic Age, derive their names from the use of stone (lithic) tools. The prefix "paleo" means ancient, "meso" means middle, and "neo" means new. The dates used in this chapter represent the earliest appearance of the periods, in Southwest Asia, which is often referred to as the cradle of civilization.

During the Neolithic Period, the cultivation of plants and domestication of animals made possible even more permanent dwelling areas. Instead of depending entirely on the skill of hunters to supply meat, livestock was bred and tended to provide such food. Instead of depending upon gathering herbs and foliage for food, vegetable gardens and fruit trees were cultivated. Both domestication of animals and cultivation of crops occurred during the Mesolithic Period, but these practices did not develop significantly until the Neolithic Period.

The farming methods during the early part of this period still did not allow completely permanent settlements. The lack of adequate tools to prepare the soil for planting prevented the use of rich fertile river valleys for cultivating purposes. The dibble stick and stone tools could not cut through the heavy sod along the banks. Consequently, the first farming was done on hill slopes through the slash and burn method. The deterioration of fallen leaves provided a blanket of compost that was easily worked with the dibble stick. Through possibly centuries of observing that vegetation grew in the open fields but not in the shade, the primitives drew the conclusion that sunlight was essential to vegetation growth. Coping with the problem of getting the nourishing rays of the sun to the soft soil, they undoubtedly tried to provide the necessary light by breaking off twigs and small branches and stripping the leaves from other branches on the tree.

Whether or not this method was experimented with, the primitives did use a crude but ingenious technique to remove the foliage obstructing the rays of the sun. They had no power saws or cross-cut saws; but perhaps they used splintered flint to cut a groove around the base of the tree, causing the life-giving sap to drain from the trunk. After the leaves had died, they started a miniature forest fire leaving only the trunk and large branches of the tree standing. This allowed enough sunlight to filter through to nourish the plants.

Such a procedure created another problem. The soft soil, especially after being churned up with the dibble stick, having no cover to protect it from the rain, washed down into the valley making the soil there richer, but because of lack of cultivating tools, of little value to the primitive. After one or two plantings, the soil had eroded so much that the slope became barren. It was then necessary to slash and burn another clump of trees and move the cultivating activities to another location.

The use of flint during the Neolithic Period made a vast improvement in tools. The more efficient tools made it possible to provide more materials to improve the protective elements of the still crude shelters. Glazing was an improvement in the pottery-making technique. The bow and arrow also became available for hunting, and as a protective weapon, during this period. The wheel, first used by the potter, was another advance in technology, which actually formed the foundation for spectacular improvements which eventually led to the Industrial Revolution thousands of years later. Other forms of technology developed so rapidly that the Neolithic Period is sometimes labeled the Stone Age Industrial Revolution.

Metal was introduced in the ensuing era, which dates from 5,000 B.C. to 3,500 B.C. It is recognized as the Cyprolithic Period, because the particular type of stone was found in Cyprus. It is also referred to as the Copper Age, because the stone was actually copper ore. When it was first introduced, the discoverers found it was a malleable form of stone. It was later discovered that it could be melted and the copper could be more easily shaped by forming molds than by hammering indentations in the copper to form crude utensils. At the close of this period, it was found that copper could be blended with tin and form bronze, which was a more durable form of metal, and harder, than copper.

The Bronze Age, dating from 3,500 B.C. to 1,200 B.C., was an era of rapid change, both technologically and socially. The new metal made it possible to improve agricultural tools. The bronze tips made the digging sticks much sharper and more durable. The plow came into use during this period. It consisted of a bronze pointed wooden wedge attached to a shaft with a handle and pulled by oxen or men. Improved methods increased agricultural production to such an extent that the tillers could supply enough food for their own use and provide for the needs of some non-agricultural workers. This meant that some of the population could be freed from subsistence farming and apply themselves to other vocations, which were mainly carried out in the villages causing an increase in the population of these centers.

However slight the trend may have been, rural to urban migration originated during the early part of the Bronze Age. As a result, the semi-permanent villages developed into established towns and cities. The size of the first cities was limited because the food surplus was meager, and the methods of transporting the farm products were crude. They did not have refrigerated trucks, trains, or planes to ship perishable produce long distances. The food had to be delivered daily, or else had to be dried or cured to preserve it. Agricultural conditions, also, determined the geographical location of cities. They had to be situated near fertile areas, where farm produce was easily accessible.

## THE INDUSTRIAL REVOLUTION

In primitive society, the members must adapt themselves to the natural environment. With the advancement of technology, man adapts the physical environment to meet his needs. The work day no longer is limited to the hours in which the sun provides light. Instead of seeking the shelter of the cave, or some other natural haven, in inclement weather, modern man can drive through rain and cold in an insulated capsule. Work can be carried on in a room with a constant temperature level, and with the same degree of light intensity, around the clock. Individuals can travel now from one place to another in a jet plane 100 times more rapidly than could be traveled by primitive modes of transportation. These technological developments, and many, many more have had a catastrophic effect on societies.

Like the stone age eras, the impact of industry on society reached significant proportions at different times in various parts of the world. The Industrial Revolution originated in England around the middle of the eighteenth century. The effect was not felt in the United States until approximately one hundred years later, following the Civil War. China was not influenced by the development of industry until after Taiwan became the center of governmental operations about the middle of the present century.

The United Sates had an advantage over England in coping with the social problems ushered in by the Industrial Revolution. The 100 years of England's experience in adjusting its institutions, established a pattern which could be followed by the United States. A disadvantage, however, was that the Industrial Revolution had been advancing at a rapid pace in England for a century when its major impact was felt by America. This meant that the social institutions had to make a much more abrupt change in America than in England. In other words, from the beginning stage of the Industrial Revolution (1750) to the modern industrialized England, covers a 240 year period, compared to 140 years the United States has been industrializing.

The adjustments the Republic of China had to make were even more phenomenal because the Industrial Revolution wielded very little influence on traditional China until the middle of the twentieth century. The industrial machinery in England had been operating for 200 years, and in America for

100 years, before its impact was felt in Taiwan. In the short span of 40 years, the Republic of China has made remarkable strides in attempting to close the technological gap between it and nations that had a much earlier start. The first stage of the Industrial Revolution is identified with the establishment of textile mills in England. It seems that a more efficient method of producing textiles could only result in improved living conditions, but this was not the case. There were no wage controls, nor governmental supervision of production methods. Consequently, the workers were exploited, the practice of child labor was abused, and the working conditions were insufferable. The centers in which the mills were located were not institutionally equipped to meet the needs of the suddenly expanded population. Because of this, living conditions were miserable.

Every phase of society was affected by this change in the method of production. The change marked the beginning of a conversion of the economy from agrarian to industrial. Such a development ushered in a change in the medium of exchange from predominately barter to money and credit. The cottage industry was replaced by factory production. The rural social institutions were undermined, and those in the factory centers were overtaxed, as a result of rural to urban migration. Migration was selective, which resulted in a brain-drain and an ever increasing exodus of skilled laborers from the rural areas. Values were changed, kinship bonds were weakened, and personal relationships were less evident. These and many other developments marked the beginning of the evolution of the tradition-bound society to mass society. The distinction between the two is measured by a comparison of their products. The former develops persons, the latter automatons.

As more and more textile mills were put into operation, more and more social problems developed. The social institutions, representing the core of social control, were designed to satisfy the needs of an agrarian economy. The rapid development of technology was unchecked by the existing social control mechanisms. As a result, the wheels of industry ground out a batch of social needs that were unmet by the social institutions. When such undesirable conditions affect a significant number of people, a social problem exists. Social unrest results, and measures are instigated to satisfy these needs.

Prior to the Industrial Revolution in England, workers had control over their products as far as both quality and quantity were concerned. From the medieval period well into the first century of the industrial era, trade and craft guilds protected the workers who belonged to them. The workers had their own tools and their own materials which enabled them to operate independently within the framework of the guild. With the establishment of the textile industry, the tools and materials were owned and furnished by the mills. The only asset provided by the worker was his skill. In order to protect this, unions formed, but they did not come into prominence until the close of the first stage of the Industrial Revolution, about 1850, although the seeds were sown during the middle of the period. The sociological significance in this development is that the close, intimate relationships of the guild were replaced by more formal, businesslike associations.

The influence of the Industrial Revolution on the social structure of America was similar to that in England in the sense that the social institutions, designed to meet the needs of a rural society, were not geared to the wheels of industry. The stages of development, however, differed. In the United States, the use of the steam engine for transportation purposes developed simultaneously with the textile mills. In addition, other types of manufacturing were operating before the textile mills became fully established. Although the early industrial development in America was quite extensive, it did not reach revolutionary proportions until around the middle of the nineteenth century.

The Civil War vigorously stimulated the Industrial Revolution in America. War accelerates industry in any nation. The momentous adjustments necessitated by the Industrial Revolution were complicated by the restructuring of society following the Civil War. A nation driven by war had to be reunited. The Southern aristocracy had to be diverted from segregated power. Slaves had to be integrated into industry, if not society. The wartorn South had to be rebuilt. Many other political and economical problems had to be dealt with at the same time the Industrial Revolution was rearranging the social order.

Social mobility during the first stage of the Industrial Revolution in America consisted mainly of residential mobility. Workers would move their families from the rural areas to the factory center in which social relationships and patterns of behavior were quite different. Whenever the economy expands, job opportunities increase. Because of this, the development of textile mills stimulated vertical mobility. There was some personal mobility at this time but it was limited mainly to the walking distance between the home and the factory. Steam powered transportation changed this.

Although the steam engine was invented almost 100 years earlier, it was not used for transportation purposes until the invention of the locomotive and the steamship around 1800. The steamship had an advantage over the locomotive in early usage because it had a natural course way provided, whereas the train required the expensive and time-consuming construction of a railway. A disadvantage of the steamship is the limitation of travel to the waterways provided by nature, with the exception of a few canals. The importance of improved transportation facilities for present purposes is to show how long-distance hauling and travel affected the structure of society. Throughout the remainder of this chapter, the traditional institutional structure of America will be used for illustrative purposes.

The use of the steam engine for inland and sea travel set off momentous repercussions through social mobility. Although there were numerous individual railway systems, especially in the northeastern part of the United States, it was not until 1869 that the East Coast was linked by rail to the West Coast. At that time, the steam locomotive replaced the horse as a source of power for traveling. The mail coach replaced the Pony Express, and the sleeping car replaced the stagecoach. All three types of social mobility, vertical, personal, and residential, were vigorously stimulated by such developments.

More importantly, steamships were making trans-Atlantic crossings in 15 days at the middle of the nineteenth century. During the latter part of that century, crossings could be made in seven days. The significant factor in these crossings was not the increased speed but the use of the steamship as an instrument of social mobility. Asian immigrants, as well as Europeans, were also flooding American shores by the middle of the nineteenth century. At first, they were welcomed as a source of cheap labor, of value to the rapidly expanding industry. However, the alarming increase in the last quarter of that century resulted in the passage of immigration laws to stem the flow. Of importance to this study is the passage of the Chinese Exclusion Act, in 1882, cutting off the Chinese immigrants because they were considered the most undesirable of the newcomers to American soil. Later the influence of southern and eastern European immigrants was curtailed for similar reasons.

The high sex ratio of European immigrants was of major importance to the mate selection process in the United States. For every 300 males coming to the American shores during the first part of the present century, there were only 100 females. Undoubtedly, those male immigrants intended to send for their betrothed or potential mates after getting established, but this did not always work out. Consequently, the demand for female marital partners outstripped the supply, resulting in a high percentage of intercultural marriages.

During the early part of the twentieth century, a phenomenal expansion of the technosphere began. One major advance was the conversion of manpower into horsepower through the electric motor. The cumbersome, air-polluting steam engine was replaced by a compact power unit. As power plants and electrical transmission systems developed, production in small factories and many times in a workshop adjacent to the home, or in the basement, became possible. Electrically powered trolley cars made local public transportation available.

More importantly, the kerosene or gas lamp was replaced by the electric light. This enabled the production of goods and the rendering of services around the clock. Shift work, whether two twelve-hour, or three eight-hour stints, disrupted home life. Social institutions had to expand their functions to meet the new demands created by the twenty-four-hour activities whether production, distribution, or other activities such as recreation. Street lights increased pedestrian traffic at nighttime and served as a deterrent to crime in the larger cities. With the Rural Electrification Administration program in 1935, the process of urbanizing rural areas was stimulated.

Telecommunications were made possible by the advancement of the use of electricity. The telegraph system transmitting messages by wires and cable served as a means of long-distance communication, even by trans-oceanic cables, before the turn or the century. The telephone extended the lines of communication criss-crossing the country and spanning oceans, making social interaction possible that never could have taken place otherwise. The home telephone has also been helpful in maintaining primary relationships with family and friends from long distances.

The impact of the automobile on traditional society as a means of local travel has revolutionized society. One of its major effects is the inversion of the city. During the earlier days of the Industrial Revolution, the owners and the top-level administrators lived near the factories and offices. Lack of adequate local transportation facilities made this location more convenient, even though the congestion and various forms of pollution were undesirable. The workers had to live some distance from the factories because of economic necessity. With the development of the automobile, the residential pattern was reversed. The factory owners could afford automobiles, which made commuting to work possible, so they shifted their residences to the more appealing physical environment of the suburbs. The workers, again because of economic necessity, moved into the congested and polluted area of the city, because the factories were more accessible.

Personal mobility, through the use of the automobile, has enabled individuals to establish new, and maintain old, relationships with others. In other words, it has expanded the geographic boundaries of neighborly relations, but not the neighborhood. For the young people, the automobile provided a mobile parlor, sans chaperone, for courting purposes.

Vertical mobility has been stimulated by the use of the automobile for community purposes. Formerly, the better occupational opportunities were limited to a confined geographical area, or else residential mobility was necessary. The car made it possible to accept positions at a higher level, some distance away, without changing residences.

Motorized homes, or mobile trailer homes, symbolize residential mobility. Their use has created a continuous flow of retirees who set up temporary residence in various parts of America to meet their needs. These range all the way from touring to making desirable climatic conditions available in different seasons. This method of living and traveling has made it possible for the retirees in America to make lengthy visits with their children and grandchildren and still maintain their independence. By parking the trailer on the lot or in the driveway of their children's home, they become neighbors rather than guests. In this way, the routine of the established home is not disturbed and the parents do not feel they are imposing.

Air travel has shrunk the world in the sense that face-to-face associations can take place on a long distance basis as easily as they could occur in the local area by the use of land transportation. It would be a hard day's drive to range out 300 miles from home and return the same day. By the jet plane, this daily range has been increased ten times. Through air travel, a New Yorker can fly to the West Coast and be home by bedtime the same day. He also can have breakfast at home, lunch in San Francisco, and dinner in Honolulu. The contact by the United States traveler, or others, with vastly different cultures has been made routine by this mode of transportation.

A short ten years after Lindbergh pioneered trans-Atlantic crossings, trans-oceanic passenger and mail flights were established in both directions from American shores spanning the world. Of importance to this book, the Pan-American China Clipper blazed a trans-Pacific airline from the West Coast to China before 1940. World War II interrupted commercial airline development, but it provided impetus to improving aircraft. At the close of the War, commercial transportation, through both domestic and trans-oceanic flights, made stupendous strides.

As the Industrial Revolution reached this stage in the United States, it was just beginning in Taiwan. This means that the textile mills, the use of the steam engines for transportation, electricity, telecommunications, the automobile, and air travel developed simultaneously in Taiwan. Although there was some lag, the developmental gap was not as great as it was in the United States.

The Industrial Revolution continues to accelerate as the cultural base is broadened. Only history will determine the terminology to be assigned to the classification of twentieth century technological advancement. Whether the various stages will be identified with automobile, electronic, computer, atomic, or space age remains to be seen. Whatever the label, the social structure is affected in a different way by each of these advancements. With changes in the social structure, the mate selection process is altered.

There are numerous reasons for the failure of pre-Communist China to industrialize. The attachment to the land is one

which often overrode all considerations of personal economic welfare. For to the Chinese, his land was not merely an investment; it was life itself. Accordingly, there was almost no sacrifice he was not prepared to make in order to avoid selling his land. (Hsu, 1981, p. 301)

Another reason is that the Chinese life is village oriented. They were reluctant to leave the familiar surroundings and break the strong neighborly ties even though staying in the village meant financial hardship. The main reason China was not sucked into the industrial stream was because the emphasis in trade was, and is, upon the relationships between buyer and seller and not the profit of the sale. Transactions were carried more in a social, rather than a business atmosphere. Whatever the reason, the industrialization of China lagged far behind many other nations.

In spite of the fact that Taiwan's first Western contact was with the Portuguese, approximately 400 years ago, and that the Dutch ruled the island for nearly half of the seventeenth century, industrialization made no noticeable impact on Taiwan until about 40 years ago.

Perhaps the most evident and consequently the most widely appreciated fact about the pre-1949 economy of China is that, despite the urgent necessity to do so, the Chinese, after a century of intimate contact with the West, failed to join the mainstream of industrialization that swept up every other major noncolonial nation. Up to World War II the largest plants, the most up-to-date machinery, and the majority of China's industrial laborers were employed in the textile industry. Yet as late as 1930, hand looms consumed about 78.5 percent of the cotton yarn on the Chinese market. In 1933, the most reliable estimates showed that China had less than two million industrial workers and of this number, less than one-tenth were employed in plants hiring ten or more workers and utilizing some form of mechanical power. (Hsu, 1981, p. 312)

Since industrialization is the main force of social change, the reluctance of traditional China to yield to this economic pressure slowed change in other segments of the society.

To this point, the chapter has compared the technosphere of America with that of traditionally bound China up until the middle of the twentieth century. It has shown the development of technology from its crudest form, in which the dibble stick was the main instrument of industry, through the gradual accumulation of the products that laid the foundation of the phenomenal plunge of the Republic of China into the unbelievable technological accomplishments resulting from its struggle for existence. Chapter 10 will discuss the social changes on Taiwan since 1950.

# SECTION III

## THE INFLUENCE OF INDUSTRIALIZATION AND URBANIZATION ON THE MATE SELECTION PROCESS IN TAIWAN

Section III is designed to serve three main purposes. The first is to show the effect of industrialization and urbanization on the social structure of the Republic of China. This is done by comparing the various spheres of the social fabric of Taiwan with those in the U.S. The outline of Chapter 10, in which this is done, follows a similar pattern to the outlines of Chapters 5 to 9, in which a comparison is made between the spheres in traditional China and the U.S. The purpose is to reveal the social gap that has to be bridged in affecting an intermarriage between a Chinese and an American-Caucasian. The present social system operating in Taiwan lies somewhere along the continuum between the traditional Chinese and modern U.S. ways of life. The comparison shows the influence of the vestigial tug of tradition on the one side and the beckoning of social innovation on the other. In this way, the social distance the Republic of China has traveled from the traditional Chinese patterns toward those in the U.S. will be revealed.

The second purpose of Section III is to analyze in detail the findings of the field study on the attitudes of Chinese college students toward intermarriage with American-Caucasians. Consideration of the mate selection mechanism as it functions in the traditional Chinese and American social environments provides an orientation for the analysis. Such a technique presents a clearer view of the mechanism as it hovers between the two societal systems.

It should be kept in mind that the research project reported in Chapter 3 is more of a pilot study than an exhaustive study of the intermarital process. The conclusions which are drawn are at different levels of scientific certainty. At one level, documentation from other studies support the conclusions. Other statements are more hypothetical. They form assumptions based on the deductive method rather than scientifically supported conclusions based upon the inductive method. For example, the summary of the field study in Chapter 3 shows that the parents of students from rural areas are much more strongly opposed to intercultural marriage between Chinese and American-Caucasians than parents in urban areas. The interference is that the rural areas of Taiwan are much more traditional bound than urban areas. This is likely true, because studies have indicated that tradition is much more prevalent in a rural society than in an urban one. But to say that this is the cause of the disapproval of such marriages in Taiwan is based upon deduction and not induction. To say definitely that intercultural marriages, specifically in Taiwan, are discouraged by tradition requires a much more detailed study than was made by using a convenient sample of college students as the respondents in the field study.

The purpose of Section III is not to present undeniable evidence that the intermarriage process in Taiwan is influenced in certain ways and to a definite extent by the findings of the study. It is rather to pose some plausible projections of the effect of social change on intercultural marriage. In other words, the results of the study are presented here mainly to indicate conclusions that would probably be drawn if a more detailed study of intercultural marriages were made in Taiwan. Although some of the statements are soundly based conclusions, others are more in the nature of tentative assumptions.

The approach used in Section III is to first show the extent to which Taiwan has yielded to the pressures of industrialization and urbanization. A statistical picture of the development of industrialization of Taiwan is first presented in Chapter 10. A discussion of the general effects of urbanization on society is then given followed by an estimate of the extent to which Taiwan has been affected. Chapter 11 treats the influence of the changed social environment on the mate selection process in Taiwan.

The third purpose of Section III is to summarize the major changes, treated throughout this book, that have contributed toward the changed attitudes regarding intercultural marriage between Chinese and American-Caucasians. These findings are set forth at the conclusion of Chapter 12 under the question, "Shall East meet West?" The answer will give some indication as to the feasibility of intercultural marriages between other nationalities.

# 10

## Industrialization
## and Urbanization of Taiwan
## since 1950

Numerous social changes since the establishment of the Republic of China in Taiwan have made Chinese society more similar to American society, which is an essential transformation if intercultural marriages are to take place between members in the two different societies. Several major results of social change in Taiwan have narrowed the gap between Chinese and American societies.

The Republic of China had no choice on developing into a highly industrialized and urbanized nation. The abandonment of the traditional way of life and the adoption of the modern and commercial social structure was essential for survival.

This chapter deals with changes brought about through industrialization and urbanization of Taiwan reflected in the technosphere, statisphere, and instisphere. In other words, this chapter deals with the changes brought about in the basic social structure of Taiwan by the phenomenal technological impact.

### TECHNOSPHERIC CHANGES

If it were not for technospheric changes in Taiwan, intercultural marriages would be few and far between. The twin processes of industrialization and urbanization have resulted in an upheaval in the Taiwan social structure. The remarkable progress in these two developments, in the short period of 40 years, has altered social relationships to an unbelievable degree. Industrialization and urbanization are two interlocked variables. Industrialization shifted the population from the sparsely settled countryside to population centers. The concentration of population in limited areas resulted in an entirely different way of life referred to as urbanism.

Industrialization, one of the major changes in the technosphere, first developed urban centers, or cities, which blossomed into metropolitan

171

centers, then the Consolidated Areas, as listed in the U.S. Census, and now in some instances, megopoli, which are masses of population stretching in one situation from Boston, Massachusetts, to the southern states. When one flies over such a population phenomenon the scenery presents a sprawling mass of residences clustered together for hundreds of miles.

Although this work, *Conversational Sociology*, cannot be labeled a monotheistic theory (i.e., claiming a single factor as the sole reason for the social changes discussed), the technospheric items are of prominent importance in the study of changed attitudes toward intercultural marriages. Consequently, changes in technology in Taiwan are considered first in the analysis of the field study for two reasons. First, technology is a prime mover in converting Taiwan from an agrarian to an industrial economy. Second, technological advances have drastically changed the mate selection process.

Earlier, a we made a brief survey of the development of technology from the earliest innovations through the catastrophic changes of the Industrial Revolution. We also discussed the influence of industrialization on society in general and in the U.S. specifically.

The first portion of the present chapter deals with the extent to which Taiwan has been industrialized and urbanized in the past 40 years, and how these processes have affected the way of life on Taiwan. The possible effect of the changes brought by these two processes on mate selection is discussed later.

Before, we pointed out that one of the major consequences of industrialization is urbanization. The second part of this chapter deals with this process as it introduces a different way of life referred to as urbanism. In the earliest stages of technological development the rural cultural characteristics were transported to the population centers gradually, with little effect on the difference between the rural and city environments. As the pace of industrialization accelerated, however, the way of life was dichotomized into rural and urban social conditions. A distinct contrast developed between the two types of cultures. But as the urbanization process increased more rapidly, the opposite trend was established and the two types of culture were blended.

Following the presentation of the general effects of urbanization on society, statistics show the extent to which urbanization has encroached upon the traditional texture of Taiwan, and the effect this has had on the mate selection process on the Island.

INDUSTRIALIZATION OF TAIWAN

Numerous social changes since World War II have made inroads into the social structure of the Republic of China. These were accelerated as major adjustments necessitated by shifting the Nationalist social institutions from the mainland to Taiwan.

In the midst of defeat and confusion on the mainland, the late Generalissimo Chiang Kai-shek had been quietly making plans for a last stand in Taiwan. The cream of the Air Force, the loyal portion of the Navy, and some of the remaining crack troops were transferred to the island along with the gold reserve of the Central Bank. Realizing the futility of peace talks with the Communists, the Generalissimo chose to retire at the beginning of 1949 just before the final offensive. (Budget, Accounting & Statistics: Executive Yuan, 1983, p. 4)

At the time Nationalist China established headquarters on Taiwan, in 1949, it was a traditionally shackled society, with little evidence of industrial development. Taiwan had been exploited by Japan during the years of World War II. Agriculture and industry on the island had dropped to a low production level by the end of the Japanese occupation, in 1945, when Taiwan was returned to China. Rice, the staple food, had also dropped to a very low production.

With the withdrawal of the Nationalist government from the mainland to Taiwan, the leaders faced the three-fold task of reconstructing the industrial complex, establishing a defense system to protect the island from Communist invasion, and making long-range plans for eventually re-uniting China. With a depleted economy, and with tradition opposing social changes, this seemed an impossible task. Perhaps this is the reason Chiang Kai-shek decided to retire from leadership rather than face the discouragement in negotiating peace with the Communists as quoted above.

Whether or not a unique salvation plan for China or the world evolved from the Generalissimo's efforts, he set industrial machinery in motion that has revolutionized the Republic of China.

As a consequence of twin processes of industrialization and urbanization, much social change has occurred in Taiwan in the past 30 years. The continuously expanding economy and resulting improvement in the living standards provides the necessary foundation for social change which proceeds in a more gradual and less apparent fashion. A new life style is now emerging with more room for individual expression and social advancement; individually and collectively there has been a qualitative improvement in social condition. (Budget, Accounting & Statistics: Executive Yuan, 1983, p. 36)

Since Taiwan had to begin its reconstruction from a depleted industrial base, as did the United States following the Civil War, expansion was very gradual during the first few years. This period is well described by Han Lih-wu in *Taiwan Today*.

Rehabilitation was difficult and slow in the early postwar days due to lack of funds and materials. The damaged power plants were repaired with reclaimed parts, as were many other industries that the Japanese had pronounced beyond repair, including the all-important railway system and sugar industry.

Commodity shortages became more critical in the late 1940's when the Communists began to overrun the China mainland and the subsequent mass evacuation of mainlanders to this island made the situation still worse.

Late in 1950 timely U.S. aid arrived. It made available materials and equipment for the rehabilitation and construction of power plants, textile mills, fertilizer factories, steel works and other important industries.

Economic and technical assistance from the United States not only quickened Taiwan's rehabilitation work, but effectively helped stabilize its economy by financing imports of large amounts of consumable goods to meet the local demand. In 1952 the upward tendency of the price index began to level off.

The government began its long-range economic development efforts in 1953 after rehabilitation had gotten well underway. Under the First Four-Year Economic Development Plan, projects to lay the groundwork for industrialization of the island were successfully implemented. An economy capable of supplying all of the basic needs of its people was in the making by 1956.

In view of the continued strength of the Taiwan economy, the United States started to phase out its economic assistance to China shortly after the turn of the decade and on June 30, 1965, the U.S. aid program was finally terminated. (Budget, Accounting & Statistics: Executive Yuan, 1983, p. 158)

The remarkable progress the Republic of China has made in industrialization is evidenced by the fact that the gross national product increased more than 100 times in less than 30 years. It "was U.S. $400 million in 1952. By the end of 1981, it has soared to U.S. $40.26 billion." At the end of 1983 the GNP of the Republic of China was more than U.S. $45 billion. This development in such an extremely short period of time disrupted the traditional patterns of the society.

The following statistics vividly reveal the stupendous strides of the Industrial Revolution in Taiwan since 1950. Each step narrowed the gap between technology in the United States and in Taiwan.

Cotton textile manufacturing has been a rapidly growing industry in Taiwan. Starting with two cotton mills at the end of the war. Taiwan has now 140 cotton mills equipped with some 2.6 million spindles and 74,598 looms.

The wool industry in Taiwan has undergone a growth no less remarkable than the cotton industry. There was only one mill with 900 spindles at the end of the war. At present, there are 61 mills with a total of 85,748 worsted spindles, 55,633 woolen spindles, 322, 272 synthetic spindles and 1,204 looms as of 1980. (Budget, Accounting & Statistics: Executive Yuan, 1983, p. 181)

In 1976 principal industrial production was valued at U.S. $16.12 billion, twenty-eight times that of 1954. (Budget, Accounting & Statistics: Executive Yuan, 1983, p. 162)

THE PROCESS OF URBANIZATION

Industrialization, in its earliest phases of development in a society, causes a shift in the population distribution pattern from rural to urban areas. In this instance, industrialization is the independent variable and urbanization is the dependent one. In turn, the concentration of population in urban centers requires a different type of social organization. Urbanization then becomes the independent variable and social change is the dependent one. Urbanization is a two-way process by which the urban way of life is disseminated. Prior to, and in the early stages of the Industrial Revolution, urbanism developed by the concentration of population in urban centers. From the early part of the present century, in the United States, urbanism has been disseminated, also, in an urban to rural flow, resulting in the development of urbanized rural areas. At the time the Republic of China was established on Taiwan, urbanism was flowing from rural areas to urban centers. It was not long after this that urbanism began to move in both directions causing a mixture of rural and urban culture in both the cities and countryside.

URBANIZATION ON TAIWAN

Urbanism differs from the rural way of life in every respect. Just to enumerate these differences, without any explanatory comments, would require pages and pages of material. Because of this, the variations in the two types of societies have been limited to a few of those for which statistics are available. Characteristics identifying urban society, discussed in this chapter, consist of high population density, low fertility and sex ratio, and the high rate of females employed in non-farm occupation. Three other differences of major importance in mate selection between the two types of societies—anonymity, the change from ascribed to achieved status, and the confusion of means and ends in urban centers—will be dealt with more fully later.

The first United States census, in 1790, listed 4 million people with only 5 percent of them living in urban areas. By 1980, those classified as urban population amounted to 95 percent of the total. In less than 200 years, the United States social structure had to adjust from one designed to meet the needs of a society that was almost totally rural to one that is almost totally urban. The rapid shift of the population in Taiwan was no less spectacular.

Because the Republic of China classifies its population more on the basis of administrative units rather than on size of urban centers, as the United States does, it is difficult to compare the two societies according to the proportion of the population living in rural or urban areas. The important point is that both societies changed rapidly from rural to urban types in a relatively short period of time.

Redistribution of the population is one of the major impacts of industrialization on society. As a consequence of this, population density differs in rural and urban societies as well as within cities. The shift of population within a society, from rural to urban areas, has necessitated a reorganization of the social structures. The needs of a sparsely settled rural geographical territory are quite different from those in a densely settled urban center.

It should be mentioned here that population density, in itself, is not the main contributing factor in urbanizing a community. For example, elite suburbs, to mention one type, are not densely populated, but the way of life there is more urban than in some crowded cities. Nor is the size of an urban center the main criterion in distinguishing between rural and urban population. For example, a city with a population of 25,000 that is 250 miles from the nearest metropolitan area will not necessarily be as urbanized as a population center of 1,000 situated within easy driving distance of a major metropolitan area.

The population density per square kilometer increased in Taiwan from 243.3 in 1954 to 520.4 in 1983. The latter figure is approximately 1,348 persons per square mile. The population density of Taipei, the largest city in Taiwan, was 8,553 per square kilometer in 1982. Based upon the same geographical area the Taipei population density was about one-fourth that in 1954. Although the comparative figures are meager, enough evidence is available to suggest, at least, that according to population density Taiwan is becoming urbanized.

The fertility rate, which is the number of births in a particular year per 1,000 females age 15–45, is another criterion indicating the extent to which a society has become urbanized. The fertility rate in Taiwan as a whole was 196 in 1954, compared to 79 in 1983 (Budget, Accounting & Statistics: Executive Yuan, 1983, p. 29). Said another way there were 2.5 times as many infants born per 1,000 females 15–45 years of age in 1954 than in 1983.

The difference in the general fertility rate in rural and urban areas of Taiwan for the years 1971 and 1983 appears in the following tabulated form.

|              | 1971 | 1983 | %Change |
|--------------|------|------|---------|
| Cities          | 105 | 70 | 35 |
| Urban Townships | 110 | 84 | 26 |
| Rural Townships | 119 | 89 | 30 |

The general fertility rate for all of Taiwan was 112 in 1971 (Budget, Accounting & Statistics: Executive Yuan, 1983, p. 30). As can be seen, the general fertility rate dropped much more rapidly in cities than in either of the other areas. One reason for this could possibly be a disproportionate number of females in the child-bearing age migrating to cities to join the work force, rather than marry and bear children.

The drastic shift in the population of Taiwan between 1954 to 1983 is shown in the *Statistical Yearbook of the Republic of China* (Budget, Accounting & Statistics: Executive Yuan, 1983).

|                                            | 1954 | 1983 |
|--------------------------------------------|------|------|
| % of Total Pop. in Farm Families           | 51.3 | 22.9 |
| % of Total Pop. in Cities of 100,000 or more | 17.0 | 50.0 |

In order to verify these estimates, available statistics of the population of Taiwan living in cities and hsiens (similar to metropolitan areas of the U.S. Census) was determined for the year 1982. According to this method of distinguishing between rural and urban population on Taiwan, the urban population represented 63 percent of the total, in 1982, compared to the above estimated total of 63.4 percent in 1983.

Regardless of the rate of change from rural to urban, the impact of industrialization and urbanization on Taiwan resulted in:

A happy combination of economic growth and well-planned social welfare policies made possible bridging the gap between the poor and the rich as well as easing the cultural and economic differences between the cities and the countryside. Along with progressing economic integration of urban and rural sectors of the economy, the cultural distinction between the urban and rural inhabitants is being obliterated because widely accessible educational opportunities in the cities and villages have opened to the young people equal opportunities for economic and social advancement. At the same time, social integration is taking place among the diverse linguistic groups and social classes thereby increasing stability and cohesion of society. (Budget, Accounting & Statistics: Executive Yuan, 1983, p. 36)

Efforts have been made in the Republic of China to slow the rural to urban migration. The government has made an intensive effort during the past ten years to stem the flow of migrants. In 1973, the government of the Republic of China launched

> a two year crash program designed to remove most of the major institutional and technical bottlenecks in agricultural development, and thereby to speed up the modernization process of the rural sector.

> The primary objective of this program was to improve the living and working conditions of farmers, who make up 40% of the population of Taiwan, and increase their income to a level comparable with that of other workers. (Budget, Accounting & Statistics: Executive Yuan, 1983, p. 154)

Other measures are being taken to encourage young people, especially, to remain in the rural areas, and thus, reduce the drain of manpower.

> The provincial government has worked out plans to develop industrial zones in rural areas to absorb the labor force. . . .

> In addition, the government is actively promoting the second phase land reform program in order to increase farm productivity. Other accelerated rural construction projects have been undertaken by the government to provide a better living environment and improve the quality of life of the farming people. (Budget, Accounting, & Statistics: Executive Yuan, 1983, p. 48)

The sex ratio, which is the number of males per 100 females, does not indicate that urbanization is affecting Taiwan according to this index. The sex ratio for all of Taiwan was 105.3 in 1954 compared to 108.5 in 1982, the sex ratio is consistently high in all of the cities in Taiwan. In fact it was 112 for all cities in 1963. In Taipei, it was 106 in 1982. According to migration statistics, the trend seems to be in the direction of females moving to urban centers. In 1982, almost 13,000 more females moved into Taipei than moved out, compared to a net immigration of 9,000 males. This indicates a slight movement of the sex ratio in the direction of urban centers.

There is a larger proportion of females in non-agricultural positions in an urban society than in a rural one. In 1954, the gainfully employed females equaled 15.8 percent of the total female population. Only 23 percent of these were in non-agricultural jobs. In 1983, there were 33.8 percent of the female population gainfully employed. Of these, 74 percent were doing non-agricultural work. These statistics indicate a significant movement of Taiwan in the direction of urbanism based on this criterion (Budget, Accounting & Statistics: Executive Yuan, 1983, p. 24).

In the discussions presented thus far in this chapter, the ground work has been provided to show the influence of technological changes on the nonmaterial culture spheres in the classification system described in Chapter 4, as well as the influence of these changes on the attitudes of college students toward intercultural marriages.

## STATISPHERIC CHANGES

Two all-inclusive concepts in the statisphere (culture and social structure) and one in the dynasphere (society) are all influenced in similar ways by industrialization and urbanization. They could easily be lumped together and treated as a unit in considering the influence of social change on them. For analytical purposes, however, it is better to consider them separately in dealing with the changes affected by industrialization and urbanization on the mate selection process of Taiwan. The discussion of the changes in the culture of Taiwan focuses on the emergence of social alternatives which weaken the traditional foundation and create subcultures. In the part of this chapter dealing with changes in the social structure, the development of cities and the adjustments in social relationships are dealt with. Changes taking place in Taiwan converting group relationships into a predominance of the secondary type are also discussed in this chapter. Two types of primary groups, the family and the peer group, are considered as they affect the mate selection process. Changes in the status and role of the female are also of importance to this discussion of cultural traits in the statisphere.

There is a striking similarity in the establishment of Chinese culture in Taiwan and the European culture planted on American soil. Both cultures are the result of a segment of culture being uprooted and then transplanted. American culture was uprooted and transplanted to a different social and physical environment a little over 200 years ago. In this process, the elements of the old culture were not completely cast out, but modified to meet the demands associated with the conception and development of a new society. The Republic of China has more recently undergone a similar experience in the transference of a segment of the population from Mainland China to Taiwan. The major difference between these two national experiences is that the Europeans migrated to America to establish a new social order, whereas the shift of the Chinese to Taiwan was to perpetuate an old social order. This means that the traditional practices of pre-Communist China are much more in evidence in the Republic of China than the traditional European practices are apparent in the United States, except in the sub-cultural pockets previously mentioned. This makes the social structure, to be discussed next, of Taiwan more rigid than that of the United States. Such a difference discourages intermarriage between members of the two societies.

The degree of traditional control is the most significant difference between the Chinese and American cultures. Social change in traditionally stable societies is evolutionary, whereas in complex modern societies it is revolutionary. In areas where social change is gradual, mate selection is little affected because social control mechanisms keep pace with the changing society. In areas where social change is rapid, however, the normative structure is weakened and the established mate selection practices are much more likely to change. Although the perpetuation of practices was more evident in traditional China, the traditional bonds are still strong as a unifying force of the Chinese in Taiwan and link the Chinese communities across the world into a single entity. President Chiang-Kuo said in his 1979 New Year's message,

> any evil force inconsistent with Chinese tradition will never be accepted or tolerated by the Chinese people. . . . We can see today that all of our compatriots at home and abroad have demonstrated with one will and one heart their absolute unity and patriotism. (Republic of China, 1979, p. 25)

In spite of the emphasis upon retaining the traditional practices, cultural innovations have been introduced in the Republic of China that have replaced some of the universal practices with social alternatives. The flow of rural population into cities has contributed toward the acceptance of innovations.

> [C]ities are the centers of political and economic control in Asian countries, and most of Asian leadership lives in them. Many of these cities are Western in origin, attitudes, and appearance. It is in the cities that the new ways of life are practiced extensively, and from them the currents of change and reform emanate. (Welty, 1984, p. 34)

Former rural dwellers have been exposed to the urban forces of social change because

> the development of new opportunities in commerce, public administration, and industry has stimulated a flow of people from the rural areas to the urban areas of Taiwan. (Ahern & Gates, 1981, p. 175)

The advantages offered by urban centers are referred to as the pull factors of migration. Such conditions as better occupational opportunities, and better educational facilities for the children, among others, attract migrants. Negative conditions such as traffic congestion, pollution, and other undesirable conditions are push factors in migration, causing some persons to move to the suburbs, or to the open country. Whatever the reason for persons moving from rural to urban areas, residential patterns evolve in some instances that develop subcultures.

> Migration to Taiwan also frequently resulted in the familiar chain pattern: early settlers induced others from their home areas to join them.

Such locally intensive migration eventually contributed to the growth of discrete, homogeneous communities that were set apart from one another by differences in speech, customs, and practices. (Ahern & Gates, 1981, p. 297)

The migration pull factors appear to be exerting more influence on females since 1950 than before.

Before 1950, most migrants had been male, in their teens, poorly educated, and unskilled. . . . Since 1950, however, more migrants have been women, their educational level has been higher, they have tended to have more work experience, and they have secured more diverse employment. They have also been upwardly mobile and have not as often settled in particular precincts. (Ahern & Gates, 1981, p. 176)

As can be seen from this quotation, the females are not settling in subcultural groups, but are intermixing with the urban residents of migrants from other villages. The migration of males is following a similar pattern. They are younger and more of them are single than the pre-1950 migrants.

SOCIAL STRUCTURAL CHANGES

In England, America, China, or wherever it strikes, industrialization revolutionizes the social structure of a traditional or an agrarian society. Social structure is a system of relationships providing a framework for society. Social structure is of importance to the study of the mate selection process because it is a network linking vital segments of a society into a unit.

The foundation of the Chinese social structure differs from that of America. Likewise, the interrelationships between the various cultural traits of each of the societies is different. Consequently, no matter how rapid the industrialization of China may be, or how extensively the urbanization process affects the social structure, the dissimilarity between Chinese and American society will be in evidence for centuries. These differences will be discussed in detail later. The purpose of this part of Chapter 10 is to show the effects of industrialization and urbanization on the total social structure.

Industrialization and motorized vehicles have played havoc with the neighborhoods, rearranging the social structures in both rural and urban communities. At one time, neighbors were bound together by a number of common interests that have been weakened by social changes. The shift from subsistence to commercial farming has taken its toll in the deterioration of neighborhoods. The dirt farmers at one time discussed their common practices and crops with one another thereby strengthening the neighborly bonds. Present-day specialized farming practices prompt the gentleman farmer to lean more heavily on the advice of the agricultural agent rather than his neighbor for advice in dealing with farming problems.

## SOCIAL GROUP CHANGES

One of the major changes in the group structure of Taiwan, as a result of urbanization, is the incidence of secondary relationships. This type of relationship develops an attitude that is individual-centered, rather than group-centered. The perspective of the individual toward the group is reversed. It is no longer what the individual can do for the group, but what the group can do for the individual. The primary group satisfies emotional needs of an individual personally. The secondary group satisfies these needs impersonally. For example, the security resulting from the knowledge that one's nation has the mightiest military force in the world is different from emotional security stemming from the comfort one mate gives to another when misfortune strikes. Likewise, financial success results in response, sometimes in a kowtowing manner, but it is inconsequential when compared to the response of a close companion. This is to say that when secondary group relationships prevail, the search for a mate too often focuses on characteristics such as the amount of wealth, the number of influential friends, or the flair for conspicuous consumption. The Chinese adjustment to the secondary type of group relationships is conducive to intermarriage with an American-Caucasian.

The main function of mate selection in traditional society was to unite two families in order to promote their consuming interests. Thus, marriages were arranged between royal families to ally two nations; two tycoons would arrange marriages between their offspring in order to broaden their financial base and increase the opportunity for forming a monopoly. In traditional China, marriages were arranged by the parents to perpetuate family interests.

> Arranging marriages for their children was one of the primary obligations of the parents. The boys must be married in order that the family line might be continued and descendants created to perpetuate the ancestral rites. Girls must be married so that they might fulfill themselves as women and strengthen the family fortunes. Gentry families were interested in making a strategic family alliance. Peasant families desired money for their daughters and were reluctant to marry them to families who owned or rented little or no land. Marriages were arranged by the families concerned. The prospective bride and groom had little to say about either the choice of their mate or the marriage arrangements. In fact, they rarely saw each other before the marriage. (Welty, 1984, p. 201)

An extreme form of arranged marriages was practiced at one time in traditional China, when mates were selected by the parents through the process of minor marriages.

Minor marriages were very important in some parts of China. . . . A woman who married in this fashion was removed from her natal family as an infant or small child and raised by her future husband's parents. The result being that husband and wife grew up under conditions as intimate as those experienced by siblings. (Ahern & Gates, 1981, p. 347)

Various theories are devised to explain such a practice. Since the observance of weddings was an elaborate and expensive occasion in traditional China, perhaps rearing an infant to a marriageable age was monetarily advantageous. Another theory is that even

families who could easily afford a major marriage sometimes chose to raise a son's wife because it was easier to educate a child than reeducate a young adult. A daughter-in-law reared from infancy could be taught to accept her mother-in-law's authority and thus did not urge family division as a way of escaping their authority. (Ahern & Gates, 1981, p. 350)

Although marriages were not arranged in traditional America, many marital partners were selected as a result of irresistible parental pressure. The acceptance of a proposal to marry was contingent upon the approval of the girl's father. The hopeful groom was interviewed by the father to determine whether or not he would be able to provide for the girl in the manner to which she had become accustomed. If the father was convinced that the proposer could make a good husband, as a provider and in other ways, consent was usually given. If the father did not approve, there would be no wedding.

When the individuals involved make their own decision as to who their future mate is to be, the emotional interests many times negate the family interests. In these cases, romance is the main determining factor, whereas in parentally arranged marriages, romance, if it is experienced at all, is a by-product of the union. The effect of industrialization and urbanization on family relationships will be dealt with more fully later, but it is helpful here to show how social changes in Taiwan have shifted, to some extent, the family's voice in mate selection to the peer group. Two major technological improvements have contributed to this development. Primary relationships are no longer limited to the immediate geographical environments. The automobile, or motorcycle in Taiwan, has made frequent face-to-face associations possible. Public transportation, such as the train and bus, have also extended the spatial distance of intimate, personal relationships.

The lot of the peasant was hard physical labor from dawn until dark. After natural light was no longer available to toil outside of the house, many peasants shifted the center of activities to the inside, where they produced handicraft to supplement their meager income. Since survival was their main interest, mate selection was based more upon the physical ability of the mate rather than upon forming alliances.

> Economic necessity forced the peasants to place more importance on obtaining a strong helpmate than upon obtaining important and influential relatives. His almost complete preoccupation with the matter of making a living determined this major concern-the efficiency of the family as a working group. The physical makeup of a wife was very important to the peasant and his family. She needed a strong back, sturdy legs, and firm hands. (Welty, 1984, p. 190)

CHANGE FROM ASCRIBED TO ACHIEVED STATUS

One of the major shifts occurring within this transition was the change from ascribed to achieved status. The ascribed status of rural areas results in a strong attachment to the land.

> [T]he people's sentimental attachment to land . . . often overrode all considerations of personal economic welfare. For the Chinese, his land was not merely an investment; it was life itself. Accordingly, there was almost no sacrifice he was not prepared to make in order to avoid selling his land. When in dire need he was more likely to mortgage his land than to sell it, even though mortgage payments over the years often ran much higher than the actual price of the land.

> When a land transaction did occur in China, the scene was marked by a most revealing contrast of moods. For the seller's family the event was like a funeral, often marked by tears; for the buyer's family it was like a wedding, usually colored by laughter. (Hsu, 1981, p. 301)

Land in rural Taiwan, as an asset, was an inheritance. In urban society, it was a commodity. In other words, at the time the Republic of China was established on Taiwan, social status, based upon land ownership, was ascribed. This was changed almost immediately. In 1951, the sale of government owned land to tenants provided an opportunity for land ownership through purchase rather than inheritance.

> By the end of 1961, a total of 96,004 hectares of public land, or 92 percent of all tenanted public land, had been sold in five successive sales to 203,531 farm families, who constituted 25 percent of all farm families in Taiwan. (Budget, Accounting & Statistics: Executive Yuan, 1983, p. 127)

The Land-to-the-Tiller Act in 1953 further converted the ownership of land from an ascribed to an achieved status.

> According to the provisions of the Act, the Government compulsorily purchased from the landlords their tenanted land . . . and then resold it

to the tillers on the same terms. . . .

After the completion of the Land-to-the-Tiller Program, the number of owner-farmer families in Taiwan increased from 36% in 1949 to 83% of all farm families in 1978. (Budget, Accounting & Statistics: Executive Yuan, 1983, pp. 127, 130)

The percentage of farms owned was still eighty-three of all farms in 1983. Although the attachment to the land is still strong in Taiwan, land is more of a commodity now than when Nationalist China's headquarters was established on Taiwan.

The measure of social status is shifting from ascribed to achieved status in other areas as well. This is especially true of females in the professional and other positions. The achievements of women in present-day Taiwan are more apparent today than when the above quote was written almost twenty years ago.

The emphasis upon status has created a need for status symbols, which in turn has led to conspicuous consumption of those who need such identification marks to establish their position of wealth. Prestigious families in the United States—such as the Fords, the Mellons, the Rockefellers—do not need a new car every year or an unaffordable mansion to prove their social position, but those who have come into a financial fortune suddenly do. There is a

difference between conspicuous consumption in China and in America. In America, it is largely personal and only incidentally ceremonial. It brings to the individual himself an aura of prestige, and is not only a token of his class standing at any point of time but also an index of his movement upward. The indices—whether Christian Dior gowns for his wife, the season's most gala debut for his daughter, or his own collection of Renaissance—are all acknowledgements of his personal worth. Consequently, he is precise about his expenditures that do not contribute to this sense and cautious about gift-making in general.

While the American engages in conspicuous consumption because he owes it to himself, the Chinese does so because he owes it to others—parents and relatives, friends and fellow townsmen. Consequently, he has less leeway in determining the extent to which he disburses his surplus. And even if he possesses no surplus, he still is forced to engage in conspicuous consumption because of its characteristically Chinese form. (Hsu, 1981, p. 314)

Expansion of employment opportunities, in addition to those offered by the factory, not only further improved the status of women but has drastically altered their social roles as wife and mother. In 1982, 48 percent of the females 15 years of age and over in Taiwan were employed in positions outside of the home. Only one-third of these were factory workers. Seven percent were in professional or administrative positions, and approximately 30 percent were in sales, clerical, or service positions. The opening of vocational and career opportunities for both sexes increases the range of intercultural mate selection through occupational propinquity.

SOCIAL ROLE

While making the adjustment to her new role, changes in the old patterns have to be made. The female factory worker has not shed the responsibilities of mother and wife. She has simply narrowed the time span in which these can be carried out.

> Though women become wage earners, they find their place in the family and their familial responsibilities are not substantially altered. Thus, some are encouraged to take part in production, but they are still subject in practice to the traditional kinds of discrimination. (Ahern & Gates, 1981, p. 210)

Nevertheless, other members of the family have to adapt their roles to fit into that of a part-time mother or wife. The father may at times be forced into the role of mother during her absence.

The role of the Chinese female has been affected more by industrialization than that of the male. Her role has traditionally been subservient to that of the male. With the availability of administrative positions to women, the sex roles are reversed in some instances. In industry, the female is often in an administrative position which places them in a role of authority over other workers, some of whom are male. In addition, her role may well be at a higher level occupationally, compared with that of her husband. These more prestigious roles develop self-respect. The female supervisor is less likely to accept a domineering husband. Also, with more opportunities for women in professional fields, her income may well be more than that of a potential marital partner. This discrepancy, in a male dominated society, would undoubtedly influence the mate selection of both sexes.

The impact of industrialization and urbanization on the very basis of the Taiwan society has been drastic. Social structure, since the middle of the twentieth century, has formed a very important part of this chapter. Adapting the social structure to accommodate the new demands called for an overhaul of the inherited social system, there was a gradual change from acquired to achieved status. This improved the status of both sexes, but mainly the female's. The peer group became more important in framing the attitudes of its members as the family was weakened by members moving into neo-local residences.

## INSTISPHERIC CHANGES

Before considering the various major social institutions individually, it will be helpful to contrast the total institutional structure of traditional China and the United States. The main difference is that in the former type, the individual institutions are tightly integrated, whereas in the latter type, they are not. As seen earlier, Confucianism permeates all aspects of Chinese life, providing a pattern of consistency in each of the major social institutions. Each reinforces the other, presenting a strong cultural front that is not easily penetrated.

On the other hand, American institutions are frequently in conflict with each other. Some business interests want a seven-day week for trading; religious interests want to "remember the Sabbath Day to keep it holy." The political party takes precedence over national interests. Religious factions are constantly at war with one another. Labor and management are frequently at the bargaining table sharpening their individual axes. Educators bring teaching to a screeching halt as they strike for more money or better conditions.

Compared to the Chinese institutions, the American institutions are not integrated, and this may weaken the social structure. Lack of cohesion in the social institutional structure makes the choice of a mate with a different cultural background more acceptable than in a society where the institutions are intertwined. In such a social environment, as the former, exogamous marriages cross over a narrow line of specific interest and not a total cultural network. Said another way, endogamy consists of marriage within the religious faith, within political parties, or between those with compatible business interests. Other matters are of much less importance.

It follows, then, that intermarriage between Chinese and Americans necessitates a weakening of the bonds linking the Chinese institutions. The extent to which this has occurred in Taiwan is the subject of discussion in the following parts of this chapter covering the individual institutions.

One of the most important changes ushered in by the Industrial Revolution was the shift of manufacturing of textiles from cottage industry to factory production. Prior to this time, the family was a production unit. The members worked together in an economic venture whatever the product, whether handicraft, textiles, or food production. Cooperation of this nature served as an economic bond solidifying the family. In addition, as long as this type of unifying activity existed, the children were exposed only to the values of the family. With the establishment of textile mills, children who worked in them were no longer limited to a common core of values in the home and homogeneous community. There were no child labor laws then, so as soon as the children in needy families were able to assume a routine task in the factory, they went to work. The hours were long and the work arduous. Such children were denied the emotional security and the valuable socialization influence of the home during the tender years of life. Children were thrust into quasi-adult economic roles, many times before they were ten years of age. The labor force statistics of the United States included those ten years and older up until the census of 1920.

The religious institution was also affected by the first stage of the Industrial Revolution. To whatever extent they might have been accepted, the Church of England, and other churches, as the Industrial Revolution developed in other countries, faced new challenges. Not only were children confronted with different values; adults also were exposed to different priorities. It was the church's responsibility to sort out these confusing and conflicting emphases on things of importance. Denying children the opportunity for adequately preparing for adulthood, should have been another concern of the church, whether or not it was accepted. The degrading of the human being through economic exploitation was another matter which was in conflict with the religious teachings that man is made in God's image.

Religious teachings lost the reinforcement of the natural influences when the individuals from the wholesome rural environment shifted to the congested cities and the depressing surrounding of the factory. The dingy, crowded nooks in a noisy, clamoring context, formed quite a contrast for the factory workers from rural areas who had been exposed to the quiet country-side, with its fresh air. They had witnessed many times the miracle of birth of animals, and the annual marvel of seeing the brown, dry grass of the pasture transformed into a lush meadow or a seed developing into a plant. The teachings of the New Testament are couched in such settings. "Consider the lilies of the field . . ." (Matt. 6:28); "Behold the fowls of the air . . ." (Matt. 6:26); and "Behold, a sower went forth to sow . . ." (Matt. 13:3); and the seed fell upon four different types of soil. The religious institution had to compensate in some way for the loss of support that nature provided in making individuals aware of God.

Although the educational institution was not affected nearly as much in the first stage as in later phases of the Industrial Revolution, there were some effects. The lack of child labor laws, and no compulsory school attendance laws, made economic assets out of some children who possibly would have attended school longer if the factories had not offered the opportunity to increase the family income. Why should time be spent in school when the only essential knowledge for an income was to know how to carry out some routine operation that could be learned the first day on the job? The first stage of the Industrial Revolution also affected this institution by introducing the first program of special education. In 1780, Robert Raikes started a special program on Sundays to teach the children who had to work in factories six days a week how to read. Although the purpose was to enable the children to read the Bible, the first Sunday school was not designed as a religious educational facility. The establishment of textile mills made education more necessary in business administration for administrators, and in engineering for mechanical engineers to establish and maintain the factories.

The political institution had to cope with the problem of an increased population which put pressure on the limited confines of the village. Extending the boundaries of the small center required redistricting and establishing new magisterial areas. Additional taxes were needed to provide service for the population of the expanding area. Also, the government had to walk a narrow line between the influential businessmen with political clout and the necessity of protecting the rights of the workers. In the cottage industry, the individual had control over the production and the price of the product. In the factory, he had control over neither. The ordinary factory worker had little job security because he could easily be replaced. The only asset he had was the little skill involved in his position, which could be learned rather easily by his replacement. Protecting the worker from exploitation and economic bondage was an additional responsibility of the political institution.

The institutional approach is used in forming the background for a study of the factors influencing decisions in regards to intermarriage between Chinese and American-Caucasians. Since social institutions are designed to meet the needs of a society, they are structured according to the demands made upon them. The complexity of the social structure of the Republic of China is demonstrated by the network of major social institutions involved in the practice of ancestor worship. "In general, the greater the opportunity for generating economic benefits from assets owned collectively by a lineage, the greater the lineage's political solidarity and ritual display" (Ahern & Gates, 1981, p. 37). Thus, the economic, family, political, and religious institutions are intermeshed in satisfying this particular need for security.

In order to function effectively, a particular social institution must conform to the patterns of the other institutions in that society. For example, an authoritarian family will not work harmoniously in a society where other institutions conform to democratic patterns. "If one interprets democratization as Taiwanization" (Ahern & Gates, 1981, p. 20), then the relentless control of the patriarchal family must of necessity be relaxed. As a society grows more complex, as is the case of the Republic of China for the past four decades, the family structure and functions are affected more and more by other institutions, causing a re-appraisal of its contemporary role in the social fabric of Taiwan. Arranging marriages, which was one of the traditional family practices (Welty, 1984, p. 201), denies the individuals involved a choice in mate selection. This practice does not harmonize with the individual's choices available in educational training, religious affiliation, political elections, and economic pursuits in Nationalist China.

As pressure is applied to the family to conform to the patterns of other institutions, it must either yield or sacrifice its effectiveness in the society. If it conforms to the societal patterns, the couple is given a choice in mate selection. If the family goes so far as to conform to the intersocietal interests of other Chinese social institutional practices such as international trade, educational exchanges with other countries, and extrasocietal political activities, the mate choice could well be influenced by these forces, thus leading to international marriages.

The installment plan has blurred the social class lines in America. One prerequisite for American marriages in the past was for the prospective husband to be in a financial position which would enable him to support the bride-to-be in the manner to which she was accustomed. This is one of the questions the pursuer had to answer when he asked the father for the hand of his daughter in marriage. Today, however, the young couple can move into a fully furnished home of their own, with a brand new automobile each, all purchased on the installment plan. With both working, the monthly payments are met without too much difficulty. In the past, the question was, "How much does it cost?" In the present, the question is, "How much are the monthly payments?"

This is not to say that each of the listed institutions performs only the function in a single major area for the institutions themselves are intermeshed in various relationships forming a particular pattern for a particular society. Each major institution has multiple functions. For example, in some societies, the family performs many functions of the religious institutions. On the other hand, as seen earlier, the original purpose of our present-day "Sunday" school was to provide secular education on Sunday to those children who had to work throughout the week. Each institution, in other words, is closely related to, and dependent upon, all other institutions.

The economic institution had to adjust from a barter base to a medium of exchange involving money. The first stage of the Industrial Revolution marked the beginning of a gradually accelerating efficiency in production. It also began the period in which the distributive function of the economic institution became more and more challenged to meet the needs of all the members of society. The differences between management and labor emerged which eventually resulted in the establishment of unions to supplement the political institution, or to apply pressure in an effort to force vested interest groups to compromise in order to benefit the workers.

When the United States broke diplomatic relations with the Republic of China in 1979 in order to normalize relations with Communist China, it severely jolted the Republic of China's political structure. President Chiang Ching-Kuo (1979) said of this development that in the last few years the U.S. government had repeatedly reaffirmed its assurances to maintain diplomatic relations with the Republic of China and to honor its treaty commitments. He added that once the U.S. government had broken its assurances and abrogated the treaty, the government could not be expected to have the confidence of free nations in the future. He concluded that although what the U.S. did was agonizing and dismaying, "we must swallow this bitter pill" (Republic of China, 1979, p. 34).

> The people of Free China replied to President Carter's unilateral breaking of formal relations with their country with an outburst of patriotic fervor. At marches and rallies, tens of thousands gave generously to a national defense fund which subsequently raised more than NT $3 billion (U.S. $750,000). Overseas Chinese communities pledged their support. (Republic of China, 1979, p. 4)

By converting its image from a friend to that of an enemy through normalization of relations with Communist China, the United States further solidified Free China within the nation itself and strengthened its bonds with Chinese communities across the world. In other words, the concept of "we" group loomed large in the ideology of Taiwan establishing an additional barrier to Taiwanese/American marriages.

# 11

## The Influence of the
## Changed Social Environment
## on the Mate Selection
## Process in Taiwan

The purpose of this chapter is to show how social change has narrowed the cultural gap between East and West and made marriages between American-Caucasians and Chinese more acceptable.

In this chapter, the technological changes are discussed first, rather than in the order of Chapters 5 through 9. The reason for this is that the technological changes have ushered in changes in the various spheres. This is not to say that technology is the sole motivating force in these changes. Rather, it is to say that the development of technology is a prime influence in bringing about social change in Taiwan.

### THE INFLUENCE OF TECHNOLOGICAL CHANGES

The influence of industrialization and urbanization has been shown according to available statistical evidence. Although much additional work needs to be done to authenticate the extent to which these two processes have influenced the social environment of Taiwan, enough evidence has been given to support the conclusion that the Republic of China has undergone dramatic social change during the past 40 years, and these changes have drastically influenced attitudes toward intercultural marriages.

With the transfer of the Nationalist governmental center from the mainland to Taiwan, necessity forced the Republic of China to plunge into the mainstream of industrialization. The massive manpower of pre-Communist China was no longer available. The population had shrunk to one percent of that on the mainland, i.e., from approximately 750 million to 7.5 million. The land area had dwindled even more. Taiwan is less than one-half of one percent the size of the area of the mainland. This means that the natural resources were reduced in similar proportions. The Republic of China had no choice but to replace the manpower with horsepower and to expand the limited natural resources with every technological means available.

The amount of social change necessitated by such a move is immeasurable. The political structure had to be re-formulated, residential patterns were turned topsy-turvy, and the economy had to be converted into a sprawling mechanism geared into an entirely different way of life. All of these changes and many, many others had an effect upon the relationships of the citizens in the newly formed Republic of China.

The task of showing the impact of each of these overwhelming social changes on the attitude toward intermarriage is interminable. Consequently, three areas in which social change seemingly took its greatest toll have been selected to consider in some detail. One of these is transportation which expands the opportunity for personal contacts. The second one is communication, which enables the bonds of primary relationships to be extended. The third one is the highly accelerated social mobility, which exposes individuals to a far different way of life than that to which they have been accustomed.

## CHANGES IN TRANSPORTATION

Prior to the middle of the twentieth century, local transportation was limited to the ox-cart or short trips on the water-ways. These modes of travel limited the number of different personal contacts an individual could make. This, in turn, confined the area of acquaintances to a very limited area.

With the shift of these crude methods of physical mobility to the automobile, bus and train, the horizons of the individual were broadened. This meant that a person could be exposed to innumerable acquaintances that would never have been met without the improved transportation facilities. Thus, meeting members of the opposite sex, who may well be considered as marital partners, was increased. More than this, the expanded circle revealed the habits and practices of a different life-style, and made the individual more tolerant of activities that differed from his or her own, which contributed to an interest in intercultural marriage. Just to give some idea of the tremendous change the Republic of China made in local transportation there were 3,900 passenger cars in 1954 compared to 687,000 in 1983, approximately 176 times the number 30 years earlier.

The automobile not only drastically increased local travel, as it improved mechanically, it became a country-wide mode of travel, which extended personal contacts even further. In addition to making personal mobility more possible, the automotive industry including the trucks, along with the train, made it possible to ship goods longer distances. This established permanent business arrangements which cemented the connection between different types of culture in various parts of the country.

Although changes in domestic social patterns are conducive to intercultural marriages, intersocietal interaction makes such relationships even more acceptable. Exports and imports require social interaction on an international basis. The value of goods Taiwan exported to the United States in 1983 was 213 times as great as the value in 1962. The value of imports from the United States by Taiwan was 40 times as great in 1983 as in 1962. Individuals in frequent contact with other cultures became accustomed to the different life-styles. Since familiarity breeds tolerance as far as culture is concerned, intermingling of Americans and Chinese increased the possibility of intercultural marriage between the natives of these two societies.

Jet travel has extended the social boundaries of Taiwan even further. Besides increasing the number of visitors to Taiwan, and from Taiwan to the United States, frequent journeys are made by business men in both directions. This serves to blend the two types of culture and makes each more acceptable to the other. There were 2.5 times the number of visitors to Taiwan from the U.S. in 1983 as there were in 1966.

Transportation has broadened the area of mate selection from the local neighborhood in Taiwan to a universal scope. Prior to the modern means of transportation in Taiwan, an individual could travel approximately 6 miles per hour by ox-cart or other crude vehicle. With the advent of the automobile and the train, the rate of travel increased to around 60 miles per hour. Through jet transportation, the approximate speed is 600 miles per hour. What this means is that in travel time the earth has shrunk to one percent of what it was prior to modern means of travel. That is, a community 600 miles away can be reached in one hour, compared to 100 hours a century or so ago.

CHANGES IN COMMUNICATION

The first form of communication, as indicated in Chapter 1, was the anticipatory level. This consisted of nothing more than a grunt or sound to which some meaning was attached. Following this, the second level of communication was the "expressive" stage in which gestures were given some meaning. The symbolic level developed with the invention of the Phoenician alphabet, about 3,500 B.C.

It was not until then that the written language came into existence. It was this medium that gave birth to communication through the mailing system. Today, there are many more sophisticated forms of communication, such as the telephone, fax machine, and radio among others.

Although letters were much slower through the mail, they served as a link between individuals until the telephone was invented. With the development of the telephone, almost instant contact was available to persons wishing to maintain relationships with one another. The use of the telephone promoted a twofold result as far as human relations were concerned. For one thing, it extended the primary association of individuals. Instead of leaning over the back fence to talk to a neighbor, who had changed residence, they could continue their primary relationship by telephone. The second thing, as this indicates, the neighborly relations could be carried out across the city or country. Although persons did not live in close proximity, as in a neighborhood, they could continue their neighborly relationship. In fact, for the most part, they could engage in a conversation by telephone more quickly than they could by visiting the neighbor across the fence. To show the extent to which this means of communication has grown, there were 57,000 telephones in use in 1957, compared to 4,855,000 in 1983.

## ACCELERATED SOCIAL MOBILITY

As indicated earlier, one form of social mobility is residential mobility. Urbanization is a two-way process by which the urban way of life is disseminated. Prior to and in the early stages of the Industrial Revolution, urbanism developed by the concentration of population in urban centers. From the early part of the present century in the United States, urbanism has been disseminated also from an urban to rural flow, resulting in the development of urbanized rural areas. At the time the Republic of China was established on Taiwan, urbanism was flowing from rural areas to urban centers. It was not long after this that urbanism began to move in both directions causing a mixture of rural and urban culture in both the cities and the countryside.

Residential mobility is one of the vehicles by which urbanism is disseminated. The flow of urbanism in one direction is seen in residential mobility, i.e., the movement of the population from the country to the city. This exposes the ruralite to a different way of life. The other direction of urbanism is seen in the city school teacher, the banker's family, or the construction worker taking up residence in the country which also exposes the ruralite to the urban way of life.

Another form of social mobility, personal mobility, has already been discussed to some extent in the section on transportation.

Another type, vertical mobility, is movement up or down on the social class scale. An expanding economy always opens opportunities for individuals to capitalize on promotions.

This affects the mate selection in two ways. For one thing, it acquaints the individual who has been promoted to a better way of life more closely akin to the American life-style. In the second place, the increased salary enables the individual to meet the additional expenses of marriage more readily.

One of the most important avenues of social mobility is ideational mobility. This exposure to a different way of life is presented through mass media, such as newspapers, periodicals, the radio, and especially the television.

Through this important method, a person can be introduced to the lifestyle of the "jet set" and to many other activities that may be strange to him or her. A person on a low level of income can see a number of people dining in an exquisite restaurant. S/he can attend professional events in this way as well and become acquainted with the life-style of "the rich and famous." All of these things prepare the Chinese in Taiwan for marriage with an American-Caucasian.

Television is an effective cultural leveler. In 1967, there were 112,000 televisions produced in Taiwan. In 1983, the number produced, 5,177,000 is 46 times that of 1962. If imported televisions are included, the number is increased significantly (Budget, Accounting & Statistics: Executive Yuan, p. 323).

The television plays an important role in acquainting members in one society with the culture of another. Through it, Chinese in Taiwan witness various phases of American culture and vice versa. Many persons who can afford a television cannot afford a trip to the United States to get a close-up view of the practices there. But they can, through television programs, become acquainted with different roles and become somewhat conditioned to the expected practices in a culture unlike their own.

Thus far, this chapter has described the bulldozing effects of industrialization and urbanization on forming the Republic of China according to its urban and rural societies, and the position Taiwan holds on this continuum. The effects of the resulting changes in transportation and communications have also been discussed at some length, showing that these two technological improvements have narrowed the gap between the cultural differences in Taiwan with those in the United States. Furthermore, the acceleration of social mobility has also been shown as a major factor in making the two cultures more similar.

This exposure to a foreign culture, especially through the mass media and intersocietal interaction, as discussed in this chapter, penetrates the endogamous armor, weakens the ethnocentric bonds, and increases the possibility of intercultural marriages.

## THE INFLUENCE OF STATISPHERIC CHANGES

The cultural traits of the statisphere perhaps offer the strongest resistance to intercultural marriage, because the category contains the deeply entrenched requisites of the marital relationship itself. The cultural traits in the statisphere dictate the patterns of the mate selection process and the acceptable qualities of the two partners in such a relationship. Social changes through industrialization and urbanization, discussed in the preceding chapter, have weakened the control of the statisphere over intercultural marriages. The causes and effects of these changes form the subject-matter of the present chapter.

From the foregoing discussion, it is evident that the urbanization process has at least set the stage to influence the selection of mates in Taiwan. The culture has become more heterogeneous, broadening the tolerance limits of practices which differ from those of traditional China. Through migration, the family ties have been weakened and the parental apron strings have been severed, causing the family image of mate selection to fade. The increased proportion of social alternatives has allowed deviations from established practices of mate selection. All of these cultural changes have increased the acceptance, if not the likelihood, of intercultural marriage.

Responses to three questions in the field study discussed in Chapter 3 reflect changes in the Chinese culture that influence the mate selection process. The answers given are based upon the supposition that the Chinese college student would marry an American-Caucasian. The cultural areas involved in the field study are the national milieu of the post-marital residence, the language the respondents would prefer their children to speak, and the customs they would prefer them to adopt.

TABLE 11.1: Desired Place of Residence If Married to an American-Caucasian by Academic Classification, Parental Income Level, and Residence of Respondent (Percent)

|  | Taiwan | U.S. | Other | No. of Respondents |
|---|---|---|---|---|
| Freshmen | 47 | 29 | 23 | 281 |
| Seniors | 38 | 46 | 16 | 204 |
| Low Income | 47 | 32 | 21 | 295 |
| High Income | 38 | 43 | 19 | 210 |
| Rural Residence | 58 | 19 | 30 | 136 |
| Urban Residence | 39 | 39 | 13 | 349 |

CHANGES IN SOCIAL STRUCTURE

Social structure, for the purposes of this presentation, is of importance because the acceptable practices of mate selection are incorporated within it. Mate selection patterns differ from culture to culture. In some societies, marriages are arranged. In others, brides are purchased. Still in others, freedom of choice is exercised by the individuals who intend to marry. Even in the last of these cases, there are certain limits within which the mate must be selected. Crossing over racial, religious, and social class boundaries is in violation of acceptable practices in most societies. Arranging marriages for their children was a primary responsibility of the parents and is interwoven into the social structure of traditional China. The parental influence in selecting their son's mate was carried to the extreme in minor marriages, "which were very common in some parts of conventional China. . . . A woman who married in this fashion was removed from her natal family as an infant or small child and raised by her future husband's parents. The result being that husband and wife grew up under conditions as intimate as those experienced by siblings" (Ahern & Gates, 1981, p. 347). The elements of the social structure in traditional China must be given a prominent position in the study of marriages between Chinese and American-Caucasians.

Likewise, in the cities, the bonds of the neighborhood are not as strong as the bonds of common interest. The weakened bonds of the locality grouping softens the homogeneous shell of the social environment and exposes individuals to different cultural practices, even in mate selection.

One of the hypotheses in the field study discussed in Chapter 3 stated that the urban social structure is more conducive to intermarriage between Chinese and American-Caucasians than the rural social structure. A comparison of some of the responses of Chinese college students whose residence is in rural areas with those in urban areas shows the validity of the hypothesis as far as the field study will permit.

The extension of the village social boundaries to marketing areas in rural traditional China which has broadened the scope of social interaction of the peasant, which extended the range of mate selection. "Standard marketing communities . . . have come to be regarded, along with the family and the village, as one of the fundamental units of traditional rural society. These marketing communities effectively set the limits to the social world of peasants, and were the units within which they intermarried" (Ahern & Gates, 1981, p. 116).

Enlarging the mate selection area, both spatially and socially, from the village to the marketing area, is an initial step in the development of a worldwide social perspective. As the range is gradually broadened, the acceptability of intermarriage between the Chinese and Americans becomes more likely.

## CHANGES IN THE SOCIAL GROUP

Within the social group, an individual is exposed to the influential forces that prepare him for a place in society. The early form of the development is mainly the result of family associations. As changes take place in the statisphere in Taiwan, however, groups outside of the home are having more and more influence in socializing the individual.

The social functions of the youngster are no longer limited to the family, or kinship, circle. The value exposure is no longer confined to those instilled by the parents; and the emotional bonds are no longer nurtured constantly by the family as is the case when spatial proximity confines the area of activity to close quarters.

These long-distance primary associations are intensified by the use of the telephone. An intimate conversation with a companion is no farther away than the nearest telephone. Although loyalty to the parents is still primary, the desire for recognition from groups outside of the family is infringing upon it. This divided loyalty lessens the familial influence on mate selection and makes intercultural marriage more acceptable.

In the urbanized society of Taiwan, the pattern is changing and the individuals involved have a stronger voice in mate selection. One reason for this change is that industrialization and urbanization in Taiwan have lessened the influence of the family in the selection of marital partners for their children. The reduction of parental pressure has increased the influence of groups outside of the family. The social group exerts a weighty influence in the mate selection process. It is through interaction of the individual within groups that the acceptable traits of a mate are described. Mass media are also influential in portraying desirable characteristics of an illusory marital companion but the primary group fractures the daydream with realism. The significant others were discussed in Chapter 7. These are the ones who determine the characteristics one should look for in selecting a marital partner. The social group, in other words, serves as an instrument of decision in the mate selection process. It carves the image of an acceptable companion. As the pressure in mate selection is shifted from the family to the peer group, the likelihood of intercultural marriage increases.

According to the field study of Chinese college students in Taiwan, presented in Chapter 3, in every instance where neither parent objected to the respondent dating an American-Caucasian, the peer would accept such a relationship, meaning that in 51 percent of the cases the parent and peer group opinions were in accord. Thirty-five percent of the responses indicated that the position of the parents raising no objections to their offspring marrying an American-Caucasian was supported by the respondent's peer group.

When the parental and peer group opinions regarding the respondent's marriage to an American-Caucasian are considered separately, in 35 percent of the responses neither parent would object to such a relationship and it would be accepted by 70 percent of the respondent's peers. This suggests, at least, that the peer group's influence is growing stronger among the Chinese college students responding to the questionnaire. This suggestion is supported by the fact that 57 percent of the respondents had discussed the possibility of marrying an American-Caucasian with a friend, compared to the smaller figure of 43 percent who had discussed the possibility with a member of the family.

Although peer group relationships may be more intimate in traditional China than those in an extended family, the parental authority takes precedence over the peer in mate selection. Since the peers of an individual are accustomed to parental authority themselves, they will exert very little pressure which is in opposition to the traditional practices. Nevertheless, as family authority is relaxed, the peer group's pressure becomes more effective in the area of mate selection.

Increased importance of the peer group also slows the pace of intergenerational interaction of the Chinese family. The peer group characterizes the present; it does not link the present with the past and the future as the inter-generational associations of the family do. The traditional bond is weakened, the kinship ties are strained, and mate selection is based more on individual preferences than on family consensus.

The overall social status provides a salient feature in the study of intermarriage of Chinese and American-Caucasians. There were two main social classes in traditional China—the ruler and the ruled, or the gentry and the peasantry. Mate selection, in China, on each of these class levels was designed to further the interests of each group. The gentry were concerned with maintaining their rights and privileges so their marital mate decisions were based upon this interest.

According to the field study presented in Chapter 3, the parents in the high income bracket had less objection to their child dating an American-Caucasian than those in the lower bracket. Sixty-one percent of these parents approved of this behavior from their child contrasted to only 56 percent in the low income bracket. As to marriage, less than half of both income groups had no objection (46 percent in the high income bracket, and 44 percent in the low).

All of these factors contributed toward the emergence of individuality among the younger generation of Taiwan society and shifted the mate selection process from family arranged marriages to individual choice. This, in turn, placed more of an emphasis on romance as a factor in mate selection.

## THE INFLUENCE OF CHANGES IN THE DYNASPHERE

The dynasphere provides the machinery by which social change takes place. Social interaction, one of the cultural traits in the dynasphere, is the life-giving mechanism of society. Without it, society could not exist, culture could not be transmitted, and human relationships would disintegrate.

Society itself is a product of social interaction. The predominant form of interaction determines the type of society that results. An authoritarian society is the product of the dominance and submission form of interaction. Cooperation gives birth to a democratic society. Accommodation encourages satellite societies. Taiwan has been mainly shaped by the dominance and submission pattern of interaction, which is the foundation stone of Confucianism.

With the establishment of the Nationalist Government on Taiwan, a new emphasis has been given to Dr. Sun Yat-sen's Three Principles of the People. Chiang Kai-shek and his son, Chiang Ching-kou, formed a coalition between the Government and the people. Through their optimistic philosophy and their strong desire to know the pulse of the people, a solid unity has been formed binding the free Chinese across the world into a contingent of loyal supporters of the Republic of China.

Our people at home and abroad have shown their soaring patriotism and wholehearted support of the government with enthusiastic and touching deeds. Scene after scene of moving stories have coalesced into page upon page of patriotic panorama revealing the unanimous anti-Communist determination of the Chinese people and attesting that the tighter the crunch of the moment, the more solidly united are the people in showing the invincible spirit of the Chinese race. (Republic of China, 1979, p. 43)

CHANGES IN INTERACTION PATTERNS

The patterns of interaction, dominance and submission, competition, conflict, cooperation, and accommodation were discussed in Chapter 6. The purpose here is to show to what extent these patterns have changed, and how they have affected the process of mate selection in Taiwan.

*Dominance and Submission*

One major effect of urbanization on Taiwan, as far as social interaction is concerned, is the replacement of the dominance and submission type by other forms of interaction. As discussed earlier, Confucianism is based upon the dominance and submission pattern of interaction as practiced in the relationships between the ruler and the ruled, parents and children, husband and wife, and the older and younger brother.

As the New Testament in Christian literature, Confucian teachings were intended for an agrarian economy. The division of labor required a dominance-submission type of interaction. The social relationships were mainly intrafamily, and within this limited circle, social interaction took place. Someone had to assume the authority in the operation of the subsistence farm and to regulate behavior. With a rigid authoritative structure, conflict was minimized. The interests and ambitions of the subservient members of the kinship group were merged into the personal characteristics of the dominant one. Since the relationships were mainly intrafamilial, the kinship structure provided a clear-cut pattern of authority which was followed without question.

With the shift from an agrarian to a market economy, the social relationships became more diversified, and the dominance-submission pattern of interaction was weakened.

> A subsistence economy had been replaced by a market economy, disturbing traditional ideas of status and creating new social roles. People in these new roles tended to interact with others on the basis of common economic, educational, religious, and political interests, rather than on the traditional basis of common place of origin and common decent. (Ahern & Gates, 1981, p. 319)

The marketing economy served as a transitional stage from the agrarian to an industrial economy. It exposed persons to relationships that were more of a secondary nature than those prevalent in the kinship group. Also, the mixture of the population in the market place served as preparation for the heterogeneity of urban society. This mixture in turn weakens the dominance-submission pattern of social interaction, making intercultural marriages more likely.

A number of forces are at work in the urbanized areas of Taiwan that are ever weakening the traditional authority of the husband over the wife. The possibility of financial independence, the higher educational level of the female, and the more ready acceptance of divorce in urban centers have all contributed toward equalizing the status of men and women.

> In terms of expressed value, Taipei household heads endorse sexual equality and believe that social prestige is and ought to be based on achievement rather than on inherited position or influence. (Ahern & Gates, 1981, p. 180)

## Competition

The pattern of interaction is changing from the dominance-submission type to competition as Taiwan becomes more urbanized. With the growth in size and in number of department stores, competition is keener than in the past, as evidenced by full-page newspaper advertisements and price-wars that occur at regular intervals. Competition is also in evidence in the political arena.

> [I]ndustrialization and urbanization have made the Taiwanese so prosperous and sophisticated that mere "tutelary" democracy is no longer either feasible or appropriate. Nonparty politicians attribute their 1977 victories to the independence of mind of the well-educated young people who make up an increasing proportion of the population and to the ease of reaching this group in urban areas through mass campaign rallies. Since local self-government began, the population of Taiwan has nearly tripled, the proportion living in cities has nearly doubled, and the occupational structure has been completely transformed. It would be remarkable, then, if the limited number of organizational channels and factional networks on which the Kuomintang has relied to get out the vote could continue to dominate completely such a rapidly expanding and drastically changing social field. (Ahern & Gates, 1981, p. 81)

Competition in the economic and political realms affects mate selection on the domestic level. With the increased participation of females in these two fields in Taiwan, the prospective husband has to have more to offer than economic security, as was the case in traditional China. In addition to this asset, if he is competing for the hand of a well-educated Chinese maiden, he must be mature emotionally, socially, and intellectually.

International trade and political ties have intensified the competitive element in mate selection for the Chinese. Americans have been exposed to the sophisticating influence of urbanism for a much longer period than the Chinese living on Taiwan. Logic would dictate that the American has an advantage over the Chinese in gaining the above-mentioned attributes of maturity. In view of the fact that studies show that marriage is more frequently the channel of upward vertical mobility for the female than for the male, a higher incidence of Chinese women marrying American men can be expected. Whether or not this is true, with the presence of Americans in Taiwan and of Chinese in America because of these international relationships, the possibility of intermarriage between the two individuals from these two different societal types increases.

Social interaction, either anticipated or eventuated, is indicated between the Chinese college students responses and American-Caucasians in the field study reported in Chapter 3. Of those answering the question, 27 percent said they had discussed with one or both parents the possibility of forming an intimate relationship with an American-Caucasian, 49 percent said they had discussed the matter with a sibling or friend, and 24 percent had not talked about he matter with anyone.

## Conflict

The third type of social interaction, conflict, is a major stumbling block in marriages between Chinese and American-Caucasians. One of the most important conflicts is caused by the difference in family loyalty. As mentioned before, whereas Americans put loyalty to the family of procreation first, the first loyalty of the Chinese is to the parents, the second is to the siblings, and the third is to the family of procreation. These deep-seated values are difficult to change. They require tolerance and understanding on the part of both partners. The gradual weaning away from the family by moving to a distant residence alleviates the problem to some extent.

## Cooperation and Accommodation

However it is done, two other types of social interaction, cooperation and accommodation, must replace conflict. As far as mate selection is concerned in Taiwan, these two substitute interaction patterns have been developed by exposure to these practices in other parts of the social structure. Cooperation through business alliances has encouraged this type of interaction in the home. Accommodation replaces conflict when the married couple place the advantages of establishing their own home as a priority over the ties to their family of orientation.

### CHANGES IN SOCIAL CONTROL

Social control is a major barrier to intercultural marriage between Taiwanese and American-Caucasians. Folkways are not too much of a hindrance because adjustments in this area are made by accommodation to the varying practices. It is no problem to become accustomed to the mate eating with chop sticks in the home if that is the preference. It is a little embarrassing, however, if the person insists on using chop sticks at a formal dinner in the United States.

The next level of social control, the mores, are more likely to cause conflict when they vary from society to society. Mores are deeply imbedded in the value system of an individual. This is especially true if the individual is a member of a close-knit family. Mores are supported by religious laws. The degree of violation of the mores depends upon the dedication of the individual to the religion, or to the authoritative source of the mores. Mores actually are more effective than laws in controlling social behavior. Mores are deeply imbedded values that, like the conscience, force individuals into certain types of behavior. They are a very effective means of social control in the rural types of societies.

Laws are the strongest form of social control. There is no accommodation to the laws. They are enacted for the purpose of protecting the members of society. A person marrying into a society where laws are different from those to which s/he has become accustomed has no other alternative but to adjust. If one is unwilling to make the adjustment, then there is no marriage. The laws are strengthened when they are supported by the mores. If they are not, the law is weakened. In many instances, the law is disobeyed or repealed by public pressure. Such a repeal, for instance, occurred with the Volstead Act through which the sale of alcohol was prevented.

CHANGES IN ANONYMITY

Urbanization breeds anonymity, a social condition in which individual identity is limited to the closest associates. In a rural area, everyone is acquainted with everyone else. They may not be intimate companions, but they know each other. Even children are identified with their families, and their reputation is the same as that of the parents. Likewise, the behavior of the offspring reflects on the family which serves to strengthen social controls.

On the other hand, anonymity in urban centers weakens social controls. Slight deviations from the norms are observed, but do not leave a lasting unfavorable imprint on the individual's character. For example, an aspiring young man may overstep the bounds of sobriety at a cocktail party. Unless he causes a ruckus, there are very few, if any, repercussions. He goes for a job interview after a good night's sleep, and this experience in no way influences the decision as to whether or not this young man should be employed. In a rural area, word gets out that the young lad is not able to hold his liquor. By the time of the job interview, the potential employer will probably be biased already. Anonymity does provide more equal employment opportunity, however, in some situations. The decision to employ, or not to employ, is based upon the qualifications of the applicant and the references of previous employers and others. The applicant that rates the highest in these respects usually is the one selected for the position. In rural areas, personal knowledge of the individual's character outranks the qualifications. For instance, suppose there are two applicants for the same job in a business enterprise in a rural area. One is a local youth that comes from a well established family in the community and is recognized as an honest, reliable, young man. His qualifications may be limited to a diploma from an unaccredited commercial college. The references of the other applicant, who hails from the city and is not personally known in the small town, also indicate that he is an honest, reliable young man. He has a Master's degree in Business Administration from a reputable university. The rural youth will have an advantage over the other candidate because of the personal knowledge of his character. The thinking is that he has enough background in business to be able to learn what he needs to know to be successful in the position.

Mates are not selected anonymously, but anonymity is a factor of varying importance in intercultural courtship patterns that may lead to marriage. It provides a cloak for dating that could not be practiced without such a protective curtain. Intimate intraracial relationships do not attract attention, because of physical similarities, as interracial association of this nature do. Even though attention is attracted in these relationships, anonymity muffles the embarrassment. Since dating is preliminary to engagement and marriage, anonymity makes possible intercultural marital relationships that could not otherwise exist.

One of the questions in the study reported in Chapter 3 was asked to determine whether the respondent would feel more embarrassed to be seen in rural or urban environments in the company of an American-Caucasian of the opposite sex. Of the 475 individuals who answered this question, 70 percent indicated they would be embarrassed to be seen in rural areas with an American-Caucasian, 49 percent said they would be embarrassed to be seen in such company in urban areas, and 45 percent suggested they would not be embarrassed in either environment with an American-Caucasian companion. About 51 percent in urban areas said they would feel comfortable dating an American-Caucasian in public. Anonymity undoubtedly is a major factor in the lack of embarrassment in these social situations.

CHANGES IN ANOMIE

Anomie is another urban characteristic that influences mate selection in Taiwan. Anomie is a condition in which social norms are weakened and means become confused with the ends. At this point, it is of value to discuss the effect of the confusion of means and ends on the mate selection process in Taiwan.

In this kind of situation, the methods of achieving goals become ends in themselves. For example, the primary purpose of endeavor for most people is to enjoy a satisfying, fulfilled life. Money is a means to this end, but for some it becomes an end in itself. They deny themselves the enjoyment of family life, the pleasantries of friendship associations, the relaxation of vacations, and many other benefits in order to amass a fortune. In the same sense, bibliolatry is practiced by those who consider the mastery of the Holy Writ as an end in itself and not a means to the abundant life for which it gives the directions. The measure of religiosity is not how much scripture can be recited from memory, but how much of it is practiced.

Perhaps a further explanation of means and ends will be helpful at this point. Means are not only methods by which goals are attained, but they also serve as intermediate goals established to reach ultimate goals. That is, education is essential to improving one's social status. Thus, education serves as a means to this end. However, education is also an intermediate goal. Social status is an important factor in selecting a mate, for the purpose of providing a home, which is an intermediate goal for the majority of people. The home, then, is the end, but it also serves as a means of becoming established in a neighborhood, which in turn becomes an intermediate goal leading to the fulfillment of an individual. It is in this sense that the means and ends become confused in urban society. The intermediate goals become primary objectives, sometimes even in the form of an obsession.

Legally, the function of marriage is to fix responsibility in order to protect society, especially to prevent any offspring from becoming wards of society. The compatibility of the couple, the purpose of the marriage, and the advisability of it are of no concern to the judiciary system. This is not to say that the means have become confused with the ends, in this event, but it is to say that the emphasis is upon the technical procedure rather than the result.

As a consequence of this, marriages are entered into, on occasion, for purposes other than forming a lifelong companionship. Any number of weddings occurs for purposes of convenience. Marriage sometimes serves as a channel of vertical mobility. This is the main objective of the bride or groom in entering into wedlock. There is no intention of establishing a permanent relationship. Marriage serves as a means of becoming legally entitled to a share of wealth. Likewise, a foreigner desiring United States citizenship will enter into a marital relationship solely for this purpose. Sometimes the person may very well be repulsive to them, but they endure this arrangement for the allotted time, become citizens, and then divorce their spouses. In these instances, marriage becomes an intermediate goal which leads to the ultimate goal. Hence, it can be said that marriage has become an end in itself.

Earlier in China, when parents arranged marriages for their children, the economic factor was an important motive. As Taiwan is being converted into an urban society, however, the young people are more and more choosing for themselves whom they will marry. The motive may or may not be of an economic nature. A study of Taipei students as early as 1967 shows that

the Chinese and Americans are nearly equally modern in respect to love as basis of choice of mate, the desire to choose one's mate independently, preference for the new (Western) style of marriage, interaction between the sexes as social gatherings, coeducation at the primary school and university level, and engagement before marriage. (Ahern & Gates, 1981, p. 173)

This quotation also indicates that intranational marriages are not as necessary in the present time as they were in the past. Confucianism previously made endogamous marriages in this respect mandatory.

The important point is that Chinese motives for marriage are changing, and that they differ from those of Americans. Among other things, the emphasis in Taiwan, as among all Chinese, is the perpetuation of the kinship group. In America, the emphasis is more on companionship between the mates. Of course, procreation is of importance in most American marriages, but it does not rank at the same level as it does in Taiwan.

In trying to analyze these answers, numerous questions are raised that could well serve as objects of future study. The majority of those responding indicated Europeans as their preference in inter-cultural marriage, while Japanese and Americans were about evenly divided as the next choice. This is surprising because the arrival in Taipei of Chinese tourists with residences in Europe is far less than those from the United States or Japan. In 1983, Chinese tourists to Taiwan living in Europe numbered 125, compared to 2,696 from Japan and 2,669 from the United States. The number of European tourists to Taiwan that same year numbered 64,365 compared to 151,618 from the United States and 595,897 from Japan.

In casual conversation with Chinese college students, it seems that romanticism is more evident in Europe than in America and may account for the naming of European intercultural marriage in preference to others. Or, possibly, the preference is based upon the recent severance of diplomatic relations with the Republic of China by the United States. This may have prejudiced the Chinese in their mate selection preferences. The strong showing of the Japanese cannot be due to racial preference. The questionnaire listed Filipinos and Koreans separately and they were selected by very few of the respondents. The tourist statistics show that twice as many Chinese with residence in Korea visited Taiwan in 1983 than Japanese. For whatever reason, only 29 percent of those responding preferred American-Caucasians as spouses.

The foregoing discussion of anonymity, the emphasis on achieved status, and anomie, give evidence of the trend in Taiwan changing from a rural to an urban society. Although the conversion is not completed, enough progress has been shown to make intermarriage between Chinese and American-Caucasians more of a possibility today than was the case forty years or so ago.

In this portion of this chapter, the influence of the changes in the dynasphere on the mate selection process in Taiwan has been discussed. The rapid and dramatic shift from an agrarian to an industrial economy with an emphasis on achieved status, has reshaped society in Taiwan. Changes in social interaction patterns and the weakening of social control were shown as advantageous in the selection of an American-Caucasian as a mate by Chinese living in Taiwan. Also, the effect of anonymity and anomie on mate selection in Taiwan were discussed. From the presentation of these forces at work in the Republic of China, it appears that intercultural marriages are becoming more and more acceptable to the Chinese in Taiwan.

## THE INFLUENCE OF CHANGES IN THE PSYCHOSPHERE

Changes in the psychospheres are at the heart of this book because attitudes are included in this classification. To change the attitudes toward intercultural marriage between two cultures as diverse as the Chinese culture of the past and that of the United States requires a remolding of attitudes in one or the other cultures or compromises by both societies.

The deep cleavage that once existed can be identified as the deeply entrenched filial piety on the part of the Chinese, which can be labeled filio-centrism. Also, the saturation of the social environment with Confucianism, and strong nationalistic bonds-or ethnocentrism-divides the Chinese Society.

### CHANGES IN SOCIETY

Little more needs to be said about the changes in Taiwan society since 1950. The various types of society that have been discussed have all affected the social structure in different ways. To list a few of these changes, would be helpful at this point.

One of the most important changes, the shift from an agrarian to an industrial society, has brought about numerous adjustments in the social fabric of Taiwan. For one thing, social relationships have changed from the primary to secondary type. The social milieu has changed from homogeneity to heterogeneity. The dispersal of the neighborhood has broadened the range of acquaintances. The change from cottage industry to the mill has weakened the family authority, and on and on.

### CHANGES IN SOCIALIZATION

One of the major changes in the psychospheres on Taiwan since 1950 is the shift from the family as the sole socialization agency to numerous, diversified groups. Such a move exposes the children and young people to different sets of values and weans them away from the family. This, in turn, weakens the traditional hold on the younger generation.

The school introduces the student to a much broader range of interests than is available in the limited confines of the home. In addition, the school opens up opportunities for the expansion of occupational endeavors. The school also emphasizes individual achievement, which encourages the student to look beyond the family for a fulfilled life.

The peer group also encourages self-expression. It offers its members freedom from family authority and plants the seeds for a different set of values. The peer group vies for the loyalty of its members and weakens the family ties. To mix with companions that exercise no authority over the individual, develops self confidence.

There are many other groups that participate in the socialization process in the present in Taiwan, compared to the past. Special interest groups in art, business, and vocational interests have an influence in socializing the young person. More will be said about socialization in the next section of this chapter, when the instisphere is dealt with.

CHANGES IN ETHNOCENTRISM

Among the major differences, racial boundaries are the most difficult to surmount. One reason for this is the ready ability to identify differences in physical appearances. More importantly, in many of the fifty states interracial marriages are in violation of the law. It is paradoxical that the foundation of such a barrier is based upon the erroneous conception of race. Since most authorities agree that race is a myth, interracial marriages based upon biological differences are in effect non-existent. The article by UNESCO (1953) on "The Nature of Race and Race Differences" states that there is no such thing as a pure race. Through social definition, however, more or less distinct lines are drawn between the races. These socially defined differences are based upon physical features such as skin color, slant of the eyes, cephalic index, hair texture, and other differences.

The following quotations from two different sources reveal ethnocentrism at its peak and pinpoint the almost unsurpassable gulf confronting a Chinese and an American contemplating marriage with one another across their national boundaries.

> Confucians sincerely believed that they were the only civilized community in the world, that all beyond the boundaries of their culture were barbarians who had nothing to give the Confucians, but to whom the Confucians had much to give. To hold such a belief is to become arrogant and contemptuous of other beliefs and cultures. One of the reasons for China's reluctance to change her way of life when first exposed to Western cultures and technology was the degree to which Confucianism had permeated Chinese life and thought. (Welty, 1984, p. 158)

> American schools seem to encourage a militant ethnocentrism. Many American school children entertain the idea that the world outside the United States is practically jungle: China is a land of inscrutable ways

and mysterious opium dens, and Africa a "dark continent" inhabited by cannibals and wild animals.

However, the Chinese, while always maintaining their own unquestioned superiority and conscious of their differences from others, never entertained the notion that their inferiors should change their ways of life.

For this reason, the Chinese attitude vis-à-vis the non-Chinese world must be characterized as *passive* superiority, in contrast to American and Western *active* superiority. (Hsu, 1981, pp. 98, 103)

*Stereotyping National and Racial Images*

Stereotyping is the wholesale assignment of characteristics observed in a few individuals to the entire category. For example, if each of the first two or three school teachers an individual meets is prim, then the stereotypist will assign the characteristic of primness to the next person who is a school teacher, even without observing the traits of that person. If the qualities assigned appeal to the stereotyper, then the assignor is prejudiced in favor of the assignee. If the qualities do not appeal to him, then the reaction is negative.

It is important to note that stereotyping in the past created a chasm between the East and the West, which according to Rudyard Kipling could never be bridged. Although cultural innovations and dissemination have narrowed the gap between these two major segments of the world, stereotyping is still in evidence.

Thinking in terms of stereotypes has influenced Americans-and others-to draw a line separating "Eastern" from "Western" types of individuals. On one side of the line, there is an "Eastern" way of life-silent, quaint, and mysterious. On the other side of the line, there is a "Western" way of life-human, normal, and understandable (Welty, 1984, p. 7).

*Prejudice*

Prejudice is an offspring of stereotyping. It simply means pre-judgment, or making a judgment before all of the facts have been considered. Racial bigots, chauvinistic pigs, and social class-conscious prigs are all products of the same prejudicial mold, which is shaped by stereotyping. Many warm, companionable relationships have been forfeited because prejudice closed the mind before the doorway of acquaintance was opened through an introduction.

Because of prejudice, more or less distinct lines have been drawn between persons with different physical characteristics classifying them as members of one of the three major races. Marriages between such categories are termed interracial. The other groupings of individuals based upon socially defined differences such as social class, religion, and ethnic background have been labeled intercultural marriages. Marriages in which mates cross over whatever degree of differences may exist between categories on the basis of physical features, as well as social characteristics, are labeled exogamous. To a lesser extent, endogamous marriages are limited to further social expectations such as age range, with the male being older and the age gap being moderate, physical stature, with the male being taller, and a myriad of other social distinctions.

Such a foundation for drawing racial boundaries is weak because the biological mixtures have made their differences in traits a matter of degree rather than kind. If it were possible to arrange the world population from one extreme to the other as far as any of the differences are concerned, there would be an unbelievable overlapping in the central portion of the array. For example, if skin color were the criterion, an arrangement from the fairest complected Caucasian to the darkest Negroid, there would be a cluster of individuals at the center which could not be distinguished between by skin color alone. The resort beaches are blanketed with deeply tanned Caucasians who could easily be labeled Negroid on the basis of skin color.

If blood is used as a criterion, at what level should the line be drawn? At one time, in one of the Western States, the United States Census listed an individual with 1/256th Indian blood as an American Indian. What this says is that the eighth generation product of interracial marriage cannot marry an American-Caucasian.

The topic "attitudes of Chinese college students toward intermarriage with American-Caucasians" has been reduced to the most feasible level of specificity. To label the subject-matter in more general terms would be misleading. To make the title more specific would involve encumbering it with details making it more of an abstract than a topic. The terms Chinese and American-Caucasian mean many things to many people. Both terms are colored with the national significance of each country, which has been hammered out in the political arena, and individual connotations have been cultivated through patriotic programs.

Both the national and racial terms in the title have been saturated with emotion resulting in a flow of prejudicial condemnation in both directions between the two nations. Among other things, the United States Chinese Exclusion Act placed a stigma upon the Chinese—who at one time were in a position of leadership among world civilizations. In addition, the early Chinese immigrants assumed roles involving dish washing, cooking for work crews, and laundering clothing, which placed them in an undesirable category and made them the butt of racially tainted jokes. Consequently, because of this stereotyped low status, some Americans would dismiss the title of this study, because it refers to "Chinese," with a prejudicial sneer.

Likewise, the term American rankles some Chinese. At one time, "America stood like a giant in the West, the embodiment of all that was good and fine in the Western Hemisphere" (Welty, 1984, p. 12). The diplomatic maneuvers of World War II, and immediately following, caused America to become gradually "associated with Western Europe. When this happened, America came to be regarded with all the old hatreds, antagonisms, suspicions, and fears with which Asians had long viewed the nations of Europe" (Welty, 1984, p. 13).

Even the term American-Caucasian, for the main part an intranational connotation, stirs the prejudices of some. To these, it may appear to be a specialized treatment of a preferential group. Such is not the case. The study is narrowed to American-Caucasians for a number of reasons. For one thing, since the population of the United States is predominantly Caucasian, the prejudice mentioned in the preceding paragraph would logically be leveled toward this majority group. For another thing, to title the work Chinese/American marriages would include marriages between native Chinese and American-Chinese, which would automatically eliminate the racial differentiation. The third reason for narrowing the title is to limit the number of marriages in the comparison and, thus, prevent confusion on the part of respondents in completing the questionnaire.

With prejudices glaring from every facet of the title of the research paper, a distinction between interracial and intercultural marriages is helpful. Interracial marriages may or may not involve intercultural factors. A Chinese born and reared in a small town in the United States would have very few cultural differences from an American-Caucasian born and reared in that same town. Likewise, intercultural marriages may or may not involve racial mixtures. Interclass, interreligious, and international marriages are all forms of intercultural marriage, but they do not necessarily constitute interracial marriages. Both types of intermarriage, however, cross over socially defined boundaries. The distinctness of these demarcations is determined by the opposition to the violation of the established social practices. The social, or religious, pressure preventing Protestant interdenominational marriages, for example, is usually not as strong as that applied to Protestant-Catholic marriages.

Because of the ambiguity of the term race, marriages crossing over whatever degree of differences may exist between categories classified on the basis of physical as well as social characteristics will be labeled intercultural marriages for the purposes of this study. Although such nomenclature is more general than interracial marriages, it lessens the stigma attached to a marital relationship which may be ideal, except for the differences in physical features.

Regardless of the attitudes toward the national and racial differences between the Republic of China and the United States, many factors have narrowed the racial and cultural gaps, and have made intercultural marriages more acceptable in modern societies than in traditional ones. Intercultural exchanges, higher educational levels, occupational propinquity, and compatibility of interests have contributed toward a greater tolerance of racial and cultural differences. In other words, social nurture is becoming more important in mate selection than biological inheritance. In fact, the mates crossing over race lines in marriage may be more compatible, because of common cultural characteristics, than those in an intraracial marriage transcending social class lines.

The field of study encompasses the traditional, as well as the modern influences, on attitudes of the Chinese college students toward intercultural marriages. The traditional culture in evidence on Taiwan at the time the Republic of China transferred its center of operations, in 1949, is compared with the culture of present-day China gleaned from recorded practices of recent years. Although the data gathered are limited to university students, family background factors such as parental authority, educational level, and income, provided by the students, broadens the cultural base of the study.

## INFLUENCE OF CHANGES IN THE INSTISPHERE

Social institutions are interdependent, which means that a change in one affects each or the others. It is not enough for a person in the American culture, for example, anticipating marriage to a citizen of the Republic of China to make certain that they will be able to make ends meet financially. They must make certain that their education is on a compatible level and that they can adjust to the other's religious and political views. Most of all, they need to determine whether or not they can live up to the expectations of the mate's family. Although this has changed some, the Chinese never lose a son through marriage. They gain a daughter.

### CHANGES IN THE FAMILY

In China, it is important to note that the role of the individual is submerged in familism, and his or her identity is lost in family loyalty. Every decision of each member of a family is based on the welfare of the total unit. The solidarity of the social entity and the strengthening of the family bonds were the main objectives of sons and daughters alike. The blending of the identity with that of the family provides another element for consideration in mate selection of the Chinese.

A Chinese thought of the interests of his family as the basis for all his judgments and decisions. What was advantageous and good for the family was permitted; what was disadvantageous and bad for the family was prohibited. The individual thought of himself as a member of a family, and he was viewed by others in the same light. The success or failure of an individual reflected upon the family and increased or decreased its prestige. The family was responsible for the acts of its individual members and was held accountable for them by the community and the government. (Welty, 1984, p. 198)

Another distinction that needs to be considered in the mate selection in a marriage between a Chinese and an American is the difference in the family patterns of authority. The Chinese family is patriarchal, meaning the father rules. The American family is a democratic form based upon companionship. Because it has some patriarchal characteristics, some designate the American family as semi-patriarchal. One of these traits is that the newly established unit is patrinymnal, it is identified by the name of the husband. Another reason for the designation is that even though more and more wives are earning salaries, the husband is still considered the main breadwinner. Also, the husband is held legally responsible for the actions and debts of his wife as well as the conduct of his juvenile children.

In the patriarchal family of China, the father was a strict disciplinarian.

Traditionally, Chinese fathers were regarded by the sons with a great deal of fear. Since untrained and undisciplined sons gave the community a bad impression of the father, Chinese fathers were often severe and inflexible in training their sons to assume their future role in society and the family. Since the father did not have the same responsibility to discipline and indoctrinate the daughter in her future family duties, the relationship between father and daughter was usually warmer and closer. (Welty, 1984, p. 200)

The role of the mother in the patriarchal family was that of "intermediary between the children, especially the son, and her husband, and she often protected them from his wrath" (Welty, 1984, p. 201).

The concern of the parents for the development of their children gives voice to the opinion that the American family is filioarchal, that is, it is ruled by the children. The children do not establish themselves as authorities, but through various subtleties, and sometimes ways that are not so subtle such as throwing tantrums, they manipulate the parents and gain their ends. Americans "not only study their children's behavior-they glorify it. Chinese did not only take their children for granted—they minimized their importance. The important thing to Americans is what parents should do for their children. To Chinese, it is what children should do for their parents" (Hsu, 1981, p. 80).

The place of residence is another important difference between Chinese and American families. The place of residence of the newly wed Chinese is the residence of the groom's parents, referred to as a patrilocal residence, whereas the American newly weds establish a home of their own, or neolocal residence. In traditional China, the patrilocal residence necessitated a tremendous, if not a traumatic, adjustment on the part of the bride.

> When she entered her new home, she was obliged to adjust to a new environment and a new set of relationships. Usually, she had not seen any of the family members before, including her husband. . . . the sudden and sharp change from a secluded, familiar life to this rather public, unfamiliar life frightened and confused her. Her most difficult adjustment was to her mother-in-law. Chinese mothers-in-law were often awe-inspiring individuals within the family. . . . Stories are told of some mothers-in-law whose nagging and cruelty drove their daughters-in-law to flee from the home and even commit suicide. (Welty, 1984, p. 202)

The family as a social institution has been treated rather extensively because it involves more of an adjustment in intercultural marriage than other social institutions require. The home is the center of life for the married couple and their children. It is of especial significance to the nonworking wife or mother. The adjustment of the wife in China is much greater than that of the husband. In America, the adjustment of both wife and husband is similar. "To the Chinese, a man's relationship with his parents is permanent" (Hsu, 1981, p. 145). "In the American way, marriage changes the entire social setting of the individual. In the Chinese way, marriage merely advances the social status of the male but changes the entire social setting of the female. While the bride has to adjust to her new surrounding, the husband's primary duties and obligations remain much the same as before" (Hsu, 1981, p. 147).

CHANGES IN THE RELIGIOUS INSTITUTION

Urbanization has resulted in the emergence of various individual needs which can be satisfied by the religious institution. Anonymity sets the stage for deviant behavior. The conduct of individuals does not reflect on the family in an environment of this type. Religiously, reinforcing the conscience encourages moral behavior. "For as he thinketh in his heart, so is he" (Prov. 23:7). The uncertainties of the day-to-day living in a secular society necessitates some form of security which is provided by religion.

> Therefore whosoever heareth these sayings of mine, and doeth them, I will liken him unto a wise man, which built his house upon a rock:
>
> And the rain descended, and the floods came, and the winds blew, and beat upon that house; and it fell not: for it was founded upon a rock. (Matt. 7:24, 25)

Recognition is hard to gain in a society in which a person is identified only through a Social Security number. "Of a truth I perceive that God is no respecter of persons: But in every nation he that feareth him, and worketh with righteousness, is accepted with him" (Acs. 10:34,35). Loneliness is characteristic of the milling crowds of a metropolis. This is offset by the promise of the constant Companion, "Lo, I am with you always, even unto the end of the world" (Matt. 28:20).

The purpose in dealing with the splintering efforts of sectarianism on the American churches is to point out a significant difference between religious attitudes of the Chinese compared to those of Americans.

> The American belongs to a church or a temple, provides for its support, attend its services, and goes to its social meetings. Protestant differentiation, in turn, compels him to be a denominationalist such as a Presbyterian or a Baptist. Yet he must not only be a Baptist, but must choose between being a Northern Baptist or a Southern Baptist. Finally, he is not only a Baptist, but he is known also as a member of the First Baptist Church of Evanston, Illinois, or the Third Baptist Church of Jonesville, Ohio, or some other. For the American way in religion is to be more and more exclusive, so that not only is God the only true God while all others are false, but I cannot rest until my particular view of God has prevailed over all others.

> The Chinese tendency is exactly the reverse. The Chinese may go to a Buddhist monastery to pray for a male heir, but he may proceed from there to a Taoist shrine where he beseeches a god to cure him of malaria. Ask any number of Chinese what their religion is and the answer of the majority will be that they have no particular religion, or that, since all religions benefit man in one way or another, they are all equally good. (Hsu, 1981, p. 254)

The problems of an interreligious marriage are commensurate with the devoutness of the adherents to the two different systems of belief. Religion would pose few problems in a marriage between a nominal Christian and a nominal Buddhist, for example. With neither person practicing their religion, the identity with the two different religious groups would have no more effect than if both were confirmed atheists. There would be more problems if the two mates were members of the same narrowly defined religious sect with the one being a devout member and the other an adherent in name only. Problems do arise when marriage takes place between two devotees whose beliefs are different even though they belong to the same religion, such as some interdenominational marriages within Christianity. Problems are more likely to occur in interreligious marriages between two staunch members of different religious types. For this reason, it will be of value to briefly compare the religious beliefs in China with those in the

United States in order to understand the hurdles involved in interreligious marriages between two devout believers. If a couple understands the differences they face in a marriage of this type and still go through with the ceremony, it means either that their religious beliefs are not too strong or that other factors offset any disadvantages of such a marriage. Because the dominant religion in the United States is Protestant-Christianity, this will be the basis for comparison with the Chinese religious environment.

The adjustment in an interreligious marriage is more easily made by the Chinese than the American-Caucasian, in an interreligious marriage, because the Chinese religion is a mixture of Confucianism, Taoism, and Buddhism. This mixture provides religious tolerance limits which exceed the tolerance limits provided by monotheistic religions, like those found in the U.S.

> By showing itself not as an exclusive religion but as a complement to other Chinese beliefs, Buddhism permeated Chinese life and became as Chinese as the native philosophies of Confucianism and Taoism. The Chinese were never thereafter at any particular period either Confucianist, Taoist, or Buddhist—they were all three simultaneously. (Welty, 1984, p. 177)

In an intermarriage between a Chinese and an American, the Chinese, in such a marriage, would simply incorporate an additional god into their concept of religion. This is born out in the survey of Chinese college students, presented in Chapter 3. The study shows that 74 percent of those responding said they would cross over religious lines in marriage. They would be more than likely unwilling, however, to forego the protection of other gods by forsaking them. The American who has been indoctrinated with the idea of one true God would have difficulty in accepting the numerous Chinese gods. For such a marriage to succeed, each mate would have to respect the religious beliefs of the other. This does not mean, however, that they would have to adopt the practices, or theology, but that they would have to tolerate them.

Since urbanization, as pointed out earlier, has ushered in a variety of needs not being met by other social institutions, religion has developed a wide diversity of beliefs designed to meet these needs. The result is a splintering of the church in the U.S. into numerous denominations, and innumerable sects.

Some feeble efforts have been made to unify the church in the U.S. but they have not been too effective. The Disciples of Christ, the only American-born major denomination, came into existence to integrate all denominations into a brotherhood. Since its founding in the early part of the nineteenth century, it not only has failed to unite the denominations, but it has itself split into the Church of Christ and the Christian Church in addition to the Disciples of Christ.

One major reason for the failure of the U.S. religious institutions to integrate society is because the moralizing is done from the pulpit instead of through action. In the American churches, the minister is the hired agent whose responsibility is to carry out the religious obligations of the congregation. In visiting the sick, the imprisoned, and the troubled, he is the representative of the congregation he serves. The conscience of the members is saved, its Christian spirit has been exemplified, and the service to Christ has been carried out. The minister has enacted the sermon, but the members continue to wallow in the stagnant pond of complacency. In order for a Christian ministry to be effective, the Christian must serve as a channel through which the religious message flows into the lives of others, and not as a reservoir that stores the message as a self-satisfying source of inspiration.

Sects form a rigid dogmatic structure that is unyielding. Their form of religion is revealed from on high, therefore, it is right—even to the letter. Some of them speak in tongues, some of them bathe the feet, and some of them handle snakes. All of these practices stem from a literal interpretation of the scriptures.

Denominations are more compromising than the sects. They are recognized by society as major religious groups than can be distinguished between by their different approaches in the interpretation of religious writings. The liberals see in the story of Jonah and the whale, for example, a lesson condemning disobedience. The conservatives read it as an account of a biological phenomenon. The proper interpretation is determined by which rendering of the account results in more complete obedience, for this is the purpose of the story.

There are numerous religious denominations in the U.S. Some have more sectarian characteristics than others. Some appeal to the intellectual class. Some have another worldly appeal that attracts the lower class. Some emphasize the mystical aspects of religion. Some involve the emotions more than others. All of them came into existence to meet a specific need that was not being met by prevailing institutions. In a heterogeneous society, the needs vary widely. A narrow interpretation of religious writings cannot satisfy all of the needs. Consequently, the interpretation must be more general, which weakens the influence of religion as an integrator of society.

This has happened in the U.S., making the adherent of religion more tolerant of other beliefs. This, coupled with the broad spectrum of religious beliefs in Taiwan, makes intermarriage between Chinese and American-Caucasians more acceptable.

CHANGES IN THE EDUCATIONAL INSTITUTION

Earlier in this book, we argued that in major universities in the U.S., the emphasis is upon the improvement of culture through research. Many humanitarian foundations provide funds to universities in order to find answers to social and medical problems. The federal government and other sources finance projects designed to unravel the mysteries of the universe.

We also wrote that the structure of the educational institutions varies from a playroom for pre-kindergarten children to the highly specialized and prestigious law schools, medical schools, and engineering schools, among others. There are special graduate programs offered by universities to supplement the efforts of all of the major social institutions. Doctorates in business administration or economics, in the family, in diplomatic relations and public administration, and in education are available. Each of these fields is further specialized at the graduate level.

Now we add that specialization in education developed much more slowly in China.

[T]he old-style Chinese schools are truly of ancient origin. The philosophy of education on which they were based flourished in China without significant change for over twenty centuries. The new-style schools were introduced from the West from about the end of the nineteenth century and did not replace the old-style schools until about the end of World War II. . . .

Furthermore, while Chinese children in modern schools learned physics and chemistry and attended physical education and craft classes, they still concentrated on reading and writing, ethics and civics, and history and geography. Until World War II, the number of Chinese students in the arts and humanities far outnumbered those in the physical sciences. (Hsu, 1981, pp. 93, 95)

As far as intermarriage between Chinese and Americans is concerned, the difference in the emphasis between the two types of educational programs is of some consequence. If two college graduates, one from China and the other from the U.S., marry and live in America, for example, although the educational levels are the same, the two degrees would not be necessarily compatible. The Chinese degree would be steeped in Confucianism, according to the old school. Even if the mate had a liberal arts degree from an American university, a common educational background would not be formed. If the United States degree is in a scientific field, the educational gap would be even wider. Another supposition is that if the Chinese mate is male, accustomed to the dominance-submission pattern of interaction, further problems would develop as the couple entered into discussions with their American friends.

Although the knowledge content of the two different educational programs is of importance, the variation in orientation from the grade school level through college is even more significant as far as intermarriage is concerned.

Old-style Chinese schools carried forward what the growing children had learned from the preschool experience, just as modern American schools attempt to further the pattern of behavior that American youngsters learn at home. Chinese children learned at home to respect their parents and tradition. In school they had the same virtues impressed on them by Confucian classics. Americans learn at home to follow their individual predilections. In school, it is true, they tare taught to cooperate, to develop sportsmanship, and so forth, but the relentless emphasis on creativity, autonomy, and progressive teaching techniques reinforces the values learned in the home. (Hsu, 1981, p. 92)

Another major educational factor that needs to be considered in intermarriage between Chinese and Americans is the differing degrees of esteem placed upon knowledge by the members of the two societies. To the American, knowledge is a means to an end. Such a person reads selectively choosing mostly those materials meeting the utilitarian needs. The Chinese read indiscriminately, mastering knowledge in many different areas of literature.

Although there are wide differences in the educational approach in Taiwan and the U.S., the emphasis upon graduate study lessens the differences, in this respect, and draws the two educational programs closer together. The professional propinquity resulting from specialized education more than offsets this disadvantage in mate selection in intercultural marriages.

## CHANGES IN THE POLITICAL INSTITUTION

The political institution is of importance in the study of intermarriage between Chinese and Americans because it is intricately interwoven with the religious and educational institutions of China through Confucianism. A combination of these three major institutions exercises heavy authority over the members of society. Religion exercises spiritual control, education through indoctrination, controls the mind, and the political institution provides the force necessary for physical control.

In America, the direct linkage of these three social institutions is not in evidence. In fact, there is a strong insistence upon the separation of church and state. This separation is so distinct that prayers are not allowed in public school classrooms. The control of the federal government over the school programs is extremely limited. The controls are sponsored by the individual states causing a wide variation in the quality of education from one state to another, thus, weakening the integrating influence at the national level.

The authoritarian type of rule ingrained in the Chinese culture for some 3,000 years cannot be shut off with the flick of a switch, as shown by the fifty years of groping for a new order. In addition, such a long-standing political influence shaped the other major social institutions. These structures also became authoritarian, which is quite a contrast to the American social institutions. Reshaping the other traditional Chinese social institutions was just as difficult as the problems faced by the transition of the political structure. The vestiges of the authoritarianism evident in the Chinese family and religious and educational institutions are quite different from their counterparts in the United States. Intermarriage between the two contrasting cultures, therefore, would call for many adjustments and possibly result in conflict.

The different attitudes of the traditional Chinese and the Americans toward government need also to be considered in analyzing the problems involved in intermarriage between members of the two societies.

> The Chinese, with his pattern of mutual dependence, maintains strong ties with his family, kin, and local group that necessarily overshadow all his relationships with the wider society. He has, therefore, little reason to look for his social and emotional security among personalities and objects in the wider world.

> The American, with his pattern of self-reliance, must unflaggingly pursue individual advancements that transcend not only his ties with his primary groups but also uproot most of this subsequent associations. His lack of security compels him to seek satisfaction of his social needs through some attachment beyond his kinship and communal scene. (Hsu, 1981, p. 205)

As Taiwan moves toward democracy, the family loyalty is shifting toward the government. Such a move brings the U.S. and Taiwan into a more compatible relationship and makes intermarriage across political boundaries more acceptable.

CHANGES IN THE ECONOMIC INSTITUTION

As mentioned earlier, the function of the economic institution is to produce and distribute goods and services. This function is carried out by technology no matter how primitive this means of providing and distributing goods and services may be. The eolith, or the dibble stick, was the first crude form of technology. Even though it was far less efficient than the modern methods of production, it did improve the production of goods.

The major shift in the economic institution of Taiwan since 1950 is the change from an agrarian to an industrial economy. This did more than change the means of providing a livelihood—it shattered the neighborhood, split up families, changed relationships from a primary to secondary nature, and transformed the life-style.

In this move, the heart of economic activities moved from the village center to the market place and then to urban areas. The major impact in the expanding economy, developed by industrialization, was the catastrophic adjustments the process necessitated in the conversion of the transported rural social structure to meet the needs of an urban society. The first movements of the population from rural to urban areas of any consequence is dated around 5,000 B.C. It may be recalled that this is the time when the cultivation of crops and the domestication of animals made it possible to establish small cities. Jarmo is considered the first city of any importance. It was located in Northern Mesopotamia with an estimated population of 5,000.

Cities gradually evolved as technology advanced, providing the mechanism to produce and distribute food, among other things, to the city dwellers. Even though the growth was gradual, the social structure was unable to adapt to meet the social needs as rapidly as technology was meeting the physical needs. It was not recognized by the authorities that the rural social structure could not adequately meet the social needs of an expanding population in a limited geographical area.

The location of cities determines to a large extent the social structure of a society. Many sites that were at first selected for defense purposes have developed into major cities. Some of these cities, at least in America, still use the designated purpose, fort, as part of their name.

Cities are also situated for commercial purposes, which affects the social structure of society. The locations of port cities have been determined by nature, but the administration of them is carried out through the social structure. Likewise, transportation breaks, points at which cargo is shifted from barges or boats to land transportation units, have developed from small centers of activity to major cities. Many other reasons for the location of cities could be given.

The point is that the sites of cities in Taiwan, like those in America, affect the social structure, which in turn influences the mate selection process. Social structure of industrialized northern Taiwan is more similar to the social structure of the northeastern United States than it is to the isolated areas on the east coast of the island. This means that a marriage between a Chinese and an American-Caucasian from industrialized areas may be more compatible than an intra-ethnic marriage of a person from the northern part of Taiwan with one on the east coast.

One consequence of urbanizing the economic structure of Taiwan was the development of one form of competition for the family loyalty which is in the form of voluntary groups which sprang up in urban centers as a result of the increasing rate of migration from rural areas. When migrants left the village and countryside, they were no longer able to draw upon the family for financial, and other forms of, assistance. In response to this newly developed need, associations were formed which offered various types of services. They assisted migrants in finding residence, granting small loans, and securing employment, among other things. They served as a haven for the migrant. Satisfying these needs through the Chinese associations made the migrant less dependent upon the family and thereby weakened the ties. The shift of dependency put the family in a different perspective, which favorably affects the decision regarding intercultural marriage. On the other hand, Chinese associations cross over international boundaries, forming strong bonds among the Chinese in foreign territories. The loyalty that binds the foreign Chinese to the Motherland through these associations discourage intercultural marriage.

CHANGES IN SOCIAL STATUS AND SOCIAL ROLE

Although there are numerous changes to the economic institution in Taiwan that could be dealt with here, such as the change from barter to a money economy, two are of extreme importance in considering the possibility or intermarriage between a Chinese and an American-Caucasian and these are social role and social status.

Urbanization of Taiwan drastically changed the social status and social role in the economic fabric, especially among the females.

Social status is an important factor to be taken into account in a contemplated intercultural marriage between a Chinese and American-Caucasian. As discussed in Chapter 5, status serves a twofold purpose. It prioritizes certain positions in society, and it is used as a measuring instrument in ranking the overall social status of individuals. Because of the practice of filial piety, a higher ranking is given to elderly persons in Taiwan than in the United States. An American-Caucasian may not be in agreement with, nor understand, the Chinese mate being more concerned with the parents than with the offspring of the mixed marriage. In order to perpetuate the family through ancestry, married persons are, also, accorded a higher status in Taiwan than in the United States. Although intercultural marriages are not arranged by the Chinese parents, filial piety applies a heavy pressure in mate selection.

Industrialization has opened opportunities for women to pursue careers outside of the home.

These enterprises, ranging from firms employing thousands of workers to family-run business employing a handful of neighbors, have provided young women with wage-earning opportunities that were previously unavailable. (Ahern & Gates, 1981, p. 184)

The women contributed to the welfare of the family and tasted financial independence, which has developed self-respect in them, and made them more discriminating in the selection of a mate.

Although a female factory worker does not enjoy a high level of prestige, she is in a socially acceptable occupation.

The sight of young women waiting for company buses in the mornings and being dropped off in the early evenings is now common place in many villages and small towns in Taiwan; it attests not only to the increasing number of factories in the outskirts of urban centers, but also to the widespread acceptance of factory work as a respectable occupation for young women. This new attitude presents a marked contrast with the prevailing view in pre-revolutionary China, when the reputation of women factory workers was often questionable. (Ahern & Gates, 1981, p. 186)

In the early stage of the Industrial Revolution on Taiwan, positions in factories affected major changes in the status of women in the family and in society.

Since social roles are intricately intertwined with social status, they are also influenced by change caused by the industrialization of Taiwan. In addition to the various kinship roles played by the female worker, she is thrust into other types of roles by her new position. She plays the role of an employee, co-worker, a novice when she first takes a position, a companion to some, and various other roles depending upon numerous factors.

Her role of factory worker requires quite a few adjustments which she has to make usually without an orientation program. She has to learn how to adapt to the requirements of the role through experience or through the advice of others. She must learn to accept responsibilities which differ from those of a housewife. Pressure to produce is applied, to which she must become inured. The secondary relationships in the factory replace, at least during working hours, those of a primary nature in the home and neighborhood.

The different social environment influences her perspective regarding relationships outside of the factory.

Rightly or wrongly, much of what female workers learn in the factory and many of the conclusions that they form there about personal relationships and about their social roles are generalized to the larger society (Ahern & Gates, 1981, p. 185).

Her horizons are extended. Although factory work is monotonous, female workers are freed from the traditional trap that rejects self-expression. Just as importantly, the range of their social relationships is broadened. After the social stratification structure had made the adjustment necessitated by the female factory worker, and society had accepted the role of the female in industry, other opportunities opened up, expanding the job market for women.

As can be seen in this discussion on the economic structure in Taiwan, coupled with the technological development there, the Taiwan and American societies are moving closer together. Although many factors in the economy appear to be conducive to intercultural marriages, others retard the movement in this direction. It should be born in mind that the rapid development of industry in Taiwan has made the economic institution more similar in this aspect of the society than reflected in any other social institution in the U.S.

The final chapter, Chapter 12, is entitled "Epilogue" and summarizes the findings of this book and the field study by identifying the similarities and differences in Taiwan and American society in an attempt to show the width of the gap separating the two as far as intercultural marriage is concerned.

# 12

## Epilogue:
## Shall the Twain Meet?

In his work "The Ballad of East and West," Rudyard Kipling wrote: "Oh, East is East, and West is West, and never the twain shall meet . . ." Kipling was evidently referring to the impossibility of bridging the wide gap existing between Eastern and Western cultures.

The pessimistic position of Rudyard Kipling was taken because he was unable to predict the technological explosion and the opportunities offered by this development. If he could have foreseen the spanning of oceans through jet flight and the linkage of various cultures through telecommunications, plus many other developments, his prediction might have been different. But Kipling was a and not a scientist.

The answer to the question, "Shall the twain meet?" simply stated is, "Someday."

The needs of all societies are similar. The way these needs are met varies. Through tracing the development of culture, in all societies, an easier and more efficient method of meeting these needs is uncovered. It then is adopted and becomes a universal within the society. It stands to reason that as these more efficient methods are revealed to other societies, they, too, will adopt them. There are some retarding forces, however, such as tradition, religion, and entrenched values, among others, that slow the adoptive process. Expediency in meeting the needs, nevertheless, whittles away at these obstacles to adoption, and gradually weakens them.

One barrier to the acceptance of new practices is the degree of success with the old ones. A farm agent from an agricultural experiment station has his efforts in promoting the raising of hybrid corn rejected, for example, because the past practices have yielded an adequate crop. Although the farm agent shows the farmer a much more abundant crop raised on the same amount of land, in the same area, the farmer is unwilling to change because the way he has done it in the past has always satisfied his needs.

The continued success of the farmer who does adopt the practice of growing hybrid corn will have an impact on the other and probably convince him to change.

Another probably more important factor promoting change is the transfer of the farmland from the conservative father, through inheritance, to the more liberal son. A young person has more opportunity to recover from mistakes than an older one and, hence, is more willing to run any risk involved in the change.

The aim of this final chapter is to summarize the influences contributing toward the changed attitudes toward intercultural marriage and to discuss some of the forces combating the acceptance of such a practice. The materials are treated in their order of appearance in this book.

To begin with, there are several findings in the field study, set forth in Chapter 3, that indicate an increasing interest in the acceptance of intercultural marriage between the Chinese and American-Caucasian.

Ethnocentrism forms a negative force in intercultural marriages. The reason for this is that it puts a high priority on the ethnic group. Ethnocentrism is actually egotism at the national level. It holds that everything of importance is the *best* in the ethnic group. This makes it difficult to accept another nation's position.

Some evidence is given in Table 3.1 (Chapter 3) that ethnocentrism has weakened to some extent in the attitudes of various college students. The Table shows that those on a higher educational level, higher income level, and those living in urban areas prefer to marry members of a Western, rather than an Eastern, type of culture. This is significant insomuch as Asians identify readily with other Asians.

There are three major factors in the establishment of ethnocentrism—race, nationalism, and religion. These three factors are taken into account in Table 3.2 (Chapter 3) in order to determine which wields the most force in retarding intercultural marriages.

The fact that all three types of intermarriage—those across racial, national, and religious boundaries—are more readily acceptable by urban, rather than rural, residents indicates that urbanization of Taiwan is taking its toll against ethnocentrism.

One measure of change in attitudes toward intercultural marriage is revealed when the objections to such marriages are shown in Table 3.6 (Chapter 3) which compares the parental objection based upon residence, educational level, and income. It shows that one-half of the parents living in urban areas had no objection to such an arrangement compared to approximately one-third in rural areas. Again, it appears that urbanization is contributing toward more acceptance of intercultural marriages.

A similar trend is shown based upon the educational level of the parents. Approximately one and one-half as many parents who both had a college degree had no objections to their daughter marrying an American-Caucasian, than those parents having six years or less of schooling (Table 3.7, Chapter 3).

This brief summary of salient points of Chapter 3 indicates that the urbanization of Taiwan has been a major contributing factor in developing a social milieu that makes intercultural marriage more acceptable in the present than in the past.

Chapter 4 presents a unique classification system developed especially for this study. An explanation of each of the categories used in the discussion of intermarriage between Chinese and the American-Caucasian is given. Also the reason for placing each cultural trait in a particular category is treated. An important aspect of that chapter is the interrelationship shown between the various aspects of the classification system through a logically closed social system set forth in the latter part of the chapter. Since each of these major divisions are discussed in Chapters 5 to 9, no additional comment is needed at this point to show how each of these concepts affects the attitudes toward intermarriage of a Chinese and an American-Caucasian. Since the major impact of social change on various spheres (statisphere, dynasphere, psychospheres, instisphere, and technosphere) in the classification system are dealt with in detail in Chapters 10 and 11, only a brief summary of Chapters 5 to 9 is given in this Epilogue.

In order for the reader to get a better understanding of each of the concepts used in this book, a composite definition, followed by a simplified definition, was given at the beginning of the discussion of each term. To some extent, in this way this book serves as an introduction to sociology.

The statisphere, discussed in Chapter 5, deals with the structural aspects of society. The first part of that chapter deals with the accumulation of culture through the testing of various possible innovations through the "battleground" of social alternatives. At this point the trait is accepted or rejected. If it is accepted, it becomes either a universal practice or a specialty. If it is rejected, then it may be modified or it may be dropped from possible usage.

It is this process that determines the stability of a society. If numerous innovative practices are introduced and accepted, the society is constantly changing. Rapid change makes predictability uncertain. Since predictability is a measure of stability, the society is considered unstable in the midst of numerous changes.

Social structure, discussed in Chapter 5, focuses on the individually centered pattern in the U.S., compared to the group-centered type in Taiwan. When the social structure is individually centered, the individual is dispensable, whereas in a group-centered structure, the individual is a vital link in a kinship group. Such a difference is of extreme importance in the mate selection process because in the first instance the family is a means to an end. In the second instance, it is an end in itself.

A major portion of Chapter 5 deals with the concept "group." A social group is the foundation of society. It is through this unit that individuals are prepared for a responsible position in society. It is through a combination of groups that neighborhoods are formed. This combination in turn enables resources to be pooled in an effort to meet social needs. Most importantly, a linkage of groups forms the social institutions which provide the bulwark of the social structure.

An extremely important development in Taiwan, as discussed in Chapter 5, is the shift in emphasis from the primary to secondary type of relationships in groups. Associations are no longer confined to the limited area of kinships or neighborhoods. Rather, they are expanded to the market place, the cities, and even across national borders. Such an expansion exposes the individual to a different way of life and a different set of values. This brings into question some of the traditional practices s/he has become accustomed to. Through this means, the individual becomes more aware, and possibly more tolerant, of the changes made necessary through cultural intermarriage.

While Chapter 5 deals with the structure of society, Chapter 6—"The Dynasphere"—deals with its functional aspects. The main focus of that chapter is the shift from an agrarian to an industrial society in Taiwan. Also, treated is the shift of population from a rural to an urban type of society. Changes in the types of interaction patterns and various methods of social control also form a part of Chapter 6.

The shift from an agrarian type of society changed functions of all of the major social institutions. The family became less of a center for interests and activities. The educational institution expanded to incorporate technological knowledge. Religion lost its appeal as an explanation of the mysterious. The economy changed from a system based upon barter to one based upon money and credit. All of these changes contributed toward a more positive attitude toward intercultural marriages.

The shift in population from rural to urban centers expanded the opportunities for social contacts, especially between the sexes. This allowed members of one sex to become acquainted with the other on a broader scale and to test the interest in differing types of values. The choice in mates expanded and the mate selection process became more receptive to intercultural marriages.

Of major importance in these changes was their influence on the interaction patterns. The dominance-submission pattern was weakened, because the opportunities for self-expression were encouraged by this development. Competition in the industrial economy spilled over into interaction patterns in the mate selection process. Accommodation became more and more acceptable as minor interests were sacrificed in order to attain major goals. Since interaction is the keynote in the marital situation, these changes contributed toward a more receptive attitude toward intercultural marriages.

The psychosphere, treated in Chapter 7, consists mainly of the socialization of the individual and the establishment of a value system. The psychosphere is the mental component of society. Socialization is the process by which attitudes are formed. When these attitudes are couched in the traditional robe of pre-Communist China, the marital practices, such as parental arrangement, are carried out. The marriages are confined to the ethnic group and to the limited circle of acquaintances.

With the development of industrialization and urbanization, however, the veil of tradition no longer hampers the mate selection process. Socialization is no longer the sole responsibility of the kinship group. There are numerous agencies that have developed out of necessity to perform this function.

One of the most significant influences is the peer group. Although individuals in this unit are similar in interests and characteristics, they form a heterogeneous group in other ways. That is to say their attitudes do not always conform. Their constant association with one another over a period of time brings these attitudes into closer harmony. Through the interaction pattern of accommodation, dealt with in Chapter 6, the members sacrifice their lesser interest—such as their interest in the family group—to gain the respect of the peer group.

One of the main contributions of the peer group is the impact it makes on the development of values. Personal values are those things of importance to the individual, whereas social values are those things of importance to society. If personal values conformed to social values, there would be no social problems. This is not always the case. Hence, there is a need for social control, which will be discussed later.

The peer group offers its members escape from parental authority. This leads, in many instances, to experimentation in various methods of need satisfaction. In other words, the peer group offers social alternatives to its members, an escape from the traditional universals.

One of the driving forces of an individual, from infancy to adulthood, is the desire for recognition. The peer group satisfies this need for the individual. Here, acceptance is offered by other members when one conforms to the peer group norms. This is especially true when these standards of behavior differ from those of the general society.

Because of those variations, which are not always in evidence, social controls are instituted to maintain or restore order. The pressure applied to bring the peer group into harmony with the main society depends upon the values involved. To illustrate this, an example of intercultural relationships is used. The study presented in Chapter 3 revealed that the approval of the peer for a Chinese dating an American-Caucasian was stronger than for marriage. Dating approval was 94 percent of the respondents compared to 69 percent who approved of marriage. Dating of an American-Caucasian would be considered in the area of the folkways, while marriage would be considered among the mores. Where intercultural marriages are considered extremely harmful to society, laws prevent such happenings.

A comparison of Tables 3.3 and 3.6 in Chapter 3 shows that the peer group looks more favorably on a Chinese dating or marrying an American-Caucasian than the parents do. This indicates that the attitude of the peer group is shifting the emphasis toward a more favorable acceptance of intercultural marriage.

Chapter 8 deals with the social institutions in Taiwan and the U.S. By way of summary of that chapter, the major changes that have contributed toward a more favorable attitude toward intercultural marriages are listed.

One important change in the family in Taiwan is the break-up of the extended type into nuclear units. Industrialization and urbanization have made inroads into family patterns. The small efficiency apartments are designed to meet the needs of workers in an urban society. They will not house three or four generations. Consequently, the extended family shrinks. This means that the responsibilities of the unit, such as baby-sitting, are shifted to other social entities. A change of this nature may be a traumatic experience for the child. A child finding security in the warmth of the extended family is now faced with confusion as it copes with a strange social environment.

Religion is the slowest institution to change. The deeply entrenched beliefs, steeped in tradition, are accepted without question. One advantage of the Taiwanese religion as far as acceptance of intercultural marriage is concerned is its mixture. Religion in Taiwan is a blend between Buddhism, Taoism, and Confucianism. This blend makes the acceptance of another religion more tolerable.

The main change in the educational system in Taiwan affecting the mate selection process is the move in the direction of specialized education. Such a program develops a common interest among individuals. The more common interest a young couple of the opposite sex has, the closer it is drawn together. Another thing, to pursue a highly specialized education will more than likely cause the individual to leave the friendly environs and disrupt the family ties. The individual is exposed to a different way of life and has her or his social horizons expanded. All of these changes contribute to a more favorable attitude toward intermarriage.

The main change in the political institution of Taiwan occurred when the center of authority was moved from Mainland China to the new location. The Republic of China had to start from scratch. It developed diplomatic relationships with Western nations and other countries of Asia. This meant the establishment of a diplomatic corps that spanned a major portion of the world. Representatives from other countries were sent to Taiwan. The result was a criss-crossing of political channels that brought about a mixture of social contacts, exposing Taiwan to a variety of cultures. Familiarity with other ways of life brought the traditional practices transported from Mainland China under question and posed changes, including the attitudes toward intercultural marriage.

The bulk of the economic institution in Taiwan is treated in Chapter 9, which deals with technology. Suffice it to say here that the major changes brought about by the shift from an agrarian to an industrial economy caused the residents of Taiwan to look more favorably on intercultural marriages.

In an attempt to give the reader a better understanding of the concepts of sociology, the impact of the development of technology is also shown in Chapter 9. Material culture is traced from the dibble stick to the state of the Industrial Revolution ending in 1950. This is by no means the end of the technological developments. Industrialization continues to mushroom in the present.

The first form of social life that could be dignified by the name "society" is represented by the roaming, food-gathering bands. The family was the only social institution needed to meet the needs of such a unit. Grubbing for food was the only economic activity and no highly specialized educational program was needed to teach this.

Through invention and discovery, food development techniques were improved. Each improvement made possible a more sedentary way of life. More permanency in settlement patterns made it possible for culture to develop at a faster pace. The hunting and fishing economy made possible the establishment of the first villages, which required an overhaul of the social organization.

It was not until the Neolithic Period, however, with the development of the domestication of animals and cultivation of crops, that the food supply was adequate to support a concentration of population in small cities.

With the end of the Stone Age, metals made their appearance improving the methods of farming and making other advances possible. Social change was still slow and the social controls were improved as these innovations were introduced.

With the birth of the Industrial Revolution about the middle of the eighteenth century, technological advances, by far, outstripped the mechanism to control the results. Even in the present day, there are wide gaps between the technological advances and the necessary mechanism to control them. For example, intercontinental ballistic missiles have placed many nations in fear of impending destruction. High powered weaponry has sent the homicide rate soaring because of lack of controls. The fatality rate in automobile accidents is a result of the inability to control the drivers of this monster of death.

The Industrial Revolution continues to accelerate as the cultural base is broadened. The question is, "Where will it all end?" It appears that a monster has been created that is intent on devouring itself.

Social change in Taiwan since 1950 can be summed up in two words—industrialization and urbanization—which are discussed in Chapter 10. The Industrial Revolution got under way in England around 1750. It was well established there as it began to make an impact on American society around 1850. One hundred years later, around 1950, it began in Taiwan. What this means is that 200 years of technological advances had been made in other parts of the world before any significant impact was made on Taiwan.

Taiwan did not have to feel its way through the earlier stages of the Industrial Revolution. It was thrust into the middle of it. Because of this, the technological progress in Taiwan occurred at a much more rapid rate than in the other two major industrial centers.

Three main factors contributed toward this accelerated expansion—transportation, telecommunications, and social mobility.

One of the first major strides in the development of transportation was the invention of the automobile. This instrument of transportation was well developed when the governmental authority was shifted to Taiwan. The importation of the product drastically changed the mode of local transportation, which was a prerequisite to the process of urbanization.

For one thing, the automobile made it possible to transport perishable goods to the cities in a much shorter time, providing a food supply for city dwellers. It also made it possible to establish a system of commerce between cities. These two factors, among others, encouraged the population shift from rural to urban centers.

Statistics show that 51 percent of the population of Taiwan was composed of farm families in 1954, compared to 22 percent in 1983. This is a change from one-half to one-fifth of the population shifting from rural to urban areas. Population in cities of 100,000 or more changed from 17 percent in 1954 to 50 percent in 1983.

Telecommunication is a second result of the Industrial Revolution that increases interaction between and among individuals. Through this method, conversations are no longer limited to those within voice range but can be carried on across the world. Crossing cultural and national boundaries becomes common place and breeds familiarity across cultural boundaries. Acquaintance with other ways of life brings questions to mind about one's own way, and may cause an individual to change.

Both the expansion of transportation and telecommunication encourages social mobility. Residential, personal, vertical, and ideational mobility—especially television—all introduce an individual to a different life-style. With each exposure to a different way of life, or any social innovation for that matter, an individual's cultural base is broadened, tolerance for the strange is increased, and the likelihood of change is greater.

The introduction of new ideas presents social alternatives, which, if adopted, may create subcultures, thereby weakening tradition. Subcultures are units of the social structure with a distinctly different life-style in which loyalty to the group is demanded, making it difficult to cross over the group boundaries. Although they are distinct entities, trade, educational systems, and political practices cause interaction between and among the subcultures causing the existing limitations to be extended.

One of the main changes brought about by industrialization and urbanization in Taiwan, as in other places, is the shift from primary to secondary group relationships. Family bonds and neighborhood ties are weakened or broken. Such influences are conducive to marriages within the cultural group. With the replacement of primary relationships by secondary associations, the interests of a person shifts from group-centered to individual-centered and the mate selection process breaks the shackles of tradition and group preference. Arranged marriages are replaced by those based upon romance and individual choice.

The institutional framework transported by Taiwan was tightly integrated. The functions of the political, economic, and educational institutions were carried out mainly by the family. Industrialization of Taiwan changed this. The political system became international, the educational system became specialized, and the economic system shifted from a family centered barter system to a money and credit economy.

The family was no longer able to meet these needs. Specialized institutions developed for this purpose. Since the needs of the child approaching the age of marriage were no longer simple, arranged marriages were no longer adequate. In other words, as the society in Taiwan moved toward complexity, the individual became more involved in making decisions.

No attempt is made here to summarize Chapter 11, because it, in itself, is a summary. It deals with the influence of social change in Taiwan on the various spheres. The changes in the technosphere, statisphere, dynasphere, psychospheres, and instisphere all show a definite trend toward a more favorable acceptance of intercultural marriage.

## CONCLUSION

An attempt has been made in this book to give a basic understanding of the key concepts in the study of sociology. The method used was to trace the development of culture from its most primitive stage to the present-day highly complex mechanism that encompasses the industrialized world.

For example, social interaction is better understood when it is viewed in its development from contact through a random selection of grunts and gestures to associations made possible through a highly sophisticated symbolic system of communication. In the first instance, social interaction is based upon mimicry. If a particular practice works for one, then it is adopted by another. The cultural base of the mimic is broadened, no matter how limited the extension. This lays a widened foundation for additional developments.

On the other hand, social interaction is defined and refined by all kinds of group associations. The degree and type of social interaction is far different in a patriarchal family than it is between two pen-pals. Social interaction in the first instance is more formal than in the second.

Other sociological terms are better understood when they are compared in different situations or at different times.

Although definitions have been hammered out for many of these concepts discussed, it should be understood that each term has a different meaning, no matter how slight, for each individual. So, social interaction for the "cave man" was direct appropriation. In a developed society, it takes place through a highly complicated legal channel.

What this is saying is that there are shady areas surrounding each definition, and that, after all, the meaning of any particular term depends upon the interpretation of the individual. Thus, the meaning of social interaction for a wrestler in a ring is quite different from the assignment of a meaning of the term in a Sunday school class.

One key issue dealt with throughout the book is the process of mate selection in intercultural marriages, especially those between Chinese and American-Caucasians. Marriage might be a means of satisfying individual needs. If the particular need is to perpetuate the family lineage, then the mate is selected on the basis of child-bearing ability. If the primary need is to select a helpmeet to assist in farm activities, then the mate is selected on the basis of physical ability, among others.

Many social changes in Taiwan have influenced the mate selection process. These have been dealt with in Chapter 11, as well as in other sections of this book. The important question addressed here is, how have these changes contributed toward meeting the needs of the individual in mate selection? A good approach in answering this question is first to determine what these needs are.

These needs are reflected in society. If a marriage or a family is to succeed, or continue to survive, it must satisfy needs that are not being met by other agencies of society. Various efforts have been made to supplement or replace the family unit. Units such as 4-H clubs, among others, are assisting economically. The government has assumed many familiar responsibilities in caring for and protecting the child. Various groups in the school have been formed to assist in the development of the child. The religious institution offers assistance in providing the child with reasons for living, among other things.

Although these are moves in the right direction, they are far from adequate. In spite of the 4-H and other economic group efforts, there is still poverty rampant across the world, including the U.S. The governmental efforts have not prevented child abuse. The educational programs are not challenging enough to prevent dropouts. And the religious efforts have not curtailed teen-age suicide, substance abuse, or dissatisfaction.

It is ironic that in spite of the stupendous progress in meeting the physical needs of members of society, very little success has been achieved in meeting the emotional needs. In the earliest stages of social development, little concern was shown for others, as the big and the strong took what they wanted. Although it is carried out in a more refined way today, business is still business, regardless of the consequences.

The problem is that the major efforts are directed toward meeting the physical needs to the neglect of emotional needs. As Ralph Waldo Emerson once said, "Things are in the saddle, and are riding mankind."

The two main emotional needs of security and recognition are paramount in importance. Physical security is offered through the police department, and other agencies. Emotional security is offered through religious and other companionate groups. Recognition stems from achievement in education and other sources.

Although these attempts to satisfy the emotional needs help some, the efforts are feeble. It seems that the function of marriage and the establishment of a family needs to do more than provide a channel to "multiply, be fruitful, and replenish the earth."

It appears that if there is agreement on this point, the question then is whether intra- or inter-cultural marriages can better satisfy these emotional needs. There are both advantages and disadvantages in each type of marriage in providing emotional security. Although an entire book could be written on each of these types of emotional security, only one or two examples will be given. Marriage within one's own culture provides security through familiarity with the expectations of the demands of marriage. When one marries others from the same culture, s/he is more likely to know what these expectations and demands are and to indicate a willingness to live up to them through marriage. Selecting a mate within the same culture does not isolate the individual from family or friends.

A disadvantage in such a union is the danger that it may be looked upon as a routine, hum-drum affair. Another disadvantage is that continued close associations with family and friends may infringe upon the marital relationships.

An advantage of an intercultural marriage is that one culture may very well compliment the other. For instance, the strong Confucian strain on the part of the Chinese may strengthen the moral fiber of the American in such an intercultural marriage. Another advantage is that new and different ways of doing things can make each experience exciting.

The main drawback of an intercultural marriage is the language barrier. Even though each mate speaks both languages fluently, it has been shown in this book that each word is embedded in the culture, and to get a complete understanding of the term one must be well-acquainted with, or even immersed, in the culture.

Recognition is a motivating force of the individual from infancy through old age. A crying baby is seeking recognition. Marriage within a culture satisfies this need by feeding the ethnocentric appetite. The mate who thinks her or his culture is best marries another with the same opinion and gains recognition of his or her ethnicity.

A disadvantage in marrying within the same culture, as far as recognition is concerned, is that the wife's identity is usually determined by the position of the husband. This is one of the vestiges of the patriarchal family still found in the American Society. This is even more true in Chinese culture. The wife becomes a member of the husband's family and her identity is absorbed by this unit.

An advantage in intercultural marriages, when dealing with recognition, is that the individual stands out as a cultural entity. This mate is often the center of attention in discussing cultural differences.

A disadvantage in intercultural marriages is that the spouse of the impending culture most of the time remains an outsider. Even though this person is accepted as a member of the family through legal channels, s/he is never fully accepted socially. No matter how hard the members of the family may try to accept her or him, they cannot surpass the deeply entrenched cultural differences.

No more needs to be said about social change in Taiwan, except to point out the main adjustments made in each of the spheres discussed. A major portion of Chapter 5—"The Statisphere"—deals with social groups, especially the shift in emphasis from primary to secondary relationships. Chapter 6—"The Dynasphere"—focuses on social interaction with particular attention paid to the weakening of the dominance-submission pattern and the increase in the competitive type.

Emphasis on socialization is placed in Chapter 7, showing how this vital process has shifted from the family to other institutions of society, especially the peer group. Chapter 8, "The Instisphere," discusses several changes. Among others, the family changed from an extended to a nuclear type, education evolved from rudimentary skills to more specialized ones, religion moved from mysticism to practical denominationalism, politics was transformed from monarchy to democracy, and the economy advanced from agrarianism to industrialization.

The influence of the technospheric social change in Taiwan is shown in Chapter 9. The main development in this respect was the acceleration of social mobility, especially the vertical type which revolutionized social relationships by changing the status of individuals from ascribed to achieved status. The expansion of transportation and telecommunications also broadened the social experiences of individuals.

Chapter 10 deals with the industrialization and urbanization in Taiwan. The changes in urbanization were brought about by industrialization, prompting the shift in population from rural to urban areas. The catastrophic changes in social organization brought about by reshuffling the population occupies a major proportion of that chapter.

The influence of the social changes, discussed in Chapters 5 to 10, on the mate selection process in Taiwan are discussed in Chapter 11. Chapter 12, "Epilogue," summarizes the influences contributing to the changed attitudes toward the mate selection process in Taiwan.

Here, then, is this book in a nutshell. The definitions of some major sociological concepts are explained as they operate in the social context of Taiwan against the backdrop of intercultural marriage.

This Epilogue was opened with the question, "Shall the twain meet?" or shall East meet West? Perhaps an appropriate conclusion would be an attempt to answer this question.

Culture is a sprawling mass of practices that are designed to meet the needs of society. The emphasis, thus far, has been on meeting the basic needs for food, clothing, and shelter. Phenomenal strides have been made in this effort. It then stands to reason if you want a path beaten to your door, you need to "build a better mousetrap."

The experience of Taiwan over the past 40 plus years has shown that the best and most expedient way of meeting needs is adopted if the new means provide better satisfaction. Taiwan plunged into the Industrial Revolution 200 years after its origin in England. Yet, in a short period of time it has closed the gap in technological development to an extremely narrow margin. In other words, the creeping cultural mass consumed the early ways of doing things in Taiwan and replaced them with an ever expanding wave of sophistication. It then appears that, as the consuming mass of culture spreads slowly to the rest of the world, the rest of the world too will succumb. This is to say that as culture expands, social universals, discussed in

Chapter 5, will no longer be defined as practices *within* a society but on a worldwide basis.

And this globalization of culture will be the result of the Industrial Revolution as well as of other social changes, such as urbanization, the Information Revolution, socioeconomic integration, and intercultural marriage. When these changes have occurred in the rest of the world, the twain shall indeed meet. Not only shall East meet West, but North will also meet South.

The outcome might look like a cultural rainbow containing a blend of cultural diversity and cultural assimilation. Whereas in a rainbow primary colors preserve their uniqueness, they also belnd with others to form a shared identity. For instance, primary colors such as blue and yellow appear in every rainbow, as does the secondary color of green, a mixture of yellow and blue. Similarly, in a cultural rainbow, all races and cutures will preserve their unique colors and ways of doing things, but they will also belnd with others to form new looks and shared ways of doing things. While some might prefer to marry within their own race or culture, many might also prefer to marry across racial or cultural boundaries, thereby creating offspring such as mestizos, mulattos, and so on. And the cultural rainbow will be reflected in the laws and structure of society as well.

# BIBLIOGRAPHY

Ahern, E. M. & Gates, H. (Eds.). (1981). *The Anthropology of Taiwanese Society*. Stanford, CA: Stanford University Press.

Buchanan, K. (1968). *The Southeast Asian World*. Garden City, NY: Doubleday.

Budget, Accounting & Statistics: Executive Yuan. (1983). *Statistical Yearbook of the Republic of China*. Taipei: Directorate-General's Office.

Cooley, C. H. (1902). *Human Nature and the Social Order*. New York: Scribner's.

Han, L. (1982). *Taiwan Today*. Taipei: Cheng Chung Book Co.

Hsu, F. L. K. (1981). *Americans and Chinese: Passage to Differences* (3rd ed.). Honolulu: University Press of Hawaii.

Thompson, F. C. (Ed.). (1934). *The New Chain-Reference Bible* (3rd ed.). Indianapolis, IN: B. B. Kirkbride.

Republic of China. (1979). *The Republic of China Is on the Move: A Report of President Chiang Ching-kou's First Year in Office*. Taipei: Kwang Hua.

Richardson, P. D. & Bauder, W. W. (1953). "Participation in Organized Activities in a Kentucky Rural Community," in *Kentucky Agricultural Experiment Station, Bulletin No. 598*, June. Lexington: University of Kentucky.

Welty, P. T. (1984). *The Asians: Their Evolving Heritage* (6th ed.). New York: Harper & Row.

# INDEX